365 DAYS OF
SPIRALIZER
RECIPES

EMMA KATIE

Check out more books by Emma Katie at:
www.amazon.com/author/emmakatie

CONTENTS

Spiralized Salad Recipes

Spiralized Soup & Stews Recipes

Spiralized Recipes with Poultry

Spiralized Recipes with Meat

Spiralized Recipes with Seafood

Spiralized Vegetarian Recipes

Spiralized Desserts

$\mathcal{D}$ESCRIPTION

Not everyone is a big fan of vegetables. The major issue with them is difficulties in prepping or chopping the vegetables. Or some people find them not so appealing. So here comes a spiral vegetable slicer or a spiralizer that makes it far easier to beautifully spiralize your vegetables making them easier to slice and appealing to eyes.

There are many brands of spiralizers in the market to choose from. Each comes with its own functions and usability. It's a lightweight kitchen tool with three major parts; collection bowl, middle part that contains the blades and the top lid with a handle attached. All these parts are made up of plastic except the blades. Mainly there are two types of spiralizers; handheld and countertop. Further, they come with different number of blades. Handheld are easy on budget but heavy on elbow grease whereas countertop are easier and quicker to use but a little bit pricier. The choice is yours.

This book consists of 365 recipes that use vegetable noodles or ribbons. To make it more interesting the book offers different combinations of vegetables with meat, seafood and poultry. You will also find plentiful recipes of soups and salads.

*As a bonus you get a **7 DAY MEAL PLAN** for healthy spiralized vegetable recipes.*

*I*NTRODUCTION

Technology is making its ways through our lives and moved into our kitchen too. There are newer types of kitchen gadgets and appliances helping food makers making it easier to get healthy food at home. A spiralizer is one such addition to the kitchen mates. Spiralizer is a magical tool that makes cutting and slicing vegetables easier and appealing.

As a matter of fact healthier diets involve more of the vegetables. But they have not always been so appealing to everyone specially the kids. Spiralizer is a simple kitchen tool to make vegetable prepping fun and easier. It is called spiralizer or spiral vegetable slicer or vegetable noodle maker. A spiral vegetable slicer allows you to create spirals or noodles of many vegetables such as, zucchini, potato, cabbage, carrots and the list goes on. These spirals are a healthy replacement of regular spaghetti noodles.

If you really want to cut on carbs and pack your meals with fruits and vegetables then the spiral vegetable slicer is the right choice for you.

What to Buy Handheld or Countertop Spiralizer?

Handheld peelers or spiralizers carry quite budget-friendly price tags but require a little more effort to make those beautiful spirals. Whereas stand spiralizers are quicker and far easier to use but they can cost a pretty penny.

What to Look For?

-   **Features**: This is something most important to take into account. Such as different shapes of blades that allow spirals of various thicknesses and shapes. The spiralizers can create spaghetti shapes, slices and spirals.
-   **Ease in use:** The spiralizer has to be user-friendly i.e. easy to use, clean and store. Stand spiralizers have easily removable components to be washed manually with scrub or in a dishwasher. Look for a compact handheld or stand spiralizer that you can tuck away neatly. Keep your storage area in mind so to fit your new kitchen gadget.
-   **Flexibility:** Make sure it's flexible in use and reliable if you are using it to make spirals of harder vegetables. So you don't have to exert much force creating ribbons of your favorite vegetables.
-   **Easy to Use:** if you're buying a handheld spiralizer you should be able to attach the vegetables easily. And then there has to be a simple lever to quickly create spirals without putting in too much force.

*B*ENEFITS OF SPIRALIZER

Time Savior

Undoubtedly saves your time by skipping chopping and slicing process to prepare the vegetables. You don't need to spend ages in kitchen to prepare a nice and healthy meal for your family. It brings down the time it takes prepping the vegetables so you just spiralize and dump vegetables into your cooking pot and you're done.

Different Blades for Different Shapes

Sizes and shapes of slices right according to your liking such as, thick or thin slices, grated or diced, wedges or noodles. This is going to spoil you with variety of choices you would have in terms of vegetable shapes.

No More Knives

If your knife using skills are not like a chef or pro, no problem. Forget about the knives and buy you a nice vegetable slicer or spiralizer. Let it do the rest.

Uniformity

The best thing about using a vegetable slicer or spiralizer is that you get a uniform produce that is hard to get manually. The same rounds of vegetables with the same thickness are quite appetizing to even the eyes too.

Easy to Maintain

Removable blades make it easy to maintain and wash after every use. You can also use a damp cloth to clean your blades instead of washing every time you use them. It doesn't require servicing as it isn't an electrical device or battery operated.

These are just a few benefits of a vegetable spiralizer out of many that you will find out after experiencing this kitchen mate.

365 Amazing Recipes of Vegetable Spiralizer

Here you go with 365 amazingly delicious recipes of vegetable spiralizer that give you best combos of vegetables with poultry, seafood and meats. There are recipes of salads, soups, stews, desserts, sandwiches, wraps, muffins, waffles, pancakes, curries, chilies and so on. On top of everything the recipes are illustrated carefully with healthy ingredients providing you all nutrients vital for a healthy body. So what to wait for? Get set Go!!

Spiralized Salad Recipes

Nutty Apple Salad

Time: 15 minutes   Servings: 4

Ingredients:

For Salad:

2 Red Delicious apples, spiralized with Blade C
2 Granny Smith apples, spiralized with Blade C
1 tablespoon fresh lemon juice
2 tablespoons walnuts, chopped

For Dressing:

2 tablespoons white balsamic vinegar
2 tablespoons olive oil
1 tablespoon Dijon mustard
1 teaspoon honey

Directions:

In a large bowl, place the apple noodles and lime juice and toss to coat.
In another bowl, mix together all salad ingredients except almonds.
Pour dressing over salad and gently toss to coat well.
Top with walnuts and serve.

Apple & Blue Cheese Salad

Time: 15 minutes   Servings: 2

Ingredients:

2 medium Gala apples, spiralized with Blade C
4 cups fresh spring mix greens

2 tablespoons Blue cheese, crumbled
2 tablespoons pecans, chopped
Balsamic vinaigrette, as required

Directions:

In a salad bowl, add all ingredients and toss to coat.
Serve immediately.

Apple & Strawberry Salad

Time: 25 minutes   Servings: 2

Ingredients:

For Dressing:

2 tablespoons extra-virgin olive oil
2 tablespoons fresh lime juice

1 tablespoon honey
Salt and freshly ground black pepper, to taste

For Salad:

2 apples, spiralized with Blade C
4 cups fresh baby greens
½ cup fresh strawberries, hulled and sliced
½ cup almonds, chopped

Directions:

In a small bowl, add all dressing ingredients and mix till well combined.
In another bowl, mix together all salad ingredients except almonds.
Pour dressing over salad and gently toss to coat well.
Top with almonds and serve.

Apple & Grapes Salad

Time: 15 minutes

Servings: 2

Ingredients:

For Salad:

1 large apple, spiralized with Blade C
½ cup seedless green grapes, halved
½ cup celery stalk, chopped
4 cups fresh baby spinach
½ cup walnuts, chopped

For Dressing:

1 tablespoon shallot, minced
3 tablespoons extra-virgin olive oil
2 tablespoons apple cider vinegar
2 tablespoons pure maple syrup
1 tablespoon water
1 teaspoon Dijon mustard

Directions:

In a large serving bowl, add all salad ingredients except walnuts and mix.
In another bowl, add all dressing ingredients and beat till well combined.
Pour dressing over salad and toss to coat well. Top with walnuts and serve.

Apple, Beet & Blueberry Salad

Time: 25 minutes

Servings: 3

Ingredients:

1 large tart apple, spiralized with Blade C
1 large golden beet, trimmed, peeled and
spiralized with Blade C
1 large red beet, trimmed, peeled and
spiralized with Blade C
1 cup fresh blueberries

1 avocado, peeled, pitted and cubed
3 tablespoons apple cider vinegar
1 tablespoon fresh lemon juice
Salt and freshly ground black pepper, to taste
Pinch of ground cinnamon

Directions:

In a large bowl, add all ingredients except cinnamon and gently, toss to coat.
Sprinkle with cinnamon and serve.

Apple, Cabbage & Berries Salad

Time: 20 minutes

Servings: 2

Ingredients:

For Salad:

2 medium apples, spiralized with Blade C
1 cup green cabbage, spiralized with Blade C
½ cup fresh mixed berries
2 cups fresh lettuce, torn
1 tablespoon fresh lemon juice

For Dressing:

2 tablespoons extra-virgin olive oil
2 tablespoons apple cider vinegar
1 teaspoon Dijon mustard
1 tablespoon honey
1 tablespoon sesame seeds
Salt and freshly ground black pepper, to taste

Directions:

In a large bowl, place all salad ingredients and gently, toss to coat.
In another bowl, add all dressing ingredients and beat till well combined.
Pour dressing over salad and gently toss to coat.
Cover the bowl and refrigerate to chill before serving.

Apple, Cabbage & Carrot Salad

Time: 20 minutes

Servings: 4

Ingredients:

For Salad:

1 Granny Smith apple, spiralized with Blade C
2 cups shredded red cabbage, spiralized with Blade C
2 cups shredded green cabbage, spiralized with Blade C
2 medium-large carrots, peeled and spiralized with Blade C

For Dressing:

2 tablespoons extra-virgin olive oil
2 tablespoons apple cider vinegar
2 teaspoons agave nectar
1 teaspoon poppy seeds
Salt and freshly ground black pepper, to taste

Directions:

In a large bowl, place all salad ingredients and gently, toss to coat.
In another bowl, add all dressing ingredients and beat till well combined.
Pour dressing over salad and gently toss to coat.
Serve immediately.

Apple, Celeriac & Fennel Salad

Time: 25 minutes   Servings: 2

Ingredients:

For Salad:

1 fennel bulb, peeled and spiralized with Blade C
1 celeriac, peeled and spiralized with Blade C
1 large apple, peeled and spiralized with Blade C
2 tablespoons fresh parsley, chopped

For Dressing:

3 tablespoons extra virgin olive oil
2 tablespoons apple cider vinegar
1 tablespoon fresh lemon juice
1 teaspoon honey
1 teaspoon Dijon mustard
Salt and freshly ground black pepper, to taste

Directions:

In a large bowl, place all salad ingredients except parsley and mix.
In another bowl, add all dressing ingredients and beat till well combined.
Pour dressing over salad and gently toss to coat.
Garnish with parsley and serve immediately.

Apple & Carrot Salad

Time: 15 minutes   Servings: 2

Ingredients:

For Salad:

1 large carrot, peeled and spiralized with Blade C
1 large apple, spiralized with Blade C
1 cup fresh cranberries
2 cups fresh baby arugula
½ cup pecans, chopped

For Dressing:

1 garlic clove, minced
2 tablespoons apple cider Vinegar
tablespoons Extra Virgin Olive Oil
1 tablespoon Honey
1 tablespoon Soy Sauce
Salt and freshly ground black pepper, to taste

Directions:

In a large serving bowl, add all salad ingredients except pecans and mix.
In another bowl, add all dressing ingredients and beat till well combined.
Pour dressing over salad and toss to coat well.
Top with pecans and serve.

APPLE & SCALLION SALAD

Time: 15 minutes   Servings: 4

Ingredients:

For Salad:

4 medium Pink Lady apples, spiralized with Blade C
½ cup scallion, chopped finely
½ cup Parmesan cheese, shredded

For Dressing:

1 small garlic clove, minced
1 tablespoon extra-virgin olive oil
2 tablespoons fresh lemon juice
1 teaspoon Dijon mustard
Salt and freshly ground black pepper, to taste

Directions:

In a large serving bowl, add all salad ingredients.
In another bowl, add all dressing ingredients and beat till well combined.
Pour dressing over salad and toss to coat well.
Serve immediately.

APPLE & BASIL SALAD

Time: 20 minutes   Servings: 2

Ingredients:

For Salad:

2 medium Fuji apples, spiralized with Blade C
1 tablespoon fresh basil, julienned
2 tablespoons walnuts, toasted and chopped

For Dressing:

1 tablespoon shallot, minced
3 tablespoons walnut oil
1 tablespoon apple cider vinegar
Salt and freshly ground black pepper, to taste

Directions:

In a large serving bowl, add all salad ingredients.
In another bowl, add all dressing ingredients and beat till well combined.
Pour dressing over salad and toss to coat well.
Serve immediately.

APPLE & GREENS SALAD

Time: 20 minutes   Servings: 6

Ingredients:

1 large bunch fresh kale, trimmed and
  chopped
Salt, to taste
1 medium apple, spiralized with Blade C
1 medium cucumber, spiralized with Blade C
4 cups fresh baby spinach

2 tablespoons olive oil
1 tablespoon apple cider vinegar
1 tablespoon mustard
2 tablespoons fresh apple juice
½ cup almonds, chopped

Directions:

In a medium bowl, add the kale and salt and with your hands, massage till leaves become tender.
In a large serving bowl, mix together kale, apple, cucumber and spinach.
In another bowl, add remaining ingredients except almonds and beat till well combined.
Pour dressing over salad and toss to coat well.
Serve immediately with the topping of almonds.

APPLE & PEAR SALAD

Time: 20 minutes   Servings: 6

Ingredients:

For Salad:

1 large, honey crisp apple, spiralized with
  Blade C
1 large Asian pear, spiralized with Blade C
1 large Bartlet pear, spiralized with Blade C
1 teaspoons fresh lemon juice
1 cup pomegranate arils
1 cup seedless red grapes, halved
1 tablespoons fresh mint leaves, minced
½ cup walnuts, chopped

For Dressing:

1/3 cup grape seed Oil
1/3 cup apple cider vinegar
2 tablespoons honey
½ teaspoon dry mustard
1 tablespoon poppy seeds
Salt and freshly ground black pepper, to taste

Directions:

In a large serving bowl, add apple and pears and drizzle with lemon juice.
Add remaining salad ingredients and toss to coat.
Pour dressing over salad and gently toss to coat.
Cover the bowl and refrigerate to chill before serving.

Pear & Spinach Salad

Time: 20 minutes   Servings: 3

Ingredients:

For Salad:

2 Bosc pears, spiralized with Blade C
5 cups fresh baby spinach
¾ cup walnuts, chopped
½ cup blue cheese, crumbled

For Dressing:

¼ cup plain Greek yogurt
3 tablespoons balsamic vinegar
1 tablespoon honey
1 teaspoon Dijon mustard
Salt and freshly ground black pepper, to taste

Directions:

In a large bowl, place all salad ingredients.
In another bowl, add all dressing ingredients and beat till well combined.
Pour dressing over salad and gently toss to coat.
Serve immediately.

Pear & Brussels Sprout Salad

Time: 20 minutes   Servings: 4

Ingredients:

For Salad:

2 Anjou pears, spiralized with Blade C
2 cups Brussels sprout, trimmed and sliced thinly
2 cups fresh kale, trimmed and chopped finely
½ cup almonds, chopped

For Dressing:

1 tablespoon shallot, minced
2 tablespoons apple cider vinegar
2 tablespoons extra-virgin olive oil
1 tablespoon pure maple syrup
1 teaspoons Dijon mustard
Salt and freshly ground black pepper, to taste

Directions:

In a large serving bowl, add all salad ingredients except walnuts and mix.
In another bowl, add all dressing ingredients and beat till well combined.
Pour dressing over salad and toss to coat well.
Top with walnuts and serve.

Cucumber Salad with Yogurt

Time: 10 minutes   Servings: 2

Ingredients:

½ cup plain Greek yogurt
1 tablespoon fresh lemon juice
2 garlic cloves, minced

1 tablespoon fresh dill, minced
Salt, to taste
2 medium cucumbers, spiralized with Blade C

Directions:

In a large serving bowl, add all ingredients except cucumbers and beat till well combined.
Add carrots and gently toss to coat well.

Cucumber & Melon Salad

Time: 15 minutes   Servings: 4

Ingredients:

For Salad:

1 large cucumber, spiralized with Blade C
1 cup avocado, peeled, pitted and cubed
2 cups honeydew melon, peeled, seeded
   and cubed
½ cup feta cheese, crumbled

For Vinaigrette:

1 tablespoon fresh mint leaves, minced
2 teaspoons pure maple syrup
1½ tablespoons balsamic vinegar
1 tablespoon extra-virgin olive oil
2 teaspoons fresh lemon juice
Salt and freshly ground black pepper, to taste

Directions:

In a large serving bowl, add all salad ingredients and mix.
In another bowl, add all dressing ingredients and beat till well combined.
Pour dressing over salad and toss to coat well.
Serve immediately.

Cucumber & Watermelon Salad

Time: 15 minutes   Servings: 6

Ingredients:

2 cucumbers, peeled and spiralized with
   Blade C
6 cups seedless watermelon, cubed
1 large red onion, chopped

1 cup feta cheese, crumbled
3 tablespoons balsamic vinegar
1 teaspoon honey

Directions:

In a large bowl, add all ingredients and toss to coat well.
Serve immediately.

Cucumber & Strawberry Salad

Time: 15 minutes

Servings: 2

Ingredients:

For Salad:

2 large cucumbers, spiralized with Blade C
2 cups fresh strawberries, hulled and sliced
4 cups fresh lettuce leaves, torn
½ cup feta cheese, crumbled

For Dressing:

1 tablespoon fresh chives, minced
1 tablespoon fresh mint leaves, minced
1 tablespoon apple cider vinegar
2 tablespoons extra-virgin olive oil
Pinch of salt
Pinch of red pepper flakes, crushed

Directions:

In a large serving bowl, add all salad ingredients except cheese and mix.
In another bowl, add all dressing ingredients and beat till well combined.
Pour dressing over salad and toss to coat well.
Top with cheese and serve.

Cucumber & Egg Salad

Time: 25 minutes

Servings: 2

Ingredients:

For Dressing:

1 garlic clove, minced
2/3 cup plain yogurt
½ tablespoon Dijon mustard
Salt and freshly ground black pepper, to taste

For Salad:

2 medium cucumbers, spiralized with Blade C
2 large hard boiled eggs, peeled and chopped
½ cup celery, chopped
1 tablespoon almonds, toasted and chopped

Directions:

In a bowl, add all dressing ingredients and beat till well combined.
In a large serving bowl, mix together cucumber, eggs and celery.
Pour dressing over salad and toss to coat well.
Top with almonds and serve.

Cucumber & Tomato Salad

Time: 20 minutes

Servings: 2

Ingredients:

2 small cucumbers, peeled and spiralized
   with Blade C
1 cup cherry tomatoes, halved

½ cup red onion, chopped
¼ cup black olives, pitted and halved
2 cups fresh baby greens

1 tablespoon extra-virgin olive oil
1 tablespoon fresh lime juice

Salt and freshly ground black pepper, to taste
¼ cup walnuts, chopped

Directions:

In a large serving bowl, add all ingredients except walnuts and toss to coat well.
Top with walnuts and serve.

CUCUMBER & GREENS SALAD

Time: 15 minutes

Servings: 2

Ingredients:

1 large cucumber, peeled and spiralized
  with Blade C
1 cup fresh baby greens, trimmed and torn
¼ cup fresh mint leaves, chopped

2 teaspoons balsamic vinegar
1 tablespoon extra-virgin olive oil
Salt and freshly ground black pepper, to taste
¼ cup pecans, chopped

Directions:

In a large serving bowl, add all ingredients except pecans and toss to coat well.
Top with pecans and serve.

CUCUMBER & RADISH SALAD

Time: 15 minutes

Servings: 4

Ingredients:

10 small radishes, trimmed and spiralized
  with Blade C
2 medium cucumbers, peeled and spiralized
  with Blade C

½ cup white vinegar
2 teaspoons white sugar
1 teaspoon mustard seeds
Salt and freshly ground black pepper, to taste

Directions:

In a large bowl, place cucumbers and radishes.
In another small bowl, add remaining ingredients and beat till well combined.
Pour vinaigrette over the salad and toss to coat.
Serve immediately!

CUCUMBER & ASPARAGUS SALAD

Time: 25 minutes

Servings: 2

Ingredients:

1 bunch asparagus, trimmed and cut into
2-inch slices
1 cup fresh spinach, torn

2 cucumbers, peeled and spiralized with
  Blade C
1 teaspoon fresh ginger, grated
2 scallions, chopped

2 tablespoons extra virgin olive oil
1½ tablespoons tamari
1/8 teaspoon cayenne pepper

Salt and freshly ground black pepper, to taste
2 tablespoons sesame seeds, toasted

Directions:

In a pan of salted boiling water, add asparagus and spinach and cook for about 2-3 minutes.

Drain and immediately place into a bowl of ice water. Drain well.

In a large serving bowl, place asparagus, spinach and cucumbers.

In another bowl, add remaining ingredients except sesame seeds and beat till well combined.

Pour ginger mixture over veggies and toss to coat well.

Top with sesame seeds and serve immediately.

CUCUMBER & VEGGIE SALAD

Time: 20 minutes

Servings: 2

Ingredients:

1 medium cucumber, peeled and spiralized with Blade C
¼ cup cherry tomatoes, halved
¼ cup black olives, pitted and halved
¼ cup orange bell pepper, seeded and chopped

2 tablespoons red onion, chopped
½ teaspoon fresh parsley, minced
½ tablespoon extra-virgin olive oil
2 tablespoons fresh lemon juice
Salt and freshly ground black pepper, to taste
1-ounce feta cheese, crumbled

Directions:

In a large serving bowl, add all ingredients except cheese and toss to coat well.

Top with cheese and serve immediately.

CUCUMBER & CARROT SALAD

Time: 25 minutes

Servings: 2

Ingredients:

For Salad:

½ cup cucumber, peeled and spiralized with Blade C
½ cup carrot, peeled and spiralized with Blade C
1 cup fresh spinach, torn
¼ cup red onion, chopped

For Dressing:

¼ cup creamy peanut butter
¼ cup warm water
1 tablespoon honey
½ tablespoon soy sauce½ teaspoon fresh ginger, minced
1 garlic clove, minced
Pinch of red pepper flakes, crushed

Directions:

In a large bowl, add all salad ingredients and mix.

In another bowl, add all dressing ingredients and beat till well combined.

Pour dressing over salad and toss to coat well. Serve immediately.

Cucumber, Onion & Pimentos Salad

Time: 20 minutes   Servings: 4

Ingredients:
6 medium cucumbers, peeled and spiralized with Blade C
1 medium sweet onion, peeled and spiralized with Blade C
1 (4-ounce) jar diced pimientos, drained
1 cup sugar
1 cup white vinegar
1 cup water
Salt and freshly ground black pepper, to taste
1 tablespoon fresh dill, minced

Directions:
In a large bowl, mix together cucumbers, onion and pimentos.
In another bowl, add remaining ingredients and beat till sugar is dissolved.
Pour dressing over salad and toss to coat well.
Serve immediately.

Cucumber & Onion Salad

Time: 20 minutes   Servings: 4

Ingredients:
3 large cucumbers, peeled and spiralized with Blade C
1 red onion, sliced thinly
¼ cup fresh lemon juice
2 tablespoons Filtered Water
2 teaspoons Raw Honey
Salt and freshly ground black pepper, to taste
2 teaspoons sesame seeds

Directions:
In a large serving bowl, place cucumbers noodles and onion.
In another bowl, add remaining ingredients except sesame seeds and beat till well combined.
Pour honey mixture over veggies and toss to coat well.
Cover and refrigerate to chill completely.
Top with sesame seeds and serve.

Cucumber Salad in Creamy Tomato Sauce

Time: 20 minutes   Servings: 2

Ingredients:
2 large cucumber, peeled and spiralized with Blade C
1 ripe avocado, peeled, pitted and sliced with Blade C
2 garlic cloves, minced
1 plum tomato, chopped
1 tablespoon scallion, chopped
1 tablespoon fresh lemon juice
Salt and freshly ground black pepper, to taste

Directions:

In a large serving bowl, place the cucumbers.

In a food processor, add remaining ingredients and pulse till smooth.

Pour avocado mixture over cucumbers and toss to coat well.

Serve immediately.

CUCUMBER & BEET SALAD IN AVOCADO SAUCE

Time: 20 minutes   Servings: 2

Ingredients:

2 medium beets, peeled and spiralized with Blade C

1 large cucumber, peeled and spiralized with Blade C

1 ripe avocado, peeled, pitted and chopped

2 garlic cloves, minced

¼ cup hemp seeds

1 tablespoon tamari

1 tablespoon walnut oil

2 tablespoons fresh lemon juice

1/8 teaspoon cayenne pepper

Salt and freshly ground black pepper, to taste

Directions:

In a large serving bowl, place the beets and cucumbers.

In a food processor, add remaining ingredients and pulse till smooth.

Pour avocado mixture over vegetables and toss to coat well.

Serve immediately.

CARROT & ONION SALAD

Time: 15 minutes   Servings: 2

Ingredients:

For Salad:

3 large carrots, peeled and spiralized with Blade C

1 onion, peeled and spiralized with Blade C

For Dressing:

1 cup fresh cilantro leaves, chopped finely

2 tablespoons fresh lemon juice

2 teaspoons pure maple syrup

1 teaspoon extra virgin olive oil

Salt, to taste

Directions:

In a large serving bowl, mix carrot and onion.

In another bowl, add all dressing ingredients and beat till well combined.

Pour dressing over salad and toss to coat well.

Serve immediately.

CARROT & BROCCOLI SALAD

Time: 20 minutes   Servings: 2

Ingredients:

1 small had broccoli with stem
2 medium carrots, peeled and spiralized
   with Blade C
¼ cup red onion, chopped
3 hard-boiled eggs, chopped
¼ cup fresh basil, chopped
1 garlic clove, minced

½ teaspoon lime zest, grated freshly
2 tablespoons extra virgin olive oil
1 tablespoon fresh lime juice
Water, as required
Salt and freshly ground black pepper, to taste
2 tablespoons pumpkin seeds, roasted

Directions:

Cut the broccoli florets into bite size pieces. Spiralized the stem with Blade C. Transfer the chopped broccoli florets and spiralized stem into a large serving bowl. Add the carrot, onion and egg into the bowl with broccoli and mix. In a food processor, add remaining ingredients except pumpkin seeds and pulse till well combined. Pour mixture over vegetables and gently, toss to coat. Garnish with pumpkin seeds and serve.

CARROT SALAD IN BASIL SAUCE

Time: 15 minutes   Servings: 2

Ingredients:

2 large carrots, peeled and spiralized with
   Blade C
1 green bell pepper, seeded and chopped
1 teaspoon fresh ginger, grated
1 garlic clove, minced

½ cup fresh cilantro leaves, chopped
2 tablespoons extra virgin olive oil
1 tablespoon fresh lemon juice
1 teaspoon tamari
2 tablespoons sesame seeds

Directions:

In a large bowl, add the carrots and bell pepper. In a food processor, add remaining ingredients except sesame seeds and pulse till smooth. Pour the dressing over carrots and toss to coat well. Top with sesame seeds and serve.

ZUCCHINI SALAD WITH MIXED VEGGIES & FRUIT

Time: 25 minutes   Servings: 4

Ingredients:

2 medium zucchinis, spiralized with Blade C
1 small apple, cored and chopped
1 small pear, cored and chopped
1 small orange bell pepper, seeded and
   sliced thinly
1 small red onion, chopped

1 small avocado, peeled, pitted and cubed
2 tablespoons fresh cilantro leaves, chopped
2 tablespoons fresh mint leaves, chopped
Salt and freshly ground black pepper, to taste
2 tablespoons fresh lemon juice

Directions:

In a large serving bowl, mix together all ingredients and toss to coat well.
Serve immediately.

Zucchini & Carrot Salad

Time: 15 minutes   Servings: 2

Ingredients:

For Salad:

- 1 medium zucchini, spiralized with Blade C
- 1 small carrot, peeled and spiralized with Blade C
- ¼ cup cherry tomatoes, halved
- ½ cup cooked chickpeas

For Dressing:

- ¼ cup mayonnaise
- 2 tablespoons maple syrup
- 1 tablespoon fresh lime juice
- 1 teaspoon extra virgin olive oil
- 2 teaspoons fresh parsley, minced
- Salt and freshly ground black pepper, to taste

Directions:

In a large serving bowl, add all salad ingredients and mix.
In another bowl, add all dressing ingredients and beat till well combined.
Pour dressing over salad and toss to coat well.
Serve immediately.

Zucchini, Squash & Cucumber Salad

Time: 20 minutes   Servings: 4

Ingredients:

For Salad:

- 1 summer squash, spiralized with Blade C
- 1 medium zucchini, spiralized with Blade C
- 1 cucumber, spiralized with Blade C
- 2 celery stock, chopped
- 1 small red onion, chopped
- ½ cup fresh cherries, pitted
- ½ cup fresh strawberries, hulled and chopped
- 2 cups fresh baby greens
- 2 tablespoons pecans, toasted and chopped

For Dressing:

- 2 tablespoons extra virgin olive oil
- 1 tablespoon fresh lime juice
- Salt and freshly ground black pepper, to taste

Directions:

In a large serving bowl, mix together all vegetables and fruit except pecans.
In another bowl, add all dressing ingredients and beat till well combined.
Pour dressing over salad and gently toss to coat.
Garnish with pecans and serve.

Zucchini & Cucumber Salad

Time: 20 minutes   Servings: 2

Ingredients:

1 medium cucumber, spiralized with Blade C
1 medium zucchini, spiralized with Blade C
½ cup red onion, chopped
3 tablespoons fresh lemon juice

1 teaspoon honey
Salt and freshly ground black pepper, to taste
1 tablespoon sesame seeds

Directions:

In a large bowl, mix together cucumber, zucchini and onion.

In another bowl, add remaining ingredients and beat till well combined.

Pour dressing over salad and gently toss to coat.

Cover and refrigerate to chill completely.

Top with sesame seeds before serving.

Zucchini & Olives Salad

Time: 20 minutes   Servings: 4

Ingredients:

4 zucchinis, spiralized
1 cup fresh baby greens
2 tablespoons black olives, pitted and halved
2 tablespoons green olives, pitted and halved
1 garlic clove, minced

½ teaspoon fresh lemon zest, grated finely
2 tablespoons fresh lemon juice
2 tablespoons extra-virgin olive oil
Salt and freshly ground black pepper, to taste
¼ cup almonds, chopped

Directions:

In a large serving bowl, mix together zucchini, greens and olives.

In another bowl, add remaining ingredients except almonds and beat till well combined.

Pour lemon mixture over veggies and toss to coat well.

Top with almonds and serve immediately

Zucchini & Berries Salad

Time: 25 minutes   Servings: 4

Ingredients:

1 large zucchini, spiralized with Blade C
1 large carrot, peeled and spiralized with Blade C
½ cup fresh strawberries, hulled and sliced
¼ cup fresh raspberries
¼ cup fresh blueberries

¼ cup fresh blackberries
2 cups fresh baby spinach
½ cup golden raisins
½ cup almonds, toasted and chopped
1 tablespoon extra-virgin olive oil
2 tablespoons fresh lime juice

Salt and freshly ground black pepper, to taste ¼ cup fresh mint leaves, chopped

Directions:

In a large serving bowl, add all ingredients except mint and toss to coat well.
Garnish with mint and serve immediately.

ZUCCHINI, PEAR & POMEGRANATE SALAD

Time: 15 minutes   Servings: 2

Ingredients:

For Salad:

2 medium zucchinis, spiralized with Blade C
1 large pear, cored and chopped
3 tablespoons fresh pomegranate arils
2 tablespoons fresh mint leaves, chopped
2 tablespoons walnuts, chopped

For Dressing:

¼ cup fresh pomegranate juice
1 teaspoon honey
2 tablespoons fresh lemon juice
1 tablespoon extra-virgin olive oil
Salt and freshly ground black pepper, to taste

Directions:

In a large serving bowl, mix together zucchini, pear and pomegranate seeds.
In another bowl, add all dressing ingredients and mix till well combined.
Pour dressing over salad and toss to coat well.
Garnish with mint and walnuts and serve immediately.

ZUCCHINI & CRANBERRY SALAD

Time: 15 minutes   Servings: 2

Ingredients:

For Salad:

2 medium zucchinis, spiralized with Blade C
4 cups romaine lettuce, torn
½ cup fresh cranberries
1 tablespoon fresh mint leaves, chopped
¼ cup walnuts, toasted and chopped

For Dressing:

1 tablespoon extra-virgin olive oil
1 tablespoon fresh lime juice
½ tablespoon honey
Salt and freshly ground black pepper, to taste

Directions:

In a large serving bowl, mix together all salad ingredients except walnuts.
In another bowl, add all dressing ingredients and beat till well combined.
Pour dressing over salad and gently toss to coat well.
Garnish with walnuts and serve immediately.

ZUCCHINI & CARROT SALAD IN PESTO SAUCE

Time: 15 minutes   Servings: 4

Ingredients:

For Salad:

2 large zucchinis, spiralized with Blade C
2 large carrots, peeled and spiralized with
   Blade C

For Pesto:

3 cups fresh spinach
4 garlic cloves, minced
¼ cup raw pumpkin seeds
3 tablespoons extra-virgin olive oil
Salt, to taste

Directions:

In a large serving bowl, mix together zucchini and carrot.
In a blender, add all pesto ingredients and pulse till smooth.
Pour pesto over salad and toss to coat well.
Serve immediately.

ZUCCHINI SALAD IN VEGGIE SAUCE

Time: 15 minutes   Servings: 2

Ingredients:

1 cup plum tomatoes, chopped
2 small red bell pepper, seeded and
   chopped
¼ cup fresh basil leaves, chopped
1 tablespoon extra-virgin olive oil

2 teaspoons fresh lemon juice
½ teaspoon honey
Salt and freshly ground black pepper, to taste
1 large zucchini, spiralized with Blade C

Directions:

In a blender, add all ingredients except zucchini and pulse till smooth.
In a large serving bowl, place zucchini.
Add sauce and mix well.
Serve immediately.

ZUCCHINI SALAD IN MANGO SAUCE

Time: 15 minutes   Servings: 4

Ingredients:

1 cup fresh mango, peeled, pitted and
   cubed
½ cup almond butter
1 teaspoon honey

2 teaspoons fresh lemon juice
2 large zucchinis, spiralized with Blade C
¼ cup almonds, chopped

Directions:

In a blender, add mango, butter, honey and lemon juice and pulse till smooth.

In a large serving bowl, place zucchini.

Add mango sauce and mix well.

Top with almonds and serve immediately.

Zucchini Salad in Spicy Butter Sauce

Time: 15 minutes   Servings: 2

Ingredients:

- 1 medium zucchini, spiralized with Blade C
- 1 medium yellow squash, spiralized with Blade C
- 1 small red bell pepper, seeded and sliced thinly
- 1 garlic clove, minced
- ½ teaspoon fresh ginger, minced
- 2 tablespoons almond butter
- ½ tablespoon soy sauce
- 1 tablespoon fresh lime juice
- ½ tablespoon Filtered Water
- ¼ teaspoon red chili powder
- Salt and freshly ground black pepper, to taste
- 1 tablespoon sesame seeds, toasted

Directions:

In a lag serving bowl, mix together zucchini, yellow squash and bell pepper.

In another small bowl, add remaining ingredients except sesame seeds and beat till well combined.

Pour sauce over vegetables and mix well.

Top with sesame seeds and serve immediately.

Zucchini & Broccoli Salad in Kale Sauce

Time: 20 minutes   Servings: 4

Ingredients:

- 3-4 zucchinis, spiralized with Blade C
- 2 garlic cloves, minced
- ½ cup broccoli florets, chopped
- 2 cups fresh kale, trimmed and torn
- ½ cup fresh cilantro leaves, chopped
- 2 tablespoons fresh lemon juice
- Salt and freshly ground black pepper, to taste

Directions:

In a large serving bowl, place the zucchini.

In a food processor, add remaining ingredients and pulse till smooth.

Pour kale mixture over zucchini and toss to coat well.

Serve immediately.

ZUCCHINI & CUCUMBER SALAD IN SWEET & SPICY SAUCE

Time: 20 minutes

Servings: 2

Ingredients:

1 zucchini, peeled and spiralized with Blade C
1 cucumber, peeled and spiralized with Blade C
¼ cup almond butter
1 tablespoon fresh lemon juice
1 tablespoon honey

1 tablespoon tamari
2 tablespoons water
1/8 teaspoon cayenne pepper, crushed
Salt and freshly ground black pepper, to taste
2 tablespoons Almonds, chopped

Directions:

In a large colander, place the zucchini and cucumber.

Arrange colander over a large bowl and keep aside for at least 15-20 minutes.

Gently, squeeze the veggies and pat dry with a paper towel.

Transfer the veggies into a large serving bowl.

In another bowl, add remaining ingredients except almonds and beat till well combined.

Pour honey mixture over veggies and toss to coat well.

Top with almonds and serve immediately.

YELLOW SQUASH SALAD IN HERB SAUCE

Time: 15 minutes

Servings: 4

Ingredients:

1½ pound summer squash, spiralized
Salt, to taste
¼ cup coconut milk
2 tablespoons fresh lemon juice
2 tablespoons extra-virgin olive oil
1 garlic clove, minced

3 tablespoons fresh parsley leaves, chopped
3 tablespoons fresh basil leaves, chopped
3 tablespoons fresh tarragon leaves, chopped
Freshly ground black pepper, to taste
¼ cup walnuts, chopped

Directions:

In a large colander, place the squash noodles and sprinkle with salt.

Arrange colander over a large bowl and keep aside for at least 15-20 minutes.

Gently, squeeze the squash and pat dry with a paper towel.

Transfer the squash into a large serving bowl.

In a food processor, add remaining ingredients except walnuts and pulse till smooth. Pour herb mixture over squash and toss to coat well.

Top with walnuts and serve.

Yellow Squash & Tomato Salad in Basil Sauce

Time: 15 minutes   Servings: 4

Ingredients:

1 pound yellow squash, spiralized
1½ cups cherry tomatoes, halved
¼ cup coconut milk
2 tablespoons extra-virgin olive oil

1 garlic clove, minced
1 cup fresh basil leaves, chopped
Salt and freshly ground black pepper, to taste

Directions:

In a large serving bowl, place the squash and tomatoes.
In a food processor, add remaining ingredients and pulse till smooth.
Pour basil mixture over vegetables and toss to coat well.
Serve immediately.

Cabbage Salad

Time: 15 minutes   Servings: 4

Ingredients:

2½ cups green cabbage, spiralized with
    Blade C
2½ cups purple cabbage, spiralized with
    Blade C
2 large scallions, chopped
¼ cup fresh parsley, chopped

1 jalapeño pepper, seeded and chopped
    finely
2 tablespoons fresh lemon juice
2 tablespoons extra-virgin olive oil
Salt, to taste
1 teaspoon fresh lemon zest, grated finely

Directions:

In a large serving bowl, add all ingredients except lemon zest and toss to coat well.
Top with lemon zest and serve.

Cabbage & Carrot Salad

Time: 15 minutes   Servings: 2

Ingredients:

For Salad:

1 large carrot, peeled and spiralized with
    Blade C
1 cup purple cabbage, spiralized with Blade C
2 cups fresh baby kale, trimmed
2 tablespoons red onion, chopped
2 tablespoons fresh mint leaves, chopped

For Dressing:

1 tablespoon extra-virgin olive oil
1 teaspoon apple cider vinegar
2 tablespoons sunflower seeds
Salt and freshly ground black pepper, to taste

Directions:

In a large serving bowl, add all salad ingredients and mix. In another bowl, add all dressing ingredients and beat till well combined. Pour dressing over salad and toss to coat well. Serve immediately.

Beet Salad

Time: 10 minutes   Servings: 2

Ingredients:

For Salad:

2 medium beets, trimmed, peeled and spiralized with Blade C
2 tablespoons feta cheese, crumbled

For Dressing:

2 tablespoons fresh orange juice
1 tablespoon extra-virgin olive oil
1 tablespoon balsamic vinegar

½ tablespoon honey
Salt and freshly ground black pepper, to taste

Directions:

In a large bowl, place the beets.
In another bowl, add all dressing ingredients and beat till well combined.
Pour dressing over salad and toss to coat well.
Serve immediately with the topping of feta cheese.

Beet & Avocado Salad

Time: 15 minutes   Servings: 2

Ingredients:

For Salad:

2 medium beets, trimmed, peeled and spiralized with Blade C
1 small avocado, peeled, pitted and chopped
1 tablespoon sesame seeds

For Dressing:

1 teaspoon fresh ginger, minced
1 garlic clove, minced
2 tablespoons fresh cilantro, minced
¼ cup fresh lemon juice

3 tablespoons extra-virgin olive oil
2 teaspoons soy sauce
2 drops liquid stevia

Directions:

In a large serving bowl, add beets and avocado.
In another bowl, add all dressing ingredients and beat till well combined.
Pour dressing over salad and toss to coat well.
Serve immediately with a topping of sesame seeds.

BEET & CARROT SALAD

Time: 25 minutes   Servings: 4

Ingredients:

- 2 large carrots, peeled and spiralized with Blade C
- 2 small red beets, trimmed, peeled and spiralized with Blade C
- 2 small yellow beets, trimmed, peeled and spiralized with Blade C
- ½ cup walnuts, chopped and divided
- 2 garlic cloves, minced
- ¼ cup fresh parsley leaves, chopped
- ¼ cup fresh basil leaves, chopped
- ½ cup walnut Oil
- Salt and freshly ground black pepper, to taste

Directions:

In a large bowl, mix together carrots and beets.

In a food processor, add ¼ cup walnuts and remaining ingredients and pulse till smooth.

Pour herb mixture over vegetables and toss to coat well.

Top with remaining walnuts and serve immediately.

BEET & SWEET POTATO SALAD

Time: 15 minutes   Servings: 4

Ingredients:

For Salad:

- 4 beets, trimmed, peeled and spiralized with Blade C
- 2 large sweet potatoes, peeled and spiralized with Blade C
- 4 scallions, chopped
- ½ cup pumpkin seeds, toasted

For Dressing:

- ½ teaspoon fresh lime zest, grated finely
- 1 garlic clove, minced
- 2 tablespoons fresh lime juice
- 1 teaspoon heavy cream
- 1 teaspoon honey
- Salt and freshly ground black pepper, to taste

Directions:

In a large bowl, mix together beets, sweet potatoes and scallions.

In another bowl, add all dressing ingredients and beat till well combined.

Pour dressing over salad and toss to coat well.

Serve immediately with a topping of pumpkin seeds.

Beet & Cashew Salad

Time: 15 minutes   Servings: 2

Ingredients:

For Salad:

2 large beets, trimmed, peeled and
    spiralized with Blade C
¼ cup fresh mint leaves, chopped
¼ cup feta cheese, crumbled
¼ cup cashews, chopped

For Dressing:

2 tablespoons balsamic vinegar
2 tablespoons extra-virgin olive oil
1 teaspoon honey
2 teaspoons Dijon mustard
Salt, to taste
Pinch of red pepper flakes, crushed

Directions:

In a large serving bowl, add all salad ingredients and mix. In another bowl, add all dressing ingredients and beat till well combined. Pour dressing over salad and toss to coat well. Serve immediately.

Beet & Pomegranate Salad

Time: 15 minutes   Servings: 2

Ingredients:

For Salad:

2 large golden beets, trimmed, peeled and
    spiralized with Blade C
¼ cup fresh pomegranate arils
2 tablespoons pumpkin seeds
¼ cup feta cheese crumbled

For Dressing:

2 tablespoons extra-virgin olive oil
1 tablespoon balsamic vinegar
1 teaspoon maple syrup
1 teaspoon Dijon mustard
Salt and freshly ground black pepper, to taste

Directions:

In a large serving bowl, add all salad ingredients and mix. In another bowl, add all dressing ingredients and beat till well combined. Pour dressing over salad and toss to coat well. Serve immediately.

Beet & Cherry Salad

Time: 20 minutes   Servings: 2

Ingredients:

For Salad:

2 medium golden beets, trimmed, peeled and spiralized with Blade C
½ pound fresh cherries, pitted and halved
2 cups fresh baby kale
¼ cup pecans, chopped
¼ goat cheese, crumbled

For Dressing:

2 teaspoons shallots, minced

¼ cup extra-virgin olive oil

2 tablespoons fresh lemon juice

2 teaspoons honey

2 teaspoons Dijon mustard

Salt and freshly ground black pepper, to taste

Directions:

In a large serving bowl, add all salad ingredients and mix.

In another bowl, add all dressing ingredients and beat till well combined.

Pour dressing over salad and toss to coat well.

Serve immediately.

Beet & Orange Salad

Time: 15 minutes   Servings: 2

Ingredients:

2 medium golden beets, trimmed, peeled and spiralized with Blade C

2 tablespoons red wine vinegar

1½ tablespoons olive oil

8-ounce canned mandarin oranges, drained, reserving 2 tablespoons of juice

1 tablespoon fresh mint leaves, chopped

Directions:

In a large bowl, place the beets.

In another bowl, add vinegar, oil and reserved orange juice and mix well.

Pour juice mixture over beet and toss to coat well and keep aside for about 15 minutes.

Top with orange and mint and serve.

Beet & Mango Salad

Time: 15 minutes   Servings: 2

Ingredients:

1 large golden beet, trimmed, peeled and spiralized with Blade C

1 mango, peeled, pitted and cubed

½ cup yellow bell pepper, seeded and sliced

1 teaspoon fresh lemon zest, grated finely

2 tablespoons sunflower seed butter

½ tablespoon fresh lemon juice

¼ teaspoon onion powder

Pinch of red pepper flakes, crushed

Pinch of powdered stevia

2 tablespoons sunflower seeds, toasted

Directions:

In a large serving bowl, add all ingredients except sunflower seeds and mix.

Serve immediately with the topping of sunflower seeds.

ZUCCHINI & CORN SALAD

Time: 35 minutes   Servings: 6

Ingredients:

For Salad:

3 ears of corn
1 teaspoon olive oil
Salt and freshly ground black pepper, to taste
2 large zucchinis, spiralized with Blade C
1 medium red onion, chopped

For Dressing:

1 teaspoon fresh lemon zest, grated finely
2 tablespoons extra-virgin olive oil
1 tablespoon balsamic vinegar
1 teaspoon honey
1 teaspoon garlic powder
½ teaspoon chili powder
Salt and freshly ground black pepper, to taste

Directions:

Preheat the grill to medium heat.
Grease the grill grate.
Drizzle the corn ears with olive oil and sprinkle with salt and black pepper.
Grill for about 15-20 minutes, flipping after every 5 minutes.
Remove from grill and keep aside to cool slightly.
Cut the kernels off.
In a large bowl, mix together zucchini, corn and onion.
In another bowl, add all dressing ingredients and beat till well combined.
Pour dressing over salad and toss to coat well.
Serve immediately.

ZUCCHINI & KIDNEY BEANS SALAD

Time: 15 minutes   Servings: 2

Ingredients:

For Salad:

2 medium zucchinis, spiralized with Blade C
1 medium avocado, peeled, pitted and cubed
½ cup red kidney beans

1 tablespoon scallion, chopped
1 tablespoon fresh cilantro leaves, chopped
1 tablespoon extra-virgin olive oil
1 tablespoon fresh lemon juice
Salt and freshly ground black pepper, to taste

Directions:

In a large serving bowl, add all ingredients and gently toss to coat well.
Serve immediately.

CARROT, ZUCCHINI & CHICKPEAS SALAD

Time: 25 minutes   Servings: 3

Ingredients:

1 large orange carrot, peeled and spiralized with Blade C
1 large red carrot, peeled and spiralized with Blade C
2 medium zucchinis, peeled and spiralized with Blade C

¼ cup fresh basil leaves, chopped
1 cup cooked chickpeas
1 tablespoon olive oil
¼ teaspoon chili powder
¼ teaspoon ground cumin
Salt and freshly ground black pepper, to taste

Directions:

In a large bowl, add all ingredients and toss to coat well.
Serve immediately.

BEET, ZUCCHINI & CHICKPEAS SALAD

Time: 25 minutes   Servings: 4

Ingredients:

1 (15-ounce) can chickpeas, rinsed and drained
1 large zucchini, peeled and spiralized with Blade C
1 large beet, trimmed, peeled and spiralized with Blade C

¼ cup olive oil
¼ cup fresh lemon juice
Salt and freshly ground black pepper, to taste
4-ounce feta cheese, crumbled

Directions:

In a large bowl, add all ingredients except cheese and toss to coat well.
Serve immediately with the topping of feta cheese.

BEET & QUINOA SALAD

Time: 25 minutes   Servings: 4

Ingredients:

2 large beets, trimmed, peeled and spiralized with Blade C
1 cup cooked quinoa
3 cups fresh baby spinach

¼ cup feta cheese, crumbled
¼ cup pecans, toasted.
2 tablespoons apple cider vinegar
Salt and freshly ground black pepper, to taste

Directions:

In a large bowl, add all ingredients and toss to coat well.
Serve immediately.

Zucchini & Quinoa Salad

Time: 25 minutes

Servings: 3

Ingredients:

2 zucchinis, peeled and spiralized with
  Blade C
½ cup prepared pesto

2 sundried tomatoes, chopped
1/3 cup cooked quinoa
2 tablespoons pine nuts

Directions:

In a bowl, add all ingredients except pine nuts and mix till well combined.
Top with pine nuts and serve.

Beet & Bacon Salad

Time: 25 minutes

Servings: 2

Ingredients:

For Salad:

2 thick bacon slices
1 large beet, trimmed, peeled and
  spiralized with Blade C
¼ cup scallion, chopped
2 tablespoons goat cheese, crumbled

For Dressing:

1 cup fresh parsley, minced
2 tablespoons fresh lemon juice
2 tablespoons avocado oil
2 teaspoons coconut sugar
Salt and freshly ground black pepper, to taste

Directions:

Heat a nonstick frying pan on medium-high heat.
Add bacon and cook for about 8-10 minutes or till crisp.
Transfer the bacon onto a paper towel lined plate to drain.
Now, chop the bacon slices
In a large serving bowl, add beet and scallion.
In another bowl, add all dressing ingredients and beat till well combined.
Pour dressing over salad and toss to coat well.
Top with the bacon and cheese and serve immediately.

Zucchini & Chicken Salad

Time: 40 minutes

Servings: 4

Ingredients:

For Salad:

2 garlic cloves, minced
2 tablespoons extra virgin coconut oil, melted
½ tablespoon soy sauce

1 tablespoon fresh lime Juice
Salt and freshly ground black pepper, to taste
2 (6-ounce) skinless, boneless chicken
  breasts, cubed

2 medium zucchinis, spiralized with Blade C
5-6 cups fresh baby greens
½ cup pecans, toasted and chopped

For Dressing:

2 tablespoons shallot, minced
1 tablespoon capers, chopped finely
1 garlic clove, minced

1 jalapeño pepper, seeded and minced
2 tablespoons fresh cilantro leaves, minced
1 teaspoon lime zest, grated freshly
¼ cup extra virgin olive oil
2 teaspoons coconut vinegar
2 tablespoons fresh lime juice
Salt and freshly ground black pepper, to taste

Directions:

Preheat the oven to 350 degrees F. Line a baking sheet with a piece of foil.
In a large bowl, mix together garlic, oil, soy sauce, lime juice, salt and black pepper.
Add chicken cubes and coat with mixture generously. Keep aside for about 15-20 minutes.
Transfer the mixture into prepared baking sheet. Bake for about 15- 20 minutes.
Transfer the chicken cubes into a large serving bowl and keep aside to cool slightly.
Add zucchini and greens. In another bowl, add all dressing ingredients and beat till well combined.
Pour dressing over salad and toss to coat well.
Top with pecans and serve immediately.

ZUCCHINI, CARROT & CHICKEN SALAD

Time: 30 minutes

Servings: 2

Ingredients:

For Salad:

1 tablespoon extra-virgin coconut oil
1 (6-ounce) skinless, boneless chicken
   breast
Salt and freshly ground black pepper, to taste
1 large zucchini, spiralized with Blade C
1 large carrot, spiralized with Blade C
2 tablespoons fresh mint leaves, chopped
2 tablespoons cashews, chopped

For Dressing:

1 garlic clove, minced
½ teaspoon fresh ginger, minced
1 jalapeño pepper, seeded and minced
2 tablespoons coconut cream
1 tablespoon almond butter
½ tablespoon honey
1 tablespoon soy sauce
1 tablespoon fresh lemon juice
Salt and freshly ground black pepper, to taste

Directions:

In a skillet, heat oil on medium heat.
Add chicken and sprinkle with salt and black pepper.
Cook for about 4-5 minutes from both sides or till chicken is done completely.
Transfer the chicken into a large plate and keep aside to cool completely.
Then shred the chicken and transfer into a large serving bowl.
Add zucchini, carrot and mint.
In another bowl, add all dressing ingredients and mix till well combined.
Pour dressing over salad and gently, mix to coat.
Top with pistachios and serve.

Zucchini, Cucumber & Chicken Salad

Time: 40 minutes   Servings: 4

Ingredients:

For Chicken:

2 garlic cloves, minced
1 tablespoon fresh thyme, chopped
2 tablespoons olive oil
2 tablespoons soy sauce
Salt and freshly ground black pepper, to taste
2 skinless, boneless chicken thighs

For Salad:

½ cup cucumber, spiralized with Blade C
½ cup zucchini, spiralized with Blade C
2 cups fresh baby greens
2 tablespoons extra virgin olive oil
2 tablespoons fresh lemon juice
Salt and freshly ground black pepper, to taste
2 tablespoons scallion, chopped

Directions:

Preheat the oven broiler. Grease a baking dish. In a large bowl, add all chicken ingredients and toss to coat well. Transfer the chicken mixture into prepared baking dish. Broil for about 20 minutes. Meanwhile in a large serving bowl, add all salad I ingredients except scallion and toss to coat well. Transfer the salad into 2 serving plates. Top with chicken thighs. Garnish with scallion and serve.

Zucchini, Asparagus & Chicken Salad

Time: 40 minutes   Servings: 4

Ingredients:

For Salad:

1 teaspoon dried rosemary, crushed
½ teaspoon ground cumin
¼ teaspoon ground coriander
Salt and freshly ground black Pepper, to taste
2 (6-ounce) skinless, boneless chicken thighs
16 baby asparagus spears, trimmed
½ tablespoon extra-virgin olive oil
2 large zucchinis, spiralized with Blade C
½ cup cherry tomatoes, halved

For Dressing:

1 small avocado, peeled, pitted and chopped
½ small cucumber, peeled and chopped
1 garlic clove, chopped
¼ cup fresh basil leaves
2 tablespoons coconut milk
1 tablespoon fresh lemon juice
Salt and freshly ground black pepper, to taste

Directions:

Preheat the grill to medium-high. Grease the grill grate. In a bowl, mix together rosemary and all spices. Add chicken thighs and rub with spice mixture generously. Keep aside for about 10 minutes. Grill the thighs for about 4-5 minutes per side or till done completely. Remove from grill and keep side for 5 minutes. With a sharp knife, cut the chicken thighs in desired size slices. Transfer the chicken into a plate. Drizzle the asparagus with oil and sprinkle with salt and black pepper. Grill the asparagus for about 2 minutes. Now cut the asparagus in 2-ich pieces. Transfer the asparagus in a large serving bowl. Add zucchini in the bowl with asparagus. For dressing, in a food processor, add all ingredients and pulse till smooth.

Pour dressing over salad and mix well.

Top with chicken slices.

Garnish with cherry tomatoes and serve immediately.

Cucumber & Chicken Salad

Time: 20 minutes   Servings: 4

Ingredients:

2 cooked skinless, boneless chicken
   Breasts, cut into bite size pieces
3 large cucumbers, spiralized with Blade C
1 avocado, peeled, pitted and cubed
10-12 black olives, pitted and halved
2 tablespoons extra-virgin olive oil

2 tablespoons fresh lemon juice
1 small red onion, chopped
1 garlic clove, minced
3 tablespoons fresh parsley leaves, chopped
Salt and freshly ground black pepper, to taste
½ cup pecans, chopped

Directions:

In a large serving bowl, mix together chicken, cucumber, avocado and olives. In a food processor, add all remaining ingredients except pecans and pulse till well combined. Pour dressing over cucumber mixture and gently toss to coat. Top with pecans and serve.

Zucchini & Turkey Salad

Time: 25 minutes   Servings: 4

Ingredients:

For Turkey:

2 teaspoons olive oil
2 garlic cloves, minced
1 pound turkey tenderloin, trimmed and cut
   into thin strips
Salt and freshly ground black pepper, to taste

For Salad:

2 medium zucchinis, spiralized with Blade C
¾ cup black olives, pitted and halved

½ cup red bell pepper, seeded and sliced
   thinly

For Dressing:

2 garlic cloves, minced
1 teaspoon dried Basil, crushed
3 tablespoons extra virgin olive oil
2 tablespoons balsamic vinegar
2 tablespoons fresh lemon juice
Salt and freshly ground black pepper, to taste

Directions:

For Turkey in a large skillet, heat oil on medium-high heat. Add garlic and sauté for about 1 minute.

Add turkey and sprinkle with salt and black pepper. Stir fry for about 5-7 minutes.

Transfer turkey into a plate. For salad in a large serving bowl, mix together all ingredients.

Add turkey and mix well.

In another small bowl, add all dressing ingredients and beat till well combined.

Pour dressing over salad and toss to coat well. Serve immediately.

CARROT, CUCUMBER & STEAK SALAD

Time: 35 minutes

Servings: 4

Ingredients:

For Steak:

1/3 cup soy sauce
1 tablespoon fresh lemon juice
Salt and freshly ground black pepper, to taste
¾ pound sirloin steak, trimmed

For Salad:

3 zucchinis, spiralized with Blade C
1 medium carrot, peeled and spiralized with Blade C

1 cucumber, spiralized with Blade C
1 red bell pepper, seeded and sliced thinly
2 garlic cloves
¼ cup fresh cilantro leaves, minced
2 tablespoons fresh lemon juice
3 tablespoons extra virgin olive oil
Salt and freshly ground black pepper, to taste
1 teaspoon sesame seeds, toasted

Directions:

For steak in a large bowl, mix together all ingredients except steak. Add steak and coat with marinade generously. Refrigerate, covered for at least 6- 8 hours. Preheat the grill to medium-high heat. Grease the grill grate. Grill the steak for about 5-6 minutes per side. Remove from grill and transfer onto a cutting board. Keep aside for about 10 minutes. With a sharp knife slice the steak according to your choice. Meanwhile in a large serving bowl, mix together zucchini, carrot, cucumber and bell pepper. In another bowl, add remaining ingredients except sesame seeds and beat till well combined. Pour dressing over vegetables and gently, toss to coat. Top with steak slices. Garnish with sesame seeds and serve.

ZUCCHINI & STEAK SALAD

Time: 25 minutes

Servings: 4

Ingredients:

For Salad:

1 (1¼ pounds) flank steak, trimmed
1 tablespoon extra-virgin olive oil
Salt and freshly ground black pepper, to taste
2 large zucchinis, spiralized with Blade C
1 red bell pepper, seeded and sliced thinly
1 orange bell pepper, seeded and sliced thinly
4 radishes, julienned
2 cups romaine lettuce, torn

1 avocado, peeled, pitted and chopped

For Dressing:

1 cup fresh cilantro, chopped
1 cup fresh parsley, chopped
2 garlic cloves, minced
2 jalapeños, seeded and chopped
¼ cup extra-virgin olive oil
¼ cup fresh lemon juice
Salt and freshly ground black pepper, to taste

Directions:

Preheat the grill to high. Grease the grill grate. Drizzle the steak with oil and sprinkle with salt and black pepper. Keep aside for about 10-15 minutes. Grill the steak for about 4-5 minutes per side or till desired doneness. Transfer into a plate and keep aside for about 5 minutes before slicing.

With a sharp knife, cut the steak into thin slices, diagonally across the grain.

Transfer the steak into a large serving bowl. Add remaining salad ingredients except avocado and mix.

In a food processor, add all dressing ingredients and pulse till smooth.

Pour dressing over salad and toss to coat well.

Top with avocado and serve immediately.

Zucchini & Salmon Salad

Time: 30 minutes   Servings: 4

Ingredients:

For Salmon:

4 (4-ounce) salmon fillets
1 tablespoon extra-virgin olive oil
Salt and freshly ground black pepper, to taste

For Salad:

2 small zucchinis, spiralized with Blade C
1 cup cherry tomatoes, halved

¼ cup black olives, pitted and sliced
3 tablespoons extra-virgin olive oil
3 tablespoon fresh lime juice
2 teaspoons fresh lime zest, grated finely
¼ cup fresh cilantro leaves, minced
Salt and freshly ground black pepper, to taste
¼ cup walnuts, toasted and chopped

Directions:

Preheat the grill to high. Grease the grill grate. Drizzle the salmon fillets with oil and sprinkle with salt and black pepper. Grill the salmon fillets for about 4 minutes per side. Remove from grill and transfer into a bowl.

In a large serving bowl, mix together zucchini, tomatoes and olives.

In another small bowl, add oil, lime juice, zest, cilantro, salt and black pepper and beat till well combined.

Pour dressing over salad and toss to coat well.

Top with salmon and walnuts and serve immediately.

Zucchini, Cucumber & Salmon Salad

Time: 20 minutes   Servings: 2

Ingredients:

½ cup grilled salmon, cut into bite size
  pieces
1 medium zucchini, spiralized with Blade C
1 medium cucumber, peeled and spiralized
  with Blade C
2 hard boiled large eggs, peeled and chopped

½ cup celery stalk, chopped
½ cup coconut milk
1 small garlic clove, minced
Salt and freshly ground black pepper, to taste

Directions:

In a large serving bowl, mix together salmon, zucchini, cucumber and celery.

In another bowl, add coconut milk, garlic and seasoning and mix till well combined.

Pour coconut milk mixture over vegetables and gently, toss to coat.

Top with chopped eggs and serve.

CARROT, CUCUMBER & COD SALAD

Time: 35 minutes   Servings: 4

Ingredients:

For Cod:

1 teaspoon ground coriander
1 teaspoon ground cumin
Salt and freshly ground black pepper, to taste
¼ cup fresh lemon juice
4 (4-ounce) cod fillets

For Salad:

1 large carrot, peeled and spiralized with Blade C
1 large cucumber, peeled and spiralized with Blade C

1 (15-ounce) can chickpeas, rinsed and drained
1 cup cherry tomatoes, quartered
1 small red onion, chopped

For Dressing:

1 garlic clove, minced
1 teaspoon fresh lemon zest, grated finely
2 tablespoons extra-virgin olive oil
2 tablespoons fresh lemon juice
¾ teaspoon curry powder
Salt and freshly ground black pepper, to taste

Directions:

Preheat the oven to 400 degrees F. Lightly, grease shallow baking dish.

For cod in a bowl, add all ingredients and toss to coat well.

Arrange the cod fillets onto prepared baking dish.

Bake for about 15 minutes.

In a large bowl, mix together all salad ingredients.

In another small bowl, add all dressing ingredients and beat till well combined.

Pour dressing over salad and toss to coat well.

Top with cod fillets and serve immediately.

ZUCCHINI & SARDINE SALAD

Time: 25 minutes   Servings: 4

Ingredients:

For Sardines:

3 garlic cloves, minced
1 teaspoon dried rosemary, crushed
¼ cup fresh lemon juice
¼ cup extra-virgin olive oil
¼ teaspoon cayenne pepper
Salt and freshly ground black pepper, to taste
1 pound fresh sardines, scaled and gutted

For Vegetables:

3-4 zucchinis, spiralized with Blade C
½ cup fresh baby arugula
¼ cup cherry tomatoes, halved
2 tablespoons black olives, pitted and halved
1 garlic clove, minced
½ teaspoon fresh lemon zest, grated finely
2 tablespoons fresh lemon juice
2 tablespoons extra-virgin olive oil
Salt and freshly ground black pepper, to taste

Directions:

For sardines in a bowl, mix together all ingredients except sardines.

Place sardines in a large shallow dish in a single layer.

Coat the sardines with garlic mixture evenly.

Cover and keep aside to marinate for at least 1 hour.

Preheat the grill to high heat.

Grease the grill grate.

Grill the sardines for about 5 minutes on direct heat, flipping once after 3 minutes.

Remove from grill and keep aside to cool.

Then, cut into bite size pieces.

Meanwhile in a large serving bowl, mix together zucchini, arugula, olives and tomatoes.

In another bowl, add remaining ingredients and beat till well combined.

Pour lemon mixture over veggies and toss to coat well.

Top with sardine pieces and serve.

Zucchini & Shrimp Salad

Time: 25 minutes   Servings: 2

Ingredients:

For Salad:

1 tablespoon extra-virgin Olive Oil

2 garlic cloves, minced

1 teaspoon fresh ginger, minced

½ pound shrimp, peeled and deveined

Salt and freshly ground black pepper, to taste

2 medium zucchinis, spiralized with Blade C

3 cups mixed fresh baby greens

1 small avocado, peeled, pitted and chopped

For Dressing:

1 tablespoon extra-virgin olive oil

1 tablespoon fresh lemon juice

1 tablespoon soy sauce

½ teaspoon honey

Pinch of red pepper flakes, crushed

Salt and freshly ground black pepper, to taste

Directions:

In a skillet, heat oil on medium heat.

Add garlic and ginger and sauté for about 1 minute.

Add shrimp and sprinkle with salt and black pepper.

Cook for about 4 minutes, flipping once after 2 minutes.

Transfer the shrimp into a large serving bowl.

Add zucchini and greens with shrimp.

In another bowl, add all dressing ingredients and beat till well combined.

Pour dressing over salad and gently toss to coat.

Garnish with avocado and serve immediately.

Spiralized Soup & Stews Recipes

CHILLED BEET SOUP

Time: 20 minutes

Servings: 4

Ingredients:

4 cups watermelon, seeded, chopped and divided
1 large tomato, seeded and chopped
1 cucumber, seeded and chopped
2 tablespoons red onion, chopped
¼ cup fresh cilantro leaves, chopped
¼ cup fresh mint leaves, chopped

½ jalapeño pepper, seeded and chopped
2 tablespoons fresh lemon juice
1 tablespoon apple cider vinegar
1 tablespoon olive oil
salt and freshly ground black pepper, to taste
2 medium beets, trimmed, peeled and spiralized with Blade C

Directions:

In a food processor, add 3 cups of watermelon and remaining ingredients except beets and pulse till smooth.
Transfer the soup into a bowl and refrigerate, covered to chill before serving.
Top with beets and remaining watermelon before serving.

CHILLED ZUCCHINI SOUP

Time: 45 minutes

Servings: 4

Ingredients:

2 tablespoons extra-virgin coconut oil
1 small onion, chopped
2 small garlic cloves, minced
1 teaspoon dried oregano, crushed
¼ teaspoon red pepper flakes, crushed

2 large zucchinis, chopped
Salt and freshly ground black pepper, to taste
2/3 cup vegetable broth
1½ cups water
1 small zucchini, spiralized with Blade C

Directions:

In a large pan, heat oil on medium heat. Add onion and sauté for about 8- 9 minutes.
Add garlic, oregano and red pepper flakes and sauté for about 1 minute.
Add chopped zucchini, salt and black pepper and cook for about 8-10 minutes, stirring occasionally.
Add broth and water and bring to a boil on high heat.
Reduce the heat to medium-low and simmer for about 10 minutes.
Remove from heat and cool slightly. In a blender, add soup in batches and pulse till smooth.
Transfer the soup into a large bowl and season with required salt and black pepper.
Refrigerate, covered to chill. Top with spiralized zucchini and serve.

Apple & Squash Soup

Time: 30 minutes   Servings: 4

Ingredients:

1 (3-pound) butternut squash, halved and seeded
2 tablespoons olive oil
Salt and freshly ground black pepper, to taste
1 shallot, minced
2 garlic cloves, minced
1 teaspoon red chili powder
2 cups vegetable broth
1 (15-ounce) can coconut milk
2 Gala apples, cored and spiralized with Blade A
1 tablespoon pumpkin seeds, toasted

Directions:

Preheat the oven to 425 degrees F. Line a baking sheet with a parchment paper.

Drizzle the cut side of squash with 1 tablespoon of oil and sprinkle with salt and black pepper.

Arrange the squash halves onto the baking sheet, cut side down.

Roast for about 45 minutes. Remove from the oven and keep aside to cool for about 10 minutes.

With a scooper, scoop out the flesh from squash halves and transfer into a bowl.

In a large pan, heat the remaining oil on medium heat. Add shallot and sauté for about 2-3 minutes.

Add garlic and chili powder and sauté for about 1 minute.

Remove from the heat and keep aside to cool slightly.

In a high speed blender, add shallot mixture, squash, broth, coconut milk, salt and black pepper and pulse till smooth. Divide the soup into serving bowls evenly.

Top with spiralized apples and pumpkin seeds and serve.

Zucchini Egg Drop Soup

Time: 30 minutes   Servings: 2

Ingredients:

1 tablespoon extra-virgin olive oil
1 teaspoon garlic, minced
1 tablespoon fresh ginger, minced
3-4 cups vegetable broth
2 tablespoons soy sauce
3 teaspoons balsamic vinegar
1 cup fresh kale, trimmed and chopped
2 large eggs, beaten
1 small zucchini, spiralized with Blade C
1 scallion, chopped
Salt and freshly ground black pepper, to taste

Directions:

In a large pan, heat oil on medium heat. Add garlic and ginger and sauté for about 1 minute.

Add broth, soy sauce and vinegar and bring to a boil.

Cook for about 4-5 minutes.

Add kale and cook for 4-5 minutes.

Slowly, add beaten eggs, stirring continuously.

Stir in zucchini, scallion and seasoning. Cook for about 3-4 minutes.

Serve hot.

Zucchini & Tomato Soup

Time: 35 minutes   Servings: 4

Ingredients:
1 tablespoon coconut oil
1 large onion, chopped
1 teaspoon dried basil, crushed
½ teaspoon ground cumin
½ teaspoon red pepper flakes, crushed
3 cups fresh tomatoes, chopped

2 cups vegetable broth
1½ cups unsweetened coconut milk
Salt and freshly ground black pepper, to taste
2 tablespoon fresh lemon juice
3 medium zucchinis, spiralized with Blade C
1 teaspoon fresh lemon zest, grated finely

Directions:
In a large pan, heat oil on medium heat. Add onion and sauté for about 3-4 minutes. Add basil and spices and sauté for about 1 minute. Add tomatoes and cook for about 1-2 minutes, crushing with the back of spoon. Add broth and bring to a boil on high heat.
Reduce the heat to low and simmer, covered for about 10 minutes.
Stir in coconut milk and simmer for about 5 minutes.
Remove from heat and keep aside to cool slightly.
In a blender, add soup in batches and pulse till smooth.
Return the soup in pan and cook for about 2-3 minutes or till heated completely.
Stir in salt, black pepper and lemon juice and remove from heat.
In serving bowls, place zucchini and top with hot soup.
Garnish with lemon zest and serve immediately.

Zucchini & Roasted Tomato Soup

Time: 45 minutes   Servings: 2

Ingredients:
10 campari tomatoes, halved
2 tablespoons olive oil, divided
Salt and freshly ground black pepper, to taste
1 onion, chopped
2 garlic cloves, minced

¼ teaspoon red pepper flakes, crushed
1 cup vegetable broth
2 tablespoons fresh basil, chopped
1 zucchini, spiralized with Blade C
2 tablespoons plain Greek yogurt

Directions:
Preheat the oven to 375 degrees F. Drizzle the tomatoes with 1 tablespoon of oil and sprinkle with salt and black pepper. Arrange the tomato halves onto a baking dish, cut side up. Roast for about 20 minutes.
Meanwhile in a large pan, heat the remaining oil on medium heat. Add onion and sauté for about 2-3 minutes. Add garlic and red pepper flakes and sauté for about 1 minute.
In a food processor, add onion mixture and roasted tomatoes and pulse till smooth.
Return the pureed soup in pan on medium heat. Add broth and basil and bring to a boil.
Reduce the heat and simmer for about 10 minutes. Add zucchini and simmer for about 2 minutes.
Stir in yogurt and simmer for about 1 minute. Season with salt and black pepper and serve hot.

Zucchini & Bok Choy Soup

Time: 35 minutes   Servings: 2

Ingredients:

7-ounce baby bok choy, trimmed and
leaves separated
½ tablespoon yellow miso paste
2 teaspoons sesame oil, divided
½ of yellow onion, sliced thinly
2 scallions, chopped (white and green parts
  separated)

1 garlic clove, minced
1 (1-inch) piece fresh ginger, minced
2 tablespoons soy sauce
4 cups vegetable broth
3½-ounce shiitake mushrooms, halved
1 large zucchini, spiralized with Blade C
½ teaspoon sesame seeds

Directions:

Rub the bok choy leaves with miso paste till covered completely.

In a large pan, heat 1 teaspoon of oil on medium-high heat.

Add the bok choy and cook for about 3 minutes per side or till charred.

Transfer the bok choy into a bowl and keep aside.

In the same pan, heat the remaining sesame oil on medium heat.

Add onion, white part of scallions, garlic and ginger and sauté for about 5 minutes.

Add soy sauce and the broth and bring to the boil.

Stir in the mushrooms and reduce the heat to low.

Simmer for about 5 minutes. Add the zucchini and cook for about 2-3 minutes.

With pasta tongs, carefully transfer the noodles into serving bowls and top with the cooked bok choy.

Pour hot soup over the veggies evenly.

Serve hot with the garnishing green part of scallions and sesame seeds.

Zucchini & Asparagus Soup

Time: 25 minutes   Servings: 2

Ingredients:

2 cups vegetable broth
2 miso soup packets
12-16 asparagus spears, trimmed and halved
1 large zucchini, spiralized with Blade C

1 teaspoon Sriracha
2 scallions, chopped
1 tablespoon sesame seeds

Directions:

In a medium pan, add 2 cups of broth and bring to a boil.

Add miso soup packets and stir to combine.

Stir in asparagus spears and bring to a boil.

Boil for about 1 minute. Reduce the heat to low and stir in zucchini noodles.

Simmer for about 4 minutes.

Stir in Sriracha and remove from heat.

Serve hot with the garnishing of sesame seeds and scallions.

SWEET POTATO SOUP

Time: 35 minutes

Servings: 2

Ingredients:

1 tablespoon olive oil
1 small onion, chopped
1 garlic clove, minced
½ teaspoon ground cumin
½ teaspoon red pepper flakes, crushed
2 cups tomatoes, chopped finely

3 cups vegetable broth
1 large sweet potato, peeled and spiralized with Blade C
1 small avocado, peeled, pitted and cubed
Salt and freshly ground black pepper, to taste
1 tablespoon fresh parsley, chopped

Directions:

In a large pan, heat oil on medium heat.
Add onion and sauté for about 4-5 minutes.
Add garlic, cumin and red pepper flakes and sauté for about 1 minute.
Add tomatoes and cook for about 2-3 minutes, crushing with the back of spoon.
Add broth and bring to a boil and cook for about 2-3 minutes.
Stir in sweet potato.
Reduce the heat to medium-low and simmer for about 6-8 minutes.
Stir in avocado, salt and black pepper and immediately remove from heat.
Garnish with parsley and serve.

CARROT SOUP

Time: 25 minutes

Servings: 4

Ingredients:

2 teaspoons olive oil
1 small white onion, chopped
2 celery stalks, chopped
2 garlic cloves, minced
Salt and freshly ground black pepper, to taste
6 cups vegetable broth

1 large carrot, peeled and spiralized with Blade C
8-ounce fresh button mushrooms, sliced thinly
3 scallions, chopped

Directions:

In a large pan, heat oil on medium heat.
Add onion, celery and garlic and sauté for about 4-5 minutes.
Add broth and bring to a boil and cook for about 1-2 minutes.
Add carrot and mushrooms and bring to a boil.
Cook for about 3-4 minutes.
Stir in scallion and cook for about 2 minutes.
Serve hot.

ONION SOUP

Time: 2 hours 15 minutes

Servings: 6

Ingredients:

3 tablespoons butter
6 medium onions, peeled and spiralized
  with Blade C
2 teaspoons brown sugar
4 garlic cloves, minced

2 tablespoons plain white flour
1 cup dry white wine
4 cups vegetable broth
2 teaspoons tamari
2 bay leaves

Directions:

In a large heavy-bottomed pan, melt the butter on low heat.

Add onion and brown sugar and stir till coated with butter completely.

Cover and cook for about 1 hour, stirring after every 15 minutes.

Add garlic and sauté for about 30 seconds.

Add the flour and stir till well combined.

Stir in white wine and bring to a just boil.

Add broth, tamari and bay leaves and simmer for about 1 hour, stirring occasionally.

Remove from the heat and discard bay leaf.

Serve hot.

RADISH & MUSHROOM SOUP

Time: 35 minutes

Servings: 2

Ingredients:

2 teaspoons olive oil
1 red onion, sliced thinly
1 garlic clove, minced
1 (1-inch) piece fresh ginger, minced
2 tablespoons soy sauce
4 cups vegetable broth

1 large Portobello mushroom cap, sliced
1 medium daikon radish, trimmed and
  spiralized with Blade C
3 cups fresh kale, trimmed and chopped
1 scallion, chopped
½ teaspoon sesame seeds

Directions:

In a large pan, heat oil on medium-high heat.

Add onion, garlic and ginger and sauté for about 5 minutes.

Add soy sauce and the broth and bring to the boil.

Stir in the mushroom caps and reduce the heat to low.

Simmer for about 5 minutes.

Add the radish and kale and cook for about 5-7 minutes.

Serve hot with the garnishing of scallions and sesame seeds.

Radish & Veggies Soup

Time: 30 minutes   Servings: 3

Ingredients:

1 tablespoon canola oil
1/3 cup scallions, chopped and divided
2 teaspoons fresh ginger, minced
2 bunches baby bok choy, trimmed and cut
    into 1-inch pieces
3¾-ounce snow peas
3½-ounce shiitake mushrooms, stems
    removed and sliced into ¼-inch slivers

Salt and freshly ground black pepper, to taste
1 medium daikon radish, trimmed and
    spiralized with Blade C
4 cups vegetable broth
1 tablespoon mirin
1 tablespoon soy sauce
1 tablespoon fresh lime juice
¼ cup fresh cilantro leaves, chopped

Directions:

In a large pan, heat oil on medium heat. Add half of scallion and ginger and sauté for about 1-2 minutes.
Add bok choy, snow peas, mushrooms, salt and pepper and cook for about 2-3 minutes.
Add broth and bring to a boil on high heat.
Add radish noodles, mirin, soy sauce and lime juice and bring to boil.
Reduce the heat to medium-low and cook for about 2 minutes.
Stir in the cilantro and remove from heat.
Serve hot with the topping of remaining scallions.

Zucchini & Tofu Soup

Time: 25 minutes   Servings: 4

Ingredients:

4 green tea bags
3 cups boiling water
2 teaspoons sesame oil
1 teaspoon fresh ginger, minced
1 cup tofu, cubed
3 cups vegetable broth

1 tablespoon miso paste
3 medium zucchinis, spiralized with Blade C
¾ cup scallions, chopped
2 teaspoons soy sauce
Freshly ground black pepper, to taste

Directions:

In a bowl, steep the tea bags in boiling water for about 3-4 minutes.
Remove the tea bags and keep the broth aside.
In a large soup pan, heat oil on medium heat and sauté ginger for about 30 seconds.
Add tofu, broth and green tea broth and bring to a boil.
Transfer 1bout 1/3 cup of the hot soup into a bowl.
Add miso paste and stir to combine.
Add miso paste mixture into soup and bring to a boil. Reduce the heat to low.
Add remaining ingredients and simmer for about 2-3 minutes.
Serve hot.

Creamy Zucchini & Tofu Soup

Time: 50 minutes

Servings: 4

Ingredients:

For Tofu:

8-ounce firm tofu
2 tablespoons low-sodium soy sauce
1 teaspoon coconut oil

For Soup:

1 teaspoon coconut oil
3 tablespoons minced shallots
3 garlic cloves, minced
1 tablespoon grated fresh ginger
1 tablespoon lemongrass, grated finely

2 teaspoons red chile paste
Salt, to taste
1 cup carrots, peeled and julienned
4 cups vegetable broth
1 (14-ounce) can unsweetened coconut milk
2 tablespoons fresh lime juice
¼ teaspoon red pepper flakes, crushed
3 scallions, chopped
2 medium zucchinis, spiralized with Blade C
1 tablespoon fresh cilantro, chopped

Directions:

In a bowl, mix together the tofu and soy sauce. In a medium frying pan, melt coconut oil on high heat. Add tofu and sauté for about 8-10 minutes or till browned from all sides. Transfer the tofu into a bowl and keep aside. For soup in a large pan, melt coconut oil on medium heat. Add the shallot and sauté for about 1 minute. Add garlic, ginger, lemongrass, red chile paste and salt and sauté for about 1 minute. Add carrots and sauté for about 2-3 minutes. Add broth, coconut milk and lime juice and bring to a simmer. Simmer for about 10 minutes. Stir in red pepper flakes and scallion and remove from the heat. Divide the zucchini noodles in serving bowls. Pour hot soup over zucchini noodles. Top with tofu and cilantro and serve.

Zucchini, Veggies & Tofu Soup

Time: 35 minutes

Servings: 4

Ingredients:

1 tablespoon extra-virgin olive oil
1 garlic clove, minced
½ teaspoon fresh ginger, minced
1 lemongrass stalk, chopped finely
Pinch of red pepper flakes, crushed
1 tablespoon Thai green curry paste
¼ cup fresh mushrooms, sliced
2 cups water
2 cups vegetable broth

1 large zucchini, peeled and spiralized with Blade C
1 cup snow peas
1 cup chopped baby bok choy, trimmed
¼ cup scallions, chopped
½ cup tofu, drained and cubed
1 tablespoon fresh lime juice
Salt and freshly ground black pepper, to taste
2 tablespoons fresh cilantro, chopped

Directions:

In a large skillet, heat oil on medium heat. Add garlic, ginger, lemongrass, red pepper flakes and curry paste and sauté for about 2 minutes. Add mushrooms and cook for about 3-4 minutes. Add water and broth and bring to a boil on high heat. Reduced the heat to medium.

Add zucchini, snow peas, bok choy, scallions, tofu, lime juice and cook for 4-5 minutes. Season with salt and pepper and remove from heat. Garnish with cilantro and serve hot.

Rutabaga, Beets & Tofu Soup

Time: 55 minutes   Servings: 4

Ingredients:

6 cups water
1 onion, sliced, reserving peel
1 tablespoon fresh ginger, chopped
1 garlic clove, chopped
1 Thai chili, halved
2 teaspoons soya sauce
8-ounce tofu, cubed
10 fresh cremini mushrooms, sliced

½ cup edamame, shelled
1 teaspoon sesame oil
1 rutabaga, spiralized with Blade C
2 small yellow beets, spiralized with Blade C
1 head Bok Choy, chopped roughly
3 scallions, chopped finely
2 tablespoons Hoisin sauce
2 tablespoons fresh cilantro, chopped

Directions:

In a large pan, add water, onion peel, ginger, garlic, Thai chili and soya sauce on high heat and bring to a boil. Reduce the heat to low and simmer, covered for about 30 minutes. Strain the broth and return into pan. Add tofu, mushrooms, edamame, sliced onion and sesame oil and bring to a boil. Cook for about 5 minutes. Add rutabaga, beets and bok choy on medium heat and cook, covered for about 5 minutes. Stir in scallions and Hoisin sauce and remove from heat. Serve hot with the garnishing of cilantro.

Turnip & Lentil Soup

Time: 55 minutes   Servings: 6

Ingredients:

2 tablespoons extra-virgin olive oil
1 medium onion, chopped
2 carrots, peeled and chopped
2 celery ribs, chopped
Salt and freshly ground black pepper, to taste
3 garlic cloves, minced
½ teaspoon dried basil
½ teaspoon dried thyme
½ teaspoon dried oregano

½ teaspoon red pepper flakes, crushed
1 (28-ounce) can diced tomatoes
2 bay leaves
1 cup red lentils, rinsed
6 cups vegetable broth
2 small turnips, peeled and spiralized with
   Blade C
2 teaspoons fresh lemon juice

Directions:

In a large pan, heat oil on medium heat. Add onion, carrot, celery, salt and black pepper and sauté for about 4-5 minutes. Add garlic, herbs and red pepper flakes and sauté for about 1 minute. Add tomatoes and stir till well combined. Add bay leaves, lentils, broth, salt and black pepper and stir well. Increase the heat to high and bring to a boil. Reduce the heat to medium-low and simmer, covered partially for about 20 minutes. Discard the bay leaves and stir in the turnip noodles. Cook for about 5-7 minutes.
Stir in lemon juice and serve hot.

BUTTERNUT SQUASH & BUTTER BEANS SOUP

Time: 35 minutes   Servings: 2

Ingredients:

2 tablespoons olive oil
½ cup carrot, peeled and chopped
½ cup red onion, chopped
½ cup celery stalk, chopped
1 tablespoons garlic, minced
¼ teaspoon red pepper flakes, crushed
Salt and freshly ground black pepper, to taste

2 teaspoons dried thyme, crushed
4 cups vegetable broth
1 (3-inch long) butternut squash, chunk, peeled and spiralized with Blade C
8 Swiss chard leaves
½ cup butter beans
1 tablespoon Parmesan cheese, grated

Directions:

In a large pan, heat oil on medium heat.
Add onion, carrot and celery and sauté for about 4-5 minutes.
Add garlic and red pepper flakes and sauté for about 1 minute.
Add broth and bring to a boil on medium-high heat.
Add squash noodles and reduce the heat to low. Simmer for about 10 minutes.
Add Swiss chard and butter beans and simmer for about 2 minutes.
Serve hot with the topping of Parmesan cheese.

BUTTERNUT SQUASH & CANNELINI BEANS SOUP

Time: 45 minutes   Servings: 6

Ingredients:

½ tablespoon extra-virgin olive oil
1 yellow onion, chopped
2 celery stalks, chopped
1 garlic clove
17-ounce canned whole, peeled tomatoes
6 cups vegetable broth
½ teaspoon dried oregano, crushed
¼ teaspoon red chili powder

1 butternut squash, peeled and spiralized with Blade C
1 large bunch fresh kale, trimmed and chopped
1 cup canned white cannelloni beans, rinsed and drained
2 teaspoons fresh chives, chopped
Salt and freshly ground black pepper, to taste
3 tablespoons Parmesan cheese, grated

Directions:

In a large pan, heat oil on medium heat. Add onions and celery and sauté for about 4-5 minutes.
Add garlic and sauté for about 1 minute. Add tomatoes and cook, chopping the tomatoes with the back of a wooden spoon. Add broth, oregano and red chili powder and bring to a boil.
Stir in squash, kale, white beans and chives and reduce the heat to low.
Simmer, covered for about 20 minutes.
Stir in salt and black pepper and remove from heat.
Serve hot with the topping of Parmesan cheese.

JICAMA & BLACK BEANS SOUP

Time: 35 minutes

Servings: 4

Ingredients:

1 tablespoon extra-virgin olive oil
1 onion, chopped
1 garlic clove, minced
1 jalapeño pepper, seeded and finely chopped
½ teaspoon ground cumin
1 teaspoon ground chili powder
¼ teaspoon smoked paprika
1 (15-ounce) can fire roasted diced tomatoes

1 (15-ounce) can black beans, rinsed and drained
6 cups vegetable broth
1 jicama, peeled and spiralized with Blade C
1 avocado, peeled, pitted and spiralized with Blade C
1 cup fresh cilantro leaves, chopped
2 tablespoons fresh lime juice
Salt and freshly ground black pepper, to taste

Directions:

In a large pan, heat oil on medium heat. Add onion and sauté for about 4-5 minutes.

Add garlic, jalapeño pepper and spices and sauté for about 1 minute.

Add tomatoes, beans and broth and bring to a boil on high heat.

Reduced the heat to medium. Add jicama, avocado, lime juice and cilantro and simmer for about 4-5 minutes.

Season with salt and pepper and serve hot.

CARROT & CANNELLINI BEANS SOUP

Time: 50 minutes

Servings: 4

Ingredients:

1 tablespoon extra-virgin olive oil
1 large celery stalk, chopped
1 small yellow onion, chopped
2 garlic cloves, minced
1 (15-ounce) can crushed tomatoes
1 tablespoon fresh thyme leaves, chopped
1 tablespoon fresh sage leaves, chopped \
1 bay leaf
Salt and freshly ground black pepper, to taste

4 cups vegetable broth
1 (15-ounce) can cannellini beans, rinsed and drained
3 cups fresh spinach
1 large carrot, peeled and spiralized with Blade C
2 cups day-old crusty whole grain bread, torn into 1-inch pieces
¼ cup Parmesan cheese, grated

Directions:

In a large pan, heat oil on medium heat. Add celery and onion and sauté for about 4-5 minutes.

Add garlic and sauté for about 1 minute. Add tomatoes, fresh herbs, bay leaf, salt, black pepper and broth and bring to a boil on medium-high heat. Stir in the beans and spinach.

Reduce the heat to low and simmer, covered for about 25 minutes.

Stir in carrot noodles and bread and simmer for about 5 minutes.

Remove from the heat and discard bay leaf.

Serve hot with the topping of Parmesan cheese.

Carrot, Zucchini & Kidney Beans Soup

Time: 35 minutes   Servings: 4

Ingredients:

2 tablespoons olive oil, chopped
1 onion, chopped
1 garlic clove, minced
1 teaspoon ground ginger
1 teaspoon ground turmeric
1 teaspoon paprika
½ teaspoon ground cinnamon
1 (15-ounce) can chopped tomatoes

¼ cup tomato paste
2 cups vegetable broth
1 zucchini, spiralized with Blade C
1 carrot, peeled and spiralized with Blade C
1 (15-ounce) can red kidney beans, rinsed
  and drained
Salt and freshly ground black pepper, to taste
2 tablespoons fresh cilantro, chopped

Directions:

In a large pan, heat olive oil on medium heat. Add celery and onion and sauté for about 4-5 minutes. Add garlic and spices sauté for about 1 minute. Add the tomatoes, tomato paste and broth and bring to a boil. Simmer for about 2-3 minutes. Add veggie noodles, beans, salt and black pepper and cook for about 4-5 minutes. Serve hot with the garnishing of cilantro.

Sweet Potato & Chickpeas Soup

Time: 55 minutes   Servings: 4

Ingredients:

1 tablespoon coconut oil
2 teaspoons ground ginger
1 teaspoons hot smoked paprika
½ teaspoons ground cinnamon
½ teaspoons freshly grated nutmeg
2 medium onions
Salt, to taste
Pinch of saffron soaked in 2 tablespoons of
  hot water
1 (14-ounce) can whole tomatoes, crushed
1 (6-oince) can tomato paste

3 cups canned chickpeas, rinsed and drained
1 cup dried lentils, soaked for overnight
  and drained
3 lemon slices
5 cups water
1 medium sweet potato, peeled and
  spiralized with Blade C
½ cup fresh cilantro, chopped
½ cup fresh parsley, chopped
Freshly ground pepper, to taste

Directions:

Steep the saffron threads in 2 tablespoons of boiled water for about 10-15 minutes.
In a large pan, melt coconut oil on medium-high heat. Add spies and sauté for about 1 minute.
Reduce the heat to medium. Add onions and salt and cook for about 10 minutes, stirring occasionally.
Add the steeped saffron water, tomatoes, tomato paste, chickpeas, lentils, lemon slices and water and bring to a boil. Reduce the heat to low and simmer, covered for about 15-25 minutes or till desired doneness.
Add the sweet potato noodles and simmer for about 5 minutes.
Season with salt and black pepper and serve hot.

Zucchini, Chickpeas & Bacon Soup

Time: 45 minutes

Servings: 6

Ingredients:

4 bacon strips
1 small onion, chopped
1 large carrot, peeled and chopped
1 celery stalk, chopped
2 garlic cloves, minced
1 tablespoon tomato paste
4 cups chicken broth

1 cup water
1 teaspoon fresh thyme
1 bay leaf
1 (14½-ounce) can chickpeas, rinsed and drained
1 large zucchini, spiralized with Blade C
¼ cup fresh parsley, chopped

Directions:

Heat a large skillet on medium-high heat. Add bacon and cook for about 8-10 minutes or till crisp. Transfer the bacon onto a paper towel lined plate to drain and then crumble it. Transfer the bacon grease into a bowl and reserve. In a large pan, heat 1 tablespoon of the reserved bacon grease on medium-high heat. Add onion, celery and carrots and sauté for about 3 minutes. Add garlic and sauté for about 30 seconds.
Stir in tomato paste, broth, water, remaining bacon grease, thyme and bay leaf and bring to a boil.
Add chickpeas and zucchini noodles and cook for about 5 minutes. Remove from the heat and discard bay leaf. Serve hot with the topping of the bacon and parsley.

Mixed Veggies & Bacon Soup

Time: 65 minutes

Servings: 6

Ingredients:

5 tablespoons olive oil, divided
4-ounces bacon slices, cut into ¼-inch pieces
1 large red onion, sliced thinly
3 garlic cloves, minced
1 tablespoon fresh basil, chopped finely
1 tablespoon fresh thyme, chopped finely
1 bay leaf
12 cups chicken broth

1 large carrot, peeled, spiralized with Blade C
1 large parsnip, peeled and spiralized with Blade C
1 medium turnip, peeled and spiralized with Blade C
8-ounce Brussels sprouts, trimmed and sliced thinly
Salt and freshly ground black pepper, to taste
2 teaspoons fresh lemon zest, grated finely

Directions:

Heat a large skillet on medium-high heat. Add bacon and cook for about 8-10 minutes or till crisp. Transfer the bacon onto a paper towel lined plate to drain and then crumble it. Transfer 2 tablespoons of the bacon grease into a large pan on medium heat. Add onion and cook for about 8-10 minutes, stirring occasionally. Add garlic and sauté for about 1 minute. Add bacon, basil, thyme, bay leaf and broth and bring to a boil. Cook for about 15 minutes. Add veggie noodles, Brussels sprouts, salt and black pepper and cook for about 3-4 minutes. Remove from heat and discard bay leaves.
Serve hot with the topping of lemon zest.

CURRIED ZUCCHINI & CHICKEN SOUP

Time: 30 minutes

Servings: 8

Ingredients:

1 tablespoon coconut oil
1 onion, chopped
2 garlic cloves, minced
1 jalapeño pepper, chopped
1½ tablespoons green curry paste
1 pound skinless, boneless chicken breasts,
   sliced thinly

6 cups chicken broth
1 (15-ounce) can full-fat coconut milk
1 red bell pepper, seeded and sliced thinly
2 tablespoons fish sauce
½ cup fresh cilantro, chopped
2 medium zucchinis, spiralized with Blade C
2 tablespoons fresh lime juice

Directions:

In a large pan, melt coconut oil on medium heat.

Add onion, carrots and mushrooms and sauté for 4-5 minutes.

Add garlic, jalapeño and curry paste and sauté for about 1 minute.

Add chicken and cook for about 3-4 minutes.

Stir in chicken broth and coconut milk and bring to a boil.

Stir in red pepper and fish sauce.

Reduce the heat to medium-low and simmer for about 5 minutes.

Stir in cilantro and remove from heat.

Divide zucchini noodles in serving bowls.

Pour hot soup over noodles.

Serve hot with the drizzling of lime juice.

ZUCCHINI, SALSA & CHICKEN SOUP

Time: 25 minutes

Servings: 4

Ingredients:

4 cups chicken broth
2 cooked chicken breasts, diced or
   shredded
3 tablespoon prepared salsa
1 jalapeño pepper, sliced
1 teaspoon garlic powder
1 teaspoon red chili powder

½ teaspoon ground cumin
Salt and freshly ground black pepper, to taste
1 tablespoon fresh lime juice
1 large zucchini, spiralized with Blade C
1 large avocado, peeled, pitted and
chopped

Directions:

In a large pan, add broth on high heat and bring to a boil.

Reduce the heat to medium-low.

Stir in remaining ingredients except zucchini and avocado and cook for about 2 minutes.

Add zucchini noodles and cook for about 2-3 minutes.

Serve hot with the topping of avocado.

Zucchini, Beans & Chicken Soup

Time: 55 minutes

Servings: 2

Ingredients:

1 teaspoon ground cumin
1 teaspoon chili powder
1 teaspoon paprika
Salt and freshly ground black pepper, to taste
1 (6-ounce) skinless, boneless chicken breast
1½ tablespoons olive oil, divided
1/3 cup red onion, chopped
2 teaspoon garlic, minced
1 small jalapeño pepper, seeded and chopped

1 teaspoon dried oregano, crushed
1 (14-ounce) can diced tomatoes
½ cup canned black beans, rinsed and drained
3 cups chicken broth
1 avocado, peeled, pitted and cubed
2 medium zucchinis, spiralized with Blade C
2 teaspoons fresh lime juice
1 tablespoon fresh cilantro, chopped

Directions:

Preheat the oven to 350 degrees. In a bowl, mix together spices, salt and black pepper. Drizzle the chicken breast with ½ tablespoon of oil and then coat with half of the spice mixture evenly. Arrange the chicken breast onto a baking sheet. Bake for about 20-25 minutes, flipping once in the middle way. Remove from the oven and keep aside to cool, then shred the chicken. Meanwhile in a large pan, heat remaining oil on medium heat. Add onion and sauté for about 4-5 minutes. Add garlic, jalapeño pepper and oregano and sauté for about 1 minute. Add tomatoes, beans and remaining spice mixture and cook for about 2 minutes. Add chicken broth and bring to a boil. Reduce the heat to low and simmer, covered for about 10-15 minutes, stirring occasionally. Add the chicken, zucchini noodles and avocado and cook for about 2-3 minutes. Stir in lime juice, cilantro, salt and black pepper and remove from heat. Serve hot.

Zucchini, Yellow Squash & Chicken Soup

Time: 65 minutes

Servings: 4

Ingredients:

2 tablespoons extra-virgin olive oil
1 medium white onion, chopped
2 medium carrots, peeled and chopped
1½ cups Portobello mushrooms, chopped
1 teaspoon dried oregano, crushed
½ teaspoon ground cumin
½ teaspoon cayenne pepper
5 cups chicken broth

3 cups cooked chicken, shredded
1 medium zucchinis, spiralized with Blade C
1 medium yellow squash, spiralized with Blade C
Salt and freshly ground black pepper, to taste
2 tablespoons fresh lime juice
¼ cup fresh parsley leaves, chopped

Directions:

In a large pan, heat oil on medium heat. Add onion, carrots and mushrooms and sauté for 4-5 minutes. Add thyme and spices and sauté for about 1 minute. Add chicken and broth and bring to a boil. Reduce the heat to low and simmer for about 30-35 minutes. Stir in zucchini, salt and black pepper and cook for about 3-4 minutes. Stir in lemon juice and parsley and immediately remove from heat. Serve hot.

YELLOW SQUASH & CHICKEN SOUP

Time: 55 minutes   Servings: 4

Ingredients:

2 tablespoons extra virgin olive oil
1 medium white onion, chopped
2 cups celery stalks, chopped
3 cups carrots, peeled and chopped
3 garlic cloves, minced

7-8 cups chicken broth
3 large yellow squash, spiralized with Blade C
2 grass fed cooked skinless, boneless chicken breasts, shredded
Salt and freshly ground black pepper, to taste

Directions:

In a large pan, heat oil on medium heat.

Add onion, celery and carrots and sauté for 4-5 minutes.

Add garlic and sauté for 1 minute.

Add broth and bring to a boil.

Reduce the heat to low and simmer, covered for about 20-25 minutes.

Stir in spiralized squash and chicken and cook for 2-3 minutes.

Season with salt and pepper and remove from heat.

Serve hot.

SWEET POTATO & CHICKEN SOUP

Time: 55 minutes   Servings: 4

Ingredients:

1 tablespoon olive oil
½ cup white onion, chopped
1 medium carrot, peeled and chopped
2 celery stalks, chopped
2 garlic cloves, minced
2 tablespoon fresh parsley, chopped
1 teaspoon fresh ginger, minced

6 cups chicken broth
1 cup sweet potato, peeled and spiralized with Blade C
1 cup cooked chicken, shredded
Salt and freshly ground black pepper, to taste
2 tablespoons fresh lemon juice

Directions:

In a large pan, heat oil on medium heat.

Add onion, carrot and celery and sauté for about 3-4 minutes.

Add garlic, ginger and parsley and sauté for 1 minute.

Add broth and bring to a boil on high heat.

Reduce the heat to low and simmer for about 15-20 minutes.

Add sweet potato and cooked chicken and simmer for about 8-10 minutes.

Stir in salt, black pepper and lemon juice and remove from heat.

Serve hot.

Carrot & Chicken Soup

Time: 35 minutes

Servings: 4

Ingredients:

2 tablespoon olive oil
½ medium red onion, chopped
2 celery stalks, chopped
2 garlic cloves, minced
Salt and freshly ground black pepper, to taste
½ teaspoon dried basil, crushed

½ teaspoon dried oregano, crushed
4 cups chicken broth
2 cups cooked chicken, shredded
1 large carrot, peeled and spiralized with Blade C

Directions:

In a large pan, heat oil on medium heat.
Add onion, celery, garlic, salt and black pepper and sauté for about 4-5 minutes.
Add broth and bring to a boil on high heat.
Add broth and herbs and bring to a boil.
Reduce the heat to low and cook for about 5-7 minutes.
Add chicken and carrot noodles and cook for about 5 minutes.
Serve hot.

Carrot, Tomato & Chicken Soup

Time: 50 minutes

Servings: 2

Ingredients:

1 tablespoon extra-virgin olive oil
1/3 cup onion, chopped
1 celery stalk, chopped
2 teaspoons garlic, minced
½ of jalapeño pepper, seeded and chopped
1 teaspoon red chili powder
1¾ cups tomatoes, chopped finely
1 teaspoon dried rosemary, crushed

3 cups chicken broth
Salt and freshly ground black pepper, to taste
3 medium carrots, peeled and spiralized with Blade C
1 cooked skinless, boneless chicken breast, shredded
1 tablespoon fresh lemon juice
1 tablespoon fresh parsley, chopped

Directions:

In a large pan, heat oil on medium heat.
Add onion and sauté for about 4-5 minutes.
Add garlic, jalapeño, rosemary and chili powder and sauté for about 1 minute.
Add tomatoes and thyme and cook for about 3 to 4 minutes.
Add broth, salt and black pepper and bring to a boil.
Reduce the heat to low and simmer, covered for about 15-20 minutes.
Stir in carrot and chicken and cook for 5 minutes.
Stir in lemon juice and parsley and remove from heat.
Serve hot.

Curried Turnip & Chicken Soup

Time: 55 minutes

Servings: 3

Ingredients:
6 cups water
2 cups of water
1 (12-ounce) chicken breast (with bones), skin discarded
2 teaspoons red curry paste
2 large turnips, peeled and spiralized with Blade C

1 red bell pepper, seeded and sliced thinly
5 scallions, chopped
Salt and freshly ground black pepper, to taste
¼ cup fresh cilantro leaves
1 lime, cut into wedges

Directions:
In a large pan, add water on medium heat and bring to a boil. Reduce the heat to low and simmer, covered for about 30 minutes. Remove the chicken and keep aside to cool and then shred it. In the pan of broth, add curry paste and stir to combine. Bring to a boil on medium-high heat. Add the turnip noodles and bell pepper and cook for about 3 minutes. Stir in the shredded chicken, scallions, salt and black pepper and cook for about 2-3 minutes. Stir in cilantro and remove from heat. Serve hot with the lime wedges.

Radish & Chicken Soup

Time: 65 minutes

Servings: 4

Ingredients:
1 tablespoon olive oil
1 small yellow onion, chopped
1 (1-inch) piece fresh ginger, minced
1 pound bone-in chicken thighs
2 chicken drumsticks
12 cups water

1 large daikon radish, trimmed and spiralized with Blade C
1 jalapeño, chopped
1 lime, cut into wedges
1 tablespoon fish sauce
1 bunch scallions, chopped
¼ cup fresh cilantro, chopped

Directions:
In a large pan, heat oil on medium heat.
Add onion and ginger and sauté for about 4-5 minutes.
Add chicken and water and bring to a boil on high heat.
Reduce the heat to low and simmer, covered for about 25 minutes.
Remove the chicken thighs and drumsticks and keep aside to cool.
Shred the meat from the thighs but leave the drumstick intact.
Return the bones from the chicken thighs into the pan.
Add fish sauce and cook for about 10-15 minutes.
Add the shredded chicken, drumsticks, radish noodles and jalapeño and cook for about 2-3 minutes.
Stir in the scallions and remove from heat.
Garnish with cilantro and serve with lime wedges.

MIXED VEGGIES & CHICKEN SOUP

Time: 55 minutes

Servings: 4

Ingredients:

2 tablespoons olive oil
1 onion, chopped
1 garlic clove, minced
½ tablespoon fresh ginger, grated
½ pound skinless, boneless chicken breast, cut into thin strips
1 tablespoon soy sauce
¼ cup chopped cilantro leaves
¼ cup fresh mint leaves, chopped
¼ cup watercress, chopped
4 cups vegetable broth

1 teaspoon red pepper flakes, crushed
½ green chili, chopped
2 medium carrots, peeled and spiralized with Blade C
1 large turnip, peeled and spiralized with Blade C
2 medium zucchini, spiralized with Blade C
1 large broccoli stem, peeled and spiralized with Blade C
Salt and freshly ground black pepper, to taste

Directions:

In a large pan, heat oil on medium heat.

Add onion, garlic and ginger and sauté for about 2-3 minutes.

Add chicken and stir fry for 4-5 minutes.

Add soy sauce, cilantro, mint and watercress and stir fry for about 1 minute.

Add broth, red pepper flakes and green chili and bring to a boil.

Add carrot, turnip, zucchini and broccoli and cook for about 10-15 minutes until done.

Season with salt and pepper and serve hot.

RUTABAGA & TURKEY SOUP

Time: 35 minutes

Servings: 6

Ingredients:

1 tablespoon olive oil
2 large carrots, peeled and chopped
1 large onion, chopped
1 large scallion, chopped finely
6 garlic cloves, minced
1½ teaspoons dried thyme, crushed
1½ teaspoons dried rosemary, crushed
1½ teaspoons dried oregano, crushed

2 teaspoons hot paprika
Salt and freshly ground black pepper, to taste
6 cups chicken broth
2 cups cooked turkey, shredded
2 cups fresh kale, trimmed and chopped
1 small rutabaga, peeled and spiralized with Blade C

Directions:

In a large pan, heat oil on medium heat.

Add carrots, onion, scallion and garlic and sauté for about 5-7 minutes.

Add garlic, herbs and seasonings and sauté for about 1 minute. Add broth and bring to a boil.

Add turkey, kale and rutabaga noodles and cook for about 10 minutes. Serve hot.

Zucchini & Turkey Soup

Time: 65 minutes

Servings: 6

Ingredients:

1 tablespoon extra-virgin olive oil
1 small yellow onion, chopped
1 cup carrots, peeled and chopped
1 cup celery stalk, chopped
1 garlic clove, minced
6 cups chicken broth

1 pound cooked turkey breast, chopped
1 teaspoon fresh parsley, chopped
½ teaspoon dried oregano, crushed
3 bay leaves
2 cups Zucchini, spiralized with Blade C
Salt and freshly ground black pepper, to taste

Directions:

In a large pan, heat oil on medium heat.

Add onion, carrot, celery and garlic and sauté for about 4-5 minutes.

Add remaining ingredients except zucchini and bring to a boil.

Reduce heat to low and simmer, covered for about 15 minutes.

Add zucchini noodles and cook for about 2-3 minutes.

Season with salt and pepper and remove from heat.

Discard bay leaf and serve hot.

Zucchini, Seaweed & Turkey Soup

Time: 25 minutes

Servings: 4

Ingredients:

4 cups vegetable broth
1 cup cooked turkey, cut into small pieces
2 cups fresh kale, trimmed and chopped
1 cup fresh shiitake mushrooms, sliced
2 tablespoons dry seaweed

1 (2-inch) piece fresh ginger, sliced thinly
2 garlic cloves, minced
Salt and freshly ground black pepper, to taste
2 medium zucchinis, spiralized with Blade C
2 teaspoons sesame oil, toasted

Directions:

In a large pan, add broth on medium heat and bring to a boil.

Add turkey, kale, mushrooms, seaweed, ginger, garlic, salt and black pepper and bring to a boil.

Reduce the heat and simmer, covered for about 3-4 minutes.

Add zucchini noodles and simmer for about 2-3 minutes.

Remove from heat.

Stir in sesame oil and serve.

YELLOW SQUASH & TURKEY MEATBALLS SOUP

Time: 55 minutes

Servings: 4

Ingredients:

For Meatballs:

¾ pound lean ground turkey
1 medium egg, beaten
½ teaspoon ground cumin
Salt and freshly ground black pepper, to taste

For Soup:

1 tablespoon extra-virgin coconut oil
1 small yellow onion, chopped
2 small carrots, peeled and chopped
3 stalks celery, chopped
3-4 garlic cloves, minced

½ teaspoon dried rosemary, crushed
½ teaspoon dried basil, crushed
½ teaspoon ground cumin
¼ teaspoon red pepper flakes, crushed
¼ teaspoon cayenne pepper
5 cups chicken broth
1 large fresh tomato, chopped finely
2 medium yellow squash, spiralized with Blade C
Salt and freshly ground black pepper, to taste
¼ cup fresh cilantro leaves, chopped
1 avocado, peeled, pitted and chopped

Directions:

In a large bowl, add all meatballs ingredients and mix till well combined. Make desired size meatballs from mixture and keep aside. In a large pan, heat oil on medium heat. Add onion, carrots and celery and sauté for 6-8 minutes. Add garlic, herbs and spices and sauté for about 1 minute. Add tomatoes and cook for 1-2 minutes. Add broth and bring to a boil. Cook for about 5 minutes. Stir in meatballs. Reduce the heat to low and simmer for about 15 minutes. Stir in squash, salt and black pepper and cook for about 3-4 minutes. Stir in cilantro and immediately remove from heat. Garnish with avocado and serve hot.

YELLOW SQUASH & BEEF SOUP

Time: 45 minutes

Servings: 2

Ingredients:

1½ tablespoons extra virgin olive oil, divided
½ pound New York strip steak, cut into bite sized pieces
Salt and freshly ground black pepper, to taste
1 small onion, chopped
3-4 garlic cloves, minced

1 cup shiitake mushrooms, chopped
1 cup fresh spinach, torn
3½ cups beef broth
2 tablespoons tamari
1 large yellow squash, spiralized with Blade C
½ cup scallion, chopped

Directions:

In a large pan, heat 1 tablespoon of oil on medium heat. Add beef and sprinkle with salt and black pepper. Cook for about 6-8 minutes or till golden brown from all sides. Transfer the beef into a bowl. In the same pan, heat remaining oil on medium heat. Add onion and sauté for about 4-5 minutes. Add garlic and sauté for about 1 minute. Add mushrooms and cook for about 3-4 minutes. Add spinach and cook for about 2 to 3 minutes. Add beef broth and tamari and bring to a boil. Reduce the heat to medium-low and simmer for about 10-15 minutes. Stir in squash, scallion, salt and black pepper and simmer for about 2-3 minutes. Remove from heat and serve hot.

ZUCCHINI & GROUND BEEF SOUP

Time: 55 minutes   Servings: 4

Ingredients:

1 tablespoon extra-virgin olive oil
¼ cup white onion, chopped
2 celery stalks, chopped
½ cup green bell pepper, seeded and chopped
½ pound ground beef
3 cups fresh tomatoes, chopped finely

4 cups beef broth
1 tablespoon fresh thyme, minced
3 medium zucchinis, spiralized with Blade C
Salt and freshly ground black pepper, to taste
1 tablespoon fresh lemon juice
½ cup scallions, chopped

Directions:

In a large pan, heat oil on medium heat. Add onion, celery and bell pepper and sauté for about 4-5 minutes. Add beef and cook for 4-5 minutes. Add tomatoes and cook for 1-2 minutes. Add broth and thyme and bring to a boil. Reduce the heat to low and simmer, covered for about 20-25 minutes. Stir in zucchini, scallion, salt and black pepper and simmer for about 2-3 minutes. Stir in lemon juice and remove from heat. Garnish with scallion and serve hot.

ZUCCHINI & BEEF MEATBALLS SOUP

Time: 50 minutes   Servings: 2

Ingredients:

For Meatballs:
1 pound extra lean ground beef
½ red onion, chopped
4-6 black olives, pitted and chopped
1 small red bell pepper, seeded and chopped
3 garlic cloves, chopped finely
2 tablespoons fresh parsley, chopped
¼ cup coconut flour
1 egg, beaten
½ teaspoon cayenne pepper
Salt and freshly ground black pepper, to taste
1 tablespoon extra-virgin olive oil

For Soup:
2 tablespoons extra-virgin olive oil
1 medium onion, chopped
2 celery stalks, chopped
1 carrot, peeled and chopped finely
2 garlic cloves, minced
7-8 cups beef broth
1½ cups fresh kale, trimmed and chopped
1 teaspoon dried oregano, crushed
Salt and freshly ground black pepper, to taste
2-3 large zucchinis, spiralized with Blade C
1 tablespoon fresh lemon juice

Directions:

For meatballs in a large bowl, add all ingredients except oil and mix till well combined. Make desired size balls from mixture. In a large skillet, heat oil on medium heat. Add meatballs in batches and cook for about 3-4 minutes or till golden brown from all sides. Transfer the meatballs into a plate and keep aside. In a large pan, heat oil on medium heat. Add onion, celery and carrot and sauté for about 4-5 minutes. Add garlic and sauté for about 1 minute. Add broth and bring to a boil. Reduce the heat to medium-low and simmer for about 3-4 minutes. Carefully, add in the meatballs and simmer, covered for about 10 minutes. Stir in kale, oregano, salt and black pepper and cook for about 2-3 minutes. Stir in zucchini and cook for about 23 minutes. Stir in lemon juice and remove from heat. Serve hot.

Zucchini & Lamb Soup

Time: 1 hour 50 minutes

Servings: 4

Ingredients:

2 tablespoons extra-virgin olive oil
2 large lamb shanks
1 medium yellow onion, chopped
2 celery stalks, chopped
2 small carrots, peeled and chopped
2 garlic cloves, minced
1 teaspoon fresh ginger, minced
½ teaspoon dried oregano, crushed
½ teaspoon dried thyme, crushed

1 teaspoon ground coriander
1½ teaspoons ground cumin
1 teaspoon cayenne pepper
2 cups tomatoes, chopped
6 cups chicken broth
3 medium zucchinis, spiralized with Blade C
Salt and freshly ground black pepper, to taste
½ cup fresh parsley, chopped

Directions:

In a large pan, heat oil on medium heat. Add shanks and cook for 6-8 minutes or till browned from all sides. Transfer the shanks into a bowl. In the same pan, add onion, celery and carrot and sauté for about 4-5 minutes. Add garlic, ginger, herbs and spices and sauté for about 1 minute. Add tomatoes and cook for about 1-2 minutes. Add cooked shanks and broth and bring to a boil.

Reduce the heat to low and simmer, covered partially for about 1½ hours.

Remove shanks from soup and shred the meat.

Stir in shredded meat, zucchini, salt and black pepper and simmer for about 3-4 minutes.

Garnish with parsley and serve hot.

Sweet Potato & Ground Pork Soup

Time: 45 minutes

Servings: 4

Ingredients:

1 tablespoon olive oil
1 teaspoon fresh ginger, minced
2 garlic cloves, minced
½ teaspoon dried thyme, crushed
½ teaspoon ground cumin
¼ teaspoon ground coriander
½ teaspoon red pepper flakes, crushed

1 pound lean ground pork
Salt and freshly ground black pepper, to taste
4 cups chicken broth
1 medium sweet potato, peeled and spiralized with Blade C
4 cups fresh spinach, torn
1 cup scallion, chopped

Directions:

In a large pan, heat oil on medium heat. Add ginger, garlic, thyme and spices and sauté for about 1 minute. Add pork and sprinkle with salt and black pepper. Cook for about 9-10 minutes, stirring and breaking with a spoon. Add broth and bring to a boil. Reduce the heat to low and simmer for about 8-10 minutes.

Add sweet potato and simmer for about 5 minutes.

Add spinach and scallion and simmer for about 3-4 minutes.

Season with salt and black pepper and serve hot.

RADISH & PORK MEATBALLS SOUP

Time: 55 minutes   Servings: 4

Ingredients:

For Meatballs:

1 pound lean ground pork
1/3 cup scallions, chopped
3 teaspoons fresh cilantro, chopped
1 teaspoon garlic, minced
1 teaspoon fresh ginger, minced
1 tablespoon soy sauce
Salt and freshly ground black pepper, to taste

For Soup:

1 teaspoon sesame oil

1 tablespoon fresh ginger, minced
2 bunches broccolini, trimmed and halved
Freshly ground black pepper, to taste
4 cups chicken broth
2 cups water
1 tablespoon fish sauce
1 tablespoon soy sauce
2 teaspoons Sriracha
3 medium daikon radishes, peeled and spiralized with Blade C
½ cup fresh cilantro leaves, chopped

Directions:

Preheat the oven to 400 degrees F. Line a baking sheet with a parchment paper. For meatballs in a large bowl, add all ingredients and mix till well combined. Make about 10-12 golf ball sized meatballs from the mixture. Arrange the balls onto prepared baking sheet in a single layer. Bake for about 18 minutes. Meanwhile in a large pan, heat oil on medium heat. Add ginger and sauté for about 1 minute. Add broccolini and pepper and cook for about 3-5 minutes. Add broth, water, fish sauce, soy sauce and Sriracha and bring to a boil. Reduce the heat to low and simmer for about 10 minutes. Add radish noodles and cook for about 3-5 minutes. Divide the soup into serving bowls and top with meatballs. Serve hot with the garnishing of cilantro.

CARROT & SAUSAGE SOUP

Time: 40 minutes   Servings: 4

Ingredients:

¾ pound sweet Italian sausage, casing removed
½ cup onion, chopped
2 garlic cloves, minced
Salt and freshly ground black pepper, to taste
4 cups curly kale, chopped

6 cups chicken broth
1 teaspoon dried oregano, crushed
1 large carrot, peeled and spiralized with Blade C
1 teaspoon red pepper flakes, crushed
¼ cup Parmesan cheese, shredded

Directions:

Heat a large pan on medium-high heat. Add sausage and cook for about 10-15 minutes, crumbling with a wooden spoon. Add onion, garlic, salt and black pepper and cook for about 3 minutes. Add kale and cook for about 1 minute. Add broth and oregano and bring to a boil on high heat. Stir in carrot noodles. Reduce the heat to low and simmer for about 5 minutes. Stir in red pepper flakes and remove from heat.
Serve hot with the topping of Parmesan cheese.

Zucchini, Pesto & Sausage Soup

Time: 40 minutes   Servings: 4

Ingredients:

For Soup:

1 tablespoon extra-virgin olive oil
4 chicken sausage links, casing removed
2 celery stalks, chopped
½ of red onion, chopped
2 garlic cloves, minced
¼ teaspoon red pepper flakes
Salt and freshly ground black pepper, to taste
6 cups chicken broth

2 medium zucchinis, spiralized with Blade C

For Pesto:

2 cups fresh basil
1 large garlic clove, chopped
2 tablespoons parmesan cheese
1 tablespoon pine nuts
1 tablespoon extra-virgin olive oil
Salt and freshly ground black pepper, to taste

Directions:

In a large pan, heat oil on medium-high heat.
Add sausage and cook for about 5 minutes, crumbling with a wooden spoon.
Add in celery, onion, garlic, red pepper flakes, salt and black pepper and cook for about 3 minutes.
Add broth and bring to a boil. Cook for about 5 minutes.
Add zucchini noodles and cook for about 3-4 minutes.
Meanwhile for pesto in a food processor, add all ingredients and pulse till smooth.
Add the pesto in the soup and stir to combine. Serve immediately.

Zucchini & Salmon Soup

Time: 30 minutes   Servings: 2

Ingredients:

2 (3-ounce) salmon fillets
Salt and freshly ground black pepper, to taste
1 tablespoon extra-virgin olive oil
2 garlic cloves, minced
1 teaspoon fresh ginger, minced

1½ cups fresh spinach, torn
2 cups fish broth
2 tablespoons soy sauce
2 medium zucchinis, spiralized with Blade C
¼ cup scallions, chopped

Directions:

Arrange a steamer basket over a pan of boiling water.
In steamer basket, place the salmon fillets and sprinkle with salt and black pepper.
Steam, covered for about 5-6 minutes. Meanwhile in a large skillet, heat oil on medium heat.
Add garlic and ginger and sauté for about 1 minute.
Add spinach and cook for about 2-3 minutes. Add broth and soy sauce and bring to a boil.
Stir in zucchini, salt and black pepper and cook for about 4-5 minutes.
Sir in salmon and scallion and remove from heat. Serve hot.

ZUCCHINI & HERRING SOUP

Time: 25 minutes

Servings: 2

Ingredients:

1 tablespoon extra-virgin olive oil
1 teaspoon fresh ginger, grated finely
2 (3-ounce) herring fillets
Salt and freshly ground black pepper, to taste
2 cups chicken broth

1 small jalapeño pepper, seeded and minced
2 medium zucchinis, spiralized with Blade C
¼ cup scallion, chopped
1 tablespoon fresh lemon juice
¼ teaspoon fresh lemon zest, grated finely

Directions:

In a large skillet, heat oil on medium-high heat. Add ginger and sauté for about 30 seconds. Add herring and sprinkle with salt and black pepper and cook for about 8 minutes, flipping once in the middle way. Meanwhile in a large pan, add broth and bring to boil on high heat. Reduce the heat to medium. Stir in jalapeño pepper and zucchini and cook for about 2-3 minutes. Stir in cooked herring, scallion, lemon juice, salt and black pepper and remove from heat. Top with lemon zest and serve hot.

ZUCCHINI & SHRIMP SOUP

Time: 25 minutes

Servings: 4

Ingredients:

2 cups chicken broth
1¾ cups unsweetened coconut milk
½ teaspoon fresh ginger, grated
1 pound shrimp, peeled and deveined

1 large zucchini, spiralized with Blade C
2 tablespoons fresh lime juice
Salt and freshly ground black pepper, to taste
3 tablespoons fresh cilantro leaves, chopped

Directions:

In a large pan, add broth and coconut milk and bring to a boil on medium-high heat. Reduce the heat to medium-low. Add shrimp and zucchini and cook for 4-5 minutes. Stir in lime juice, salt and black pepper and remove from heat. Garnish with cilantro and serve hot.

MIXED VEGGIE STEW

Time: 60 minutes

Servings: 4

Ingredients:

2 tablespoons olive oil
1 yellow onion, chopped
2 large garlic cloves, minced
¼ teaspoon red pepper flakes, crushed
1 medium zucchini, spiralized with Blade C
1 medium yellow squash, spiralized with Blade C
2 red bell peppers, seeded and sliced thinly

1 cup eggplant, julienned
Salt and freshly ground black pepper, to taste
1 (28-ounce) can whole peeled tomatoes with juice
1 tablespoon fresh oregano, chopped
½ cup vegetable broth
1 bay leaf
¼ cup fresh basil, chopped

Directions:

In a large pan, heat oil on medium heat. Add onion, garlic and red pepper flakes and sauté for about 4-5 minutes. Add zucchini, squash, bell pepper, eggplant, salt and black pepper and cook for about 7-10 minutes. With your hands, crush the tomatoes in the pan. Stir in tomato juice from can, oregano, bay leaf and bring to a boil on high heat. Reduce the heat to low and simmer for about 10-15 minutes. Stir in basil and cook for about 1 minute. Discard the bay leaf and serve hot.

Carrot, Celeriac & Beans Stew

Time: 45 minutes   Servings: 2

Ingredients:

1 large carrot, peeled and spiralized with Blade C
1 medium celeriac, peeled and spiralized with Blade C
1 tablespoon olive oil
1 small onion, minced
3 garlic cloves, minced
4 cups vegetable broth

1½ cups canned chickpeas, rinsed and drained
1 teaspoon thyme, crashed
1 teaspoon marjoram, crashed
½ teaspoon smoked paprika
½ teaspoon ground turmeric
1 cup fresh spinach, torn
¼ cup nutritional yeast
Salt and freshly ground black pepper, to taste

Directions:

In a large pan, heat oil on medium heat. Add onion, garlic and red pepper flakes and sauté for about 4-5 minutes. Add garlic and sauté for about 1 minute. Add the broth, chickpeas, herbs and spices and bring to a boil on high heat. Add carrot and celeriac noodles and reduce the heat to medium-low. Simmer, covered for about 10 minutes. Stir in spinach and simmer for about 5 minutes. Stir in the nutritional yeast, salt and black pepper and remove from the heat.

Rutabaga & Beans Stew

Time: 60 minutes   Servings: 4

Ingredients:

1 large rutabaga, peeled and spiralized with Blade C
2½ tablespoons olive oil, divided
Salt and freshly ground black pepper, to taste
1 cup celery stalk, chopped
1 cup carrot, peeled and chopped
½ cup white onion, chopped
4 garlic cloves, minced
1 teaspoon dried basil, crushed
1 teaspoon dried oregano, crushed
½ teaspoon cayenne pepper

½ teaspoon ground cumin
3 cups fresh spinach, torn
3 cups vegetable broth
2 cups tomatoes, chopped
1½ cups canned navy beans, rinsed and drained
2 tablespoons fresh lemon juice

Directions:

Preheat the oven to 425 degrees F. Line a baking dish with parchment paper. In a bowl, add rutabaga noodles, 1 tablespoon of oil, salt and black pepper and toss to coat well. Arrange the rutabaga noodles onto the prepared baking dish. Bake for about 15-20 minutes. Meanwhile in a large pan, heat remaining oil on medium heat. Add celery, carrot and onion and sauté for about 5-7 minutes. Add garlic, herbs and spices and sauté for about 1 minute. Add spinach and cook for about 1-2 minutes. Add broth, tomatoes and beans and bring to a boil. Reduce the heat to low and simmer for about 20-30 minutes. Stir in lemon juice, salt and black pepper and remove from heat. Divide the rutabaga noodles in 4 serving bowls. Pour stew over rutabaga noodles evenly and serve.

BUTTERNUT SQUASH & BEANS STEW

Time: 50 minutes

Servings: 6

Ingredients:

1 tablespoon extra-virgin olive oil
1 onion, chopped
1 celery stalk, chopped
1 carrot, peeled and chopped
2 garlic cloves, minced
1 Serrano pepper, seeded and chopped
½ teaspoon dried thyme, crushed
½ teaspoon dried basil, crushed
½ teaspoon ground cumin
½ teaspoon smoked paprika

1 (15-ounce) can diced tomatoes with juice
5 cups vegetable broth
1 butternut squash, peeled and spiralized with Blade C
3 cups fresh spinach, trimmed and chopped
1 cup canned navy beans, rinsed and drained
¼ cup scallion, chopped
Salt and freshly ground black pepper, to taste
2 tablespoons fresh lemon juice

Directions:

In a large pan, heat oil on medium heat. Add onions, celery and carrot and sauté for about 4-5 minutes. Add garlic, Serrano pepper, herbs and spices and sauté for about 1 minute. Add tomatoes and cook, crushing with the back of a wooden spoon. Add broth and bring to a boil. Stir in squash and beans and reduce the heat to low. Simmer, covered for about 15 minutes. Stir in spinach and scallion and simmer for about 5 minutes. Stir in salt, black pepper and lemon juice and remove from heat. Serve hot.

ZUCCHINI & CHICKEN STEW

Time: 65 minutes

Servings: 4

Ingredients:

2½ tablespoons olive oil, divided
2½ pound boneless chicken, cubed
Salt and freshly ground black pepper, to taste
1 large carrot, peeled and sliced thinly|
1 large white onion, chopped
1 medium red bell pepper, seeded and cut into thin strips

1 medium orange bell pepper, seeded and cut into thin strips
2 garlic cloves, minced
2 Serrano pepper, seeded and chopped
2 cups fresh tomatoes, chopped finely
2 cups chicken broth
2 large zucchinis, spiralized with Blade C
¼ cup fresh cilantro leaves, chopped

Directions:

In a large pan, heat 2 tablespoons of oil on medium heat. Add chicken and sprinkle with salt and black pepper and cook for about 8-10 minutes. Transfer the chicken into a large plate. In the same pan, add carrot, onion and bell peppers and sauté for about 3-4 minutes. Add garlic and Serrano pepper and sauté for about 1 minute. Add tomatoes and cook for about 1-2 minutes, crushing with the back of a wooden spoon. Add broth and chicken and bring to a boil. Reduce the heat to low and simmer for about 20-25 minutes. Add zucchini, salt and black pepper and cook for about 23 minutes. Stir in cilantro, salt and black pepper and remove from heat. Serve hot.

RUTABAGA & BEEF STEW

Time: 2 hours 15 minutes   Servings: 4

Ingredients:

1 tablespoon extra-virgin coconut oil
1 pound beef stew meat, trimmed and cubed
Salt and freshly ground black pepper, to taste
2 celery stalks, chopped
1 large onion, chopped
2 garlic cloves, minced
10-12 fresh tomatoes, chopped finely

½ cup tomato puree
2½ cups water
1 teaspoon dried oregano, crushed
1 teaspoon dried thyme, crushed
½ teaspoon cayenne pepper
6 small rutabagas, peeled and spiralized with Blade C

Directions:

In a large pan, heat oil on medium-high-heat. Add beef and sprinkle with salt and black pepper and cook for about 4-5 minutes or till browned from all sides. Transfer the beef into a plate. In the same pan, add celery and onion and sauté for 4-5 minutes. Add garlic and sauté for about 1 minute. Add tomatoes and cook for about 1-2 minutes, crushing with the back of a wooden spoon. Add beef and remaining ingredients except rutabaga noodles and bring to a boil. Reduce the heat to low and simmer, covered for about 2 hours. Meanwhile, arrange a steamer basket in a pan of boiling water. Place the rutabaga noodles in steamer basket and sprinkle with salt. Steam, covered for about 4-5 minutes. Divide rutabaga noodles into serving bowls and top with beef mixture and serve.

SWEET POTATO & BEEF STEW

Time: 1 hour 40 minutes   Servings: 6

Ingredients:

2 pound beef stew meat, trimmed and cubed
2 tablespoons all-purpose flour
2 tablespoons butter
2 large onions, chopped
4 garlic cloves, minced
1 teaspoon fresh ginger, minced
2 cups dry red wine
2 cups beef broth

4 large carrots, peeled and chopped into coins
2 bay leaves
1 teaspoon dried oregano, crushed
Salt and freshly ground black pepper, to taste
2 medium sweet potatoes, peeled and spiralized with Blade C
½ cup fresh basil, chopped

Directions:

Coat the beef cubes with flour evenly. In a large pan, melt butter on medium-high heat. Add beef in batches and cook for about 4-5 minutes or till browned from all sides. Transfer the beef into a plate. Add onions, garlic and ginger and sauté for about 5 minutes. Add wine and scrape the brown bits from to bottom of the pan. Add beef and remaining ingredients except sweet potato noodles and basil and bring to a boil. Reduce the heat to low and simmer, covered for 1½-2 hours. Stir in sweet potato noodles and basil and simmer for about 8-10 minutes. Serve hot.

ZUCCHINI, SQUASH & BEEF STEW

Time: 1 hour 30 minutes   Servings: 4

Ingredients:

½ tablespoon olive oil
1 pound beef stew meat, cubed
Salt and freshly ground black pepper, to taste
1 medium onion, chopped
4 celery stalks, chopped
2 large carrots, peeled and chopped
2 garlic cloves, minced
1 Serrano pepper, chopped
2 bay leaves
1 teaspoon dried thyme, crushed

1 teaspoon ground coriander
2 teaspoons ground cumin
½ teaspoon cayenne pepper
2 cups tomatoes, chopped finely
5 cups chicken broth
2 tablespoons tamari
2 large zucchinis, spiralized with Blade C
2 yellow squash, spiralized with Blade C
½ cup fresh cilantro, chopped

Directions:

In a large pan, heat oil on medium heat. Add beef and sprinkle with salt and black pepper and cook for about 4-5 minutes or till browned from all sides. Transfer the beef into a bowl. In the same pan, add onion, celery and carrots and sauté for about 4-5 minutes. Add garlic, Serrano pepper, bay leaves, thyme and spices and sauté for about 1 minute. Add tomatoes and cook for about 2-3 minutes. Add beef, broth and tamari and bring to a boil. Reduce the heat to low and simmer, covered partially for about 40 minutes. Uncover and simmer for about 25-30 minutes. Stir in zucchini, squash, salt and black pepper and cook for about 4-5 minutes. Garnish with cilantro and serve hot.

ZUCCHINI & LAMB STEW

Time: 1 hour 50 minutes   Servings: 4

Ingredients:

2 tablespoons canola oil, divided
1 pound lamb stew meat, trimmed and cubed
Salt and freshly ground black pepper, to taste
1 small onion, chopped
2 carrots, peeled and chopped
2 celery stalks, chopped
2 garlic cloves, minced

1 (15-ounce) can diced tomatoes
½ tablespoon smoked paprika
3 cups chicken broth
2 tablespoons tomato paste
4 medium zucchinis, spiralized with Blade C
2 tablespoons fresh lemon juice
¼ cups fresh parsley leaves, chopped

Directions:

In a large pan, heat oil on medium heat. Add lamb and sprinkle with salt and black pepper and cook for about 4-5 minutes or till browned completely. Transfer the lamb into a bowl. In the same pan, heat remaining oil on medium heat. Add onion, carrots and celery and sauté for about 5-6 minutes. Add garlic and sauté for about 1 minute. Add tomatoes and paprika and cook for about 2-3 minutes, crushing with the back of spoon. Add lamb, broth and tomato paste and bring to a boil on high heat. Reduce the heat to low and simmer, covered for about 1½ hours or till desired thickness. Uncover and stir in zucchini and cook for about 4-5 minutes. Stir in lemon juice, salt and black pepper and remove from heat. Garnish with parsley and serve.

ZUCCHINI & MACKEREL STEW

Time: 40 minutes   Servings: 4

Ingredients:

1 tablespoon olive oil
1 yellow onion, chopped
4 garlic cloves, minced
½ teaspoon dried oregano, crushed
1 teaspoon ground cumin
½ teaspoon ground coriander
½ teaspoon cayenne pepper
4 cups fresh tomatoes, chopped finely

¼ cup black olives, pitted and sliced
1 tablespoon capers
2 cups fish broth
1 pound mackerel, cubed
1 pound zucchini, spiralized with Blade C
Salt and freshly ground black pepper, to taste
2 tablespoons fresh lemon juice
¼ cup fresh cilantro, chopped

Directions:

In a large pan, heat oil on medium heat. Add onion and sauté for about 4-5 minutes. Add garlic, oregano and spices and sauté for about 1 minute. Add tomatoes and cook for about 1-2 minutes. Add olives, capers and broth and bring to a boil. Reduce the heat to medium-low and simmer for about 10 minutes. Stir in fish and cook for about 3-4 minutes. Stir in zucchini, salt and black pepper and cook for about 2-3 minutes. Stir in lemon juice and cilantro and immediately remove from heat. Serve hot.

POTATO & COD STEW

Time: 50 minutes   Servings: 6

Ingredients:

2 teaspoons olive oil
4 large carrots, peeled and chopped
1 large onion, chopped
3 garlic cloves, minced
½ teaspoon dried rosemary, crushed
Salt and freshly ground black pepper, to taste

4 cups chicken broth
2 pound potatoes, peeled and spiralized with Blade C
1 (15-ounce) can diced tomatoes with juice
1 (6-ounce) can tomato sauce
1 pound cod fillets

Directions:

In a large pan, heat oil on medium heat. Add onion and carrots and cook, covered for about 6-8 minutes, stirring occasionally. Add garlic, rosemary, salt and black pepper and sauté for about 1 minute.

Add broth and bring to a boil. Reduce the heat to low and simmer, covered for about 8-10 minutes. Stir in potato noodles, with juices and tomato sauce and bring to a gentle simmer. Simmer for about 4-5 minutes. Stir in the cod and simmer for about 4-5 minutes.

Zucchini, Corn & Shrimp Stew

Time: 50 minutes   Servings: 4

Ingredients:

2 tablespoons olive oil
1 large onion, chopped
2 garlic cloves, minced
2 poblano peppers, seeded and chopped
Salt and freshly ground black pepper, to taste

1 (28-ounce) can diced tomatoes with juice
2 cups fish broth
1 pound medium shrimp, peeled and deveined
1 large zucchini, spiralized with Blade C
2 cups frozen corn kernels, thawed

Directions:

In a large pan, heat oil on medium-high heat. Add onion, garlic, poblano peppers, salt and black pepper and cook for about 10-12 minutes, stirring occasionally. Add the tomatoes with juice and cook and cook for about 10-12 minutes, stirring occasionally. Add broth and bring to a boil on medium heat. Add shrimp, zucchini and corn and simmer for about 5-6 minutes. Serve hot.

Zucchini & Seafood Stew

Time: 50 minutes   Servings: 6

Ingredients:

¼ cup olive oil
1 medium yellow onion, chopped finely
1 celery stalk, chopped finely
1 medium red bell pepper, seeded and chopped finely
1 small carrot, peeled and chopped finely
1 garlic clove, chopped finely
2 tablespoons tomato paste
2 large tomatoes, seeded and chopped finely
1 zucchini, spiralized with Blade C

4 cups fish broth
8-ounce swordfish, cut into 1-inch pieces
8-ounce small shrimp, peeled and deveined
1 pound mussels, cleaned
1 pound calamari bodies and tentacles, bodies cut into $1/_2$-inch rings
1 lb. clam, cleaned
$1/_2$ cup almonds, toasted and chopped finely
¼ cup fresh parsley leaves, chopped
Salt and freshly ground black pepper, to taste

Directions:

In a large Dutch oven, heat olive oil on medium heat. Add onion, celery, bell pepper, carrot and garlic and cook for about 12 minutes, stirring occasionally. Add tomato paste and cook for about 2 minutes. Add tomatoes and cook, stirring for about 2 minutes. Add broth and bring to a boil. Add the seafood and cook covered for about 7 minutes, shaking the pan occasionally. Gently, stir in zucchini noodles and cook covered for about 3-4 minutes, shaking the pan occasionally. Stir in almonds, parsley, salt and black pepper and remove from heat. Serve hot.

Spiralized Recipes with Poultry

Zucchini with Scrambled Eggs

Time: 25 minutes

Servings: 2

Ingredients:

2 medium zucchinis, spiralized with Blade C
Salt, to taste
1 tablespoon plus ½ teaspoon olive oil, divided
1 tablespoon almond flour

1 garlic clove, minced
3 eggs
Freshly ground black pepper, to taste
¼ cup fresh cilantro leaves, chopped

Directions:

In a colander place zucchini noodles and sprinkle with salt. Keep aside for at least 20 minutes. Drain well and pat dry with a paper towel. Meanwhile in a non-stick skillet, mix ½ teaspoon of oil, almond flour and a pinch of salt on medium heat. Cook for about 1 minute, stirring continuously. Remove from heat and keep aside. In another skillet, heat remaining oil on medium heat. Add zucchini noodles and cook for about 1-2 minutes. Transfer the zucchini noodles into a bowl. In the same skillet, add garlic and sauté for about 1 minute. Add eggs and cook, stirring for about 2-3 minutes. Stir in zucchini noodles and cilantro and cook for to about 2 minutes. Top with toasted almond flour and serve.

Zucchini & Shrimp with Scrambled Eggs

Time: 35 minutes

Servings: 2

Ingredients:

2 tablespoons olive oil, divided
2 large eggs
1 cup small broccoli florets
1 small onion, chopped
1 medium red bell pepper, seeded and chopped
1 teaspoon garlic, minced
1 teaspoon fresh ginger, minced

6-8 Jumbo shrimp, peeled and deveined
Salt and freshly ground black pepper, to taste
1 teaspoon coconut vinegar
3 tablespoons tamari
1 teaspoon honey
2 medium zucchinis, spiralized with Blade C
½ teaspoon black sesame seeds, toasted

Directions:

In a small skillet, heat 1 teaspoon of oil on medium heat. Add eggs and cook, stirring for about 2-3 minutes. Remove from heat and keep aside. In a large skillet, heat remaining oil on medium heat. Add broccoli and cook for about 3-4 minutes. Add onion, bell pepper, garlic and ginger and cook for about 2-3 minutes. Stir in shrimp, salt and black pepper and cook for about 2 minutes. Meanwhile in a bowl, mix together, vinegar, tamari and honey. Add scrambled eggs, zucchini noodles and honey mixture in the skillet and cook for about 2-3 minutes. Top with sesame seeds and serve.

CHEESY SCRAMBLED POTATOES & EGGS

Time: 25 minutes   Servings: 2

Ingredients:

1 tablespoon olive oil
2 small potatoes, peeled and spiralized with
   Blade C
5 eggs

½ cup avocado, peeled, pitted and cubed
½ cup feta cheese, crumbled
2 tablespoons fresh cilantro leaves, chopped

Directions:

In a large skillet, heat oil on medium heat. Add potatoes and cook, tossing occasionally for about 8-10 minutes. Add eggs and cubed avocado and cook for about 1-2 minutes, stirring continuously. Add feta and cook stirring for about 1-2 minutes. Garnish with cilantro and serve.

BEET OMELET

Time: 30 minutes   Servings: 2

Ingredients:

2 tablespoons olive oil, divided
2 small beets, peeled and spiralized with
   Blade C
4 large eggs

Salt and freshly ground black pepper, to taste
1 small avocado, peeled, pitted and cubed
1 scallion, chopped

Directions:

In a large skillet, heat 1 tablespoon of oil on medium heat. Add beet noodles and cook for about 6-7 minutes. Remove from heat and keep aside. Meanwhile in a bowl, add eggs and seasoning and beat well. In a large frying pan, heat remaining oil on medium heat. Add beaten eggs and with a wooden spoon, spread the eggs towards the edges of pan. Cook for about 1-2 minutes. Place bees and avocado over eggs. Carefully, fold the omelet over the beet noodles and avocado and cook for about 2 minutes. Top with scallions and serve.

ZUCCHINI & KALE FRITTATA

Time: 40 minutes   Servings: 4

Ingredients:

1 tablespoon olive oil
1 garlic clove, minced
3 cups fresh kale, trimmed and chopped

1 large zucchini, spiralized with Blade C
Salt and freshly ground black pepper, to taste
12 egg whites, beaten

Directions:

Preheat the oven to 375 degrees F. In an oven proof skillet, heat oil on medium heat. Add garlic and sauté for about 1 minute. Add kale and cook for 3-4 minutes or till just wilted. Transfer half of kale into a plate. Place the zucchini noodles over kale evenly and top with remaining kale. Sprinkle with salt and black pepper and spread beaten egg whites over kale evenly. Cook for about 2 minutes. Transfer the skillet into oven and bake for about 15-18 minutes.

Cheesy Zucchini & Spinach Frittata

Time: 40 minutes

Servings: 4

Ingredients:

12 egg whites
Salt and freshly ground black pepper, to taste
2 teaspoons olive oil
1 garlic clove, minced

3 cups fresh baby spinach, chopped
1 large zucchini, spiralized with Blade C
2-ounce feta cheese, crumbled

Directions:

Preheat the oven to 375 degrees F. In a large bowl, add egg whites, salt and pepper and beat. In an oven proof skillet, heat oil on medium heat. Add garlic and sauté for about 1 minute. Add spinach and cook for about 2-3 minutes. Transfer half of spinach into a bowl. Place zucchini over spinach evenly. Spread remaining spinach over zucchini and top with egg white mixture evenly. Sprinkle with cheese evenly and slightly push into egg whites. Bake for about 15-20 minutes or till top becomes golden brown.

Squash & Spinach Frittata

Time: 40 minutes

Servings: 2

Ingredients:

½ cup egg whites
4 eggs
1 large yellow squash, spiralized with Blade C and sliced into 3-inch pieces.
1 tablespoon olive oil

2 garlic cloves, minced
2 cups fresh spinach, chopped
1 cup red bell pepper, seeded and chopped
Salt and freshly ground black pepper, to taste

Directions:

Preheat the oven to 350 degrees F. In a large bowl, add egg whites, eggs and seasoning and beat till well combined. Stir in squash noodles and keep aside. In a large oven proof skillet, heat oil on medium heat. Add garlic and sauté for about 1 minute. Add spinach and bell peppers and cook for about 3-4 minutes. Stir in egg mixture. Transfer the skillet into oven and bake for about 20 minutes.

Sweet Potato with Eggs

Time: 45 minutes

Servings: 4

Ingredients:

1 tablespoon canola oil
¼ cup white onion, chopped
2 garlic cloves, minced
1 Serrano pepper, seeded and chopped
¼ teaspoon ground cumin
¼ teaspoon red pepper flakes, crushed

2 cups fresh tomatoes, chopped finely
1 large sweet potato, peeled and spiralized with Blade C
Salt and freshly ground Black Pepper, to taste
4 eggs
2 tablespoons fresh basil leaves, chopped

Directions:

Preheat the oven to 375 degrees F. In a large skillet, heat oil on medium heat. Add onion and sauté for about 3-4 minutes. Add garlic, Serrano pepper, cumin and red pepper flakes and sauté for about 1 minute. Add tomatoes and cook for about 2-3 minutes. Add sweet potato noodles, salt and black pepper and cook for about 6-7 minutes. Transfer the sweet potato mixture into 4 large ramekins evenly. Crack 1 egg in each ramekin over sweet potato mixture and sprinkle with salt and black pepper. Bake for about 10-15 minutes or till desired doneness. Garnish with basil and serve.

CHEESY SWEET POTATO & EGGS

Time: 55 minutes   Servings: 4

Ingredients:

2 tablespoons olive oil
1 onion, sliced
1 large sweet potato, peeled and spiralized
   with Blade C

2 garlic cloves, minced
8 eggs
Salt and freshly ground black pepper, to taste
2-ounce feta cheese, crumbled

Directions:

Preheat the oven to 350 degrees F. In an oven proof skillet, heat oil on medium heat. Add onion and sauté for about 4 minutes. Add garlic and sauté for about 1 minute. Add sweet potato noodles and cook for about 8-10 minutes. Carefully, crack the eggs over sweet potato noodles evenly and sprinkle with salt and black pepper. Bake for about 20 minutes. Remove from oven and sprinkle with cheese evenly. Bake for about 5 minutes more.

SWEET POTATO, SPINACH & CHICKEN WITH EGGS

Time: 25 minutes   Servings: 2

Ingredients:

1 tablespoon sunflower oil
½ small white onion, chopped
1 garlic clove, minced
2 medium sweet potatoes, peeled and
spiralized with Blade C

¼ teaspoon cayenne pepper
Salt and freshly ground black pepper, to taste
1 cup cooked chicken, chopped finely
2 cups fresh spinach, chopped
2 eggs

Directions:

In a large skillet, heat oil on medium heat. Add onion and sauté for about 3-4 minutes. Add garlic and sauté for about 1 minute. Add sweet potato and seasoning and cook for about 4-5 minutes. Add chicken and spinach and cook for about 3-4 minutes. Carefully, crack the eggs over sweet potato mixture. Sprinkle each egg with salt and black pepper. Cover the skillet and cook for about 2-3 minutes or till desired doneness.

POTATO WITH EGGS

Time: 45 minutes

Servings: 4

Ingredients:

2 tablespoons olive oil
2 large potatoes, peeled and spiralized with Blade C
1 white onion, chopped

2 garlic cloves, minced
Salt and freshly ground black pepper, to taste
8 eggs

Directions:

Preheat the oven to 350 degrees F. In a large oven proof skillet, heat oil on medium heat. Add potato noodles and onion and cook for about 8-9 minutes. Add garlic and cook for 1 minute. Carefully, crack the eggs over sweet potato mixture evenly. Transfer the skillet into oven. Bake for about 20-25 minutes.

ZUCCHINI & SWEET POTATO WITH EGGS

Time: 35 minutes

Servings: 2

Ingredients:

2 tablespoons olive oil, divided
1 medium sweet potato, peeled and spiralized with Blade C

1 medium zucchini, spiralized with Blade C
4 eggs
Salt and freshly ground black pepper, to taste

Directions:

In a large skillet, heat 1½ tablespoons of oil on medium heat. Add sweet potato noodles and cook for about 3-4 minutes. Add zucchini noodles and cook for about 2-3 minutes. Carefully, make a well in the center of vegetables. Pour remaining oil in the well. Carefully, crack the eggs in the well. Cover the skillet and cook for about 2-3 minutes or till desired doneness. Sprinkle with salt and black pepper and serve.

ZUCCHINI & CHICKEN WITH EGGS

Time: 25 minutes

Servings: 2

Ingredients:

2 tablespoon olive oil, divided
4 small zucchinis, spiralized with Blade C
1 cup cooked chicken breast, cut into bite size pieces

Salt and freshly ground black pepper, to taste
4 eggs
2 tablespoons fresh cilantro leaves, chopped

Directions:

In a large skillet, heat 1 tablespoon of oil on medium-high heat. Add zucchini and cook for about 3-4 minutes. Add chicken, salt and black pepper and cook for about 1 minute. Carefully, make 2 wells in the middle of zucchini mixture. Pour remaining oil in the wells. Carefully, crack 2 eggs in each well and sprinkle with salt and black pepper. Cover the skillet and cook for about 2-3 minutes or till desired doneness. Garnish with cilantro and serve.

Sweet Potato & Poached Eggs

Time: 45 minutes   Servings: 4

Ingredients:

2 medium sweet potatoes, peeled and spiralized with Blade C
4 tablespoons olive oil, divided

1 teaspoon red chili powder
Salt and freshly ground black pepper, to taste
4 large eggs

Directions:

Preheat the oven to 450 degrees F. Line a baking sheet with parchment paper. Place the sweet potato noodles in prepared baking sheet. Drizzle with 2 tablespoons of oil and sprinkle with seasoning. Bake for about 30 minutes, tossing once after 15 minutes. Meanwhile in large pan, boil water on medium-high heat and then, reduce the heat to medium. Crack 1 egg in a bowl and carefully pour the egg into the pan of boiling water. Repeat with the remaining eggs. Cook for about 2-3 minutes or till desired doneness. Place poached eggs over sweet potato noodles and serve.

Sweet Potato & Chicken with Fried Eggs

Time: 40 minutes   Servings: 4

Ingredients:

3 tablespoons olive oil, divided
2 garlic cloves, minced and divided
1 large sweet potato, peeled and spiralized with Blade C
1 small white onion, chopped
1 red bell pepper, seeded and chopped
1 green bell pepper, seeded and chopped

½ teaspoon dried thyme, crushed
¼ teaspoon cayenne pepper
Salt and freshly ground black pepper, to taste
½ cup cooked chicken, shredded
4 eggs
1 tablespoon fresh cilantro, chopped

Directions:

In a large skillet, heat 1 tablespoon of oil on medium heat. Add 1 garlic clove and sauté for about 1 minute. Add sweet potato noodles and cook for about 6-8 minutes. Transfer sweet potato noodles into a plate. Meanwhile in another skillet, heat 1 tablespoon of oil on medium heat. Add onion, bell peppers, thyme, remaining garlic and seasoning and cook for about 4-5 minutes. Stir in chicken and transfer the chicken mixture over sweet potato noodles. In a frying pan, heat remaining oil on low heat. Carefully, crack the eggs and cook for about 3-4 minutes. Spoon the hot oil over whites till set, but spoon the oil over yolks only a couple of time. Top the chicken and sweet potato with fried eggs. Garnish with fresh cilantro and serve.

Jicama with Fried Eggs

Time: 45 minutes   Servings: 4

Ingredients:

1 large jicama, peeled and spiralized with Blade C
5 tablespoons olive oil, divided

1 teaspoon cayenne pepper
Salt and freshly ground black pepper, to taste
4 large eggs

Directions:

Preheat the oven to 400 degrees F. Lightly grease 2 baking sheets. Arrange jicama noodles in prepared baking sheets. Drizzle with 2 tablespoons of oil and sprinkle with spices. Bake for about 30 minutes, flipping once after 15 minutes. Meanwhile in a large frying pan, heat remaining oil on low heat. Carefully, crack the eggs and cook for about 3-4 minutes. Spoon the hot oil over whites till set, but spoon the oil over yolks only a couple of time. Top the jicama with fried eggs and serve immediately.

ZUCCHINI WITH FRIED EGGS

Time: 20 minutes   Servings: 2

Ingredients:

2½ tablespoons extra virgin olive oil, divided
4 eggs
1 large zucchini, spiralized with Blade C

Salt and freshly ground black pepper, to taste
1 tablespoon soy sauce
1 tablespoon fresh parsley, chopped

Directions:

In a large frying pan, heat 2 tablespoons of oil on low heat. Carefully, crack the eggs and cook for about 3-4 minutes. Spoon the hot oil over whites till set, but spoon the oil over yolks only a couple of time. Meanwhile place zucchini noodles in a micro wave safe bowl. Sprinkle with salt and black pepper and microwave on High for about 1 minute. Drizzle with ½ tablespoon of oil and soy sauce and microwave for about 1 minute more. Transfer zucchini in a large serving plate and top with fried eggs. Garnish with parsley and serve.

CHEESY ZUCCHINI WITH FRIED EGGS

Time: 20 minutes   Servings: 2

Ingredients:

2 tablespoons olive oil, divided
1 garlic clove, minced
2 large zucchinis, spiralized with Blade C
¼ teaspoon red pepper flakes, crushed

Salt and freshly ground black pepper, to taste
2 tablespoons mozzarella cheese, grated
4 eggs

Directions:

In a large skillet, heat 1 tablespoon of oil on medium heat. Add garlic and sauté for about 1 minute. Add zucchini, red pepper flakes, salt and black pepper and cook for about 3-4 minutes. Transfer the zucchini mixture into 2 large serving plates. Immediately, sprinkle with cheese evenly. Meanwhile in a large frying pan, heat remaining oil on medium heat. Crack the eggs in skillet one by one. Cook for about 2-3 minutes or till desired doneness. Place the eggs over zucchini. Sprinkle each egg with salt and black pepper and serve.

Sweet Potato Buns with Fruit

Time: 25 minutes   Servings: 2

Ingredients:

1½ tablespoons butter, divided
1 large sweet potatoes, peeled and
  spiralized with Blade C
Salt and freshly ground black pepper, to taste
1 egg

¼ cup peanut butter
½ small banana, peeled and sliced
4 fresh strawberries, hulled and sliced
1 teaspoon honey

Directions:

In a large skillet, melt ½ tablespoon of butter on medium heat. Add sweet potato noodles and sprinkle with salt and black pepper and cook for about 6-8 minutes. Transfer the sweet potato noodles into a bowl. Add egg and mix well. Transfer the mixture into 2 (6-ounce) ramekins, half way full. Cover the ramekins with wax paper. Now, place a weight over noodles to press firmly down. Refrigerate for at least 15-20 minutes. In a large skillet, melt remaining butter on medium-low heat. Carefully, transfer the sweet potato patties into skillet and cook for about 3-4 minutes. Flip the side and cook for about 2-3 minutes more. Place patties in serving plate. Spread peanut butter over patties evenly. T Top with banana slices and strawberries. Drizzle with honey and serve.

Sweet Potato Buns Sandwich

Time: 45 minutes   Servings: 2

Ingredients:

3 tablespoons olive oil, divided
1 garlic clove, minced
2 medium sweet potatoes, peeled and
spiralized with Blade C
Salt and freshly ground black pepper, to taste
2 eggs, beaten

1 medium onion, sliced into rings
1 medium avocado, peeled, pitted and sliced
3 tablespoons butter, softened
4 tomato slices
8 fresh baby spinach leaves

Directions:

In a large skillet, heat 1 tablespoon of oil on medium heat. Add garlic and sauté for about 1 minute. Add sweet potato noodles and sprinkle with salt and black pepper and cook for about 6-8 minutes. Transfer the sweet potato mixture into a bowl. Add beaten eggs and mix well. Transfer the mixture into 4 ramekins, half way full. Cover the ramekins with wax paper. Now, place a weight over noodles to press firmly down. Refrigerate for at least 20 minutes. Meanwhile in a skillet, heat ¼ tablespoon of oil on medium heat. Add onion and sprinkle with salt and black pepper and sauté for about 4-5 minutes. Transfer the onion into a plate and keep aside. In the same skillet, add tomato slices and sear for about 1 minute per side. Transfer the tomato slices into a plate and keep aside. In a bowl, add avocado and butter and with a fork, mash till well combined. In a large skillet, heat remaining oil on medium-low heat. Carefully, transfer the sweet potato bun into skillet and cook for about 3-4 minutes. Flip the side and cook for about 2-3 minutes more. In a serving plate place 1 bun. Spread avocado mixture over all buns. Place spinach leaves over buns and top with onion rings and tomato slices evenly. Cover with other bun. Repeat with remaining buns. Secure with a toothpick before serving.

Zucchini Buns Sandwich with Chicken

Time: 25 minutes

Servings: 2

Ingredients:

For Buns:

2 tablespoons olive oil, divided
2 garlic cloves, minced
3 large zucchinis, spiralized with Blade C
Salt and freshly ground black pepper, to taste
2 large eggs, beaten
2 egg whites, beaten
For Avocado Mash:
1 avocado, peeled, pitted and chopped

1½ tablespoons fresh parsley leaves, minced
Pinch of salt
Pinch of red pepper flakes, crushed

For Sandwiches:

2 red onion slices
2 large tomato slices
4-ounce cooked chicken breast, chopped
2 romaine lettuce leaves, torn

Directions:

In a large skillet, heat 1 tablespoon of oil on medium heat. Add garlic and sauté for about 1 minute. Add zucchini and sprinkle with salt and black pepper and cook for about 3-4 minutes. Transfer the zucchini mixture into a bowl. Immediately, add beaten eggs and egg whites and mix well. Transfer the mixture into 2 large ramekins, half way full. Cover the ramekins with wax paper. Now, place a weight over wax paper to press firmly down. Refrigerate for at least 20 minutes. In a large skillet, heat remaining oil on medium-low heat. Carefully, transfer the zucchini bun into skillet and cook for about 2-3 minutes per side. Transfer the buns into a plate. Meanwhile in a bowl, add all mash ingredients and with a fork, mash till smooth and creamy. Preheat the grill to medium heat. Grease the grill grate. Grill onion slices for 2 minutes, flipping once after 1 minute. Grill the tomato slices for 1 minute, flipping once after 30 seconds. In a serving plate place 1 bun. Spread avocado mash over buns evenly. Place 1 onion slices over mash, followed by half of chicken, 1tomato slice and half of torn lettuce. Cover with other bun. Repeat with remaining buns. Secure with a toothpick before serving.

Sweet Potato & Zucchini Patties

Time: 60 minutes

Servings: 4

Ingredients:

1 large egg
¼ teaspoon ground cumin
½ teaspoon red pepper flakes, crushed
Salt and freshly ground black pepper, to taste
¼ cup butter, melted
2 tablespoons almond flour

1 large zucchini, spiralized with Blade C and chopped
1 large sweet potato, peeled, spiralized with Blade C and chopped
2 tablespoons fresh cilantro leaves, chopped

Directions:

Preheat the oven to 375 degrees F. Line 2 baking sheets with greased parchment papers. In a large bowl, add egg and spices and beat well. Add butter and flour and mix till well combined. Add remaining ingredients and mix till well combined. With ½ cup of mixture make a patty. Repeat with the remaining mixture. Arrange the patties onto prepared baking sheets in a single layer. Bake for about 10 minutes. Reduce the temperature of oven to 350 degrees F. Bake for about 15 minutes. Carefully, flip the side of patties and bake for about 15 minutes.

Carrot & Zucchini Patties

Time: 25 minutes   Servings: 4

Ingredients:
1 medium zucchini, spiralized with Blade C
1 medium carrot, peeled and spiralized with Blade C
4-5 scallions, chopped
2 small eggs, beaten
½ cup almond flour

¼ teaspoon ground cumin
¼ teaspoon red pepper flakes, crushed
1 teaspoon ground turmeric
Salt and freshly ground black pepper, to taste
2 tablespoons extra virgin olive oil

Directions:
In a large bowl, add all ingredients except oil and mix till well combined. In a large skillet, heat ½ tablespoon of oil on medium-high heat. Place ¼ of the mixture in oil and gently press down like a patty. Cook for about 5-6 minutes, flipping once after 3 minutes. Repeat with the remaining oil and veggie mixture.

Sweet Potato Muffins

Time: 50 minutes   Servings: 3

Ingredients:
1½ tablespoons olive oil, divided
1 garlic clove, minced
1 large sweet potato, peeled and spiralized with Blade C

Salt and freshly ground black pepper, to taste
3 cups fresh spinach, torn
12 egg whites, beaten lightly

Directions:
Preheat the oven to 375 degrees F. Grease a 6 cups of a muffin tin. In a large skillet, heat oil on medium heat. Add garlic and sauté for about 1 minute. Add sweet potato noodles and sprinkle with salt and black pepper and cook for about 6-8 minutes. Transfer the sweet potato mixture into a plate and keep aside. In the same skillet, add spinach and cook for about 3-4 minutes. Add egg whites in prepared muffin cups, about ½-inch full. Place sweet potato noodles over egg whites, followed by spinach and remaining egg whites evenly. Bake for about 20 minutes.

Carrot & Zucchini Loaf

Time: 75 minutes   Servings: 4

Ingredients:
2 tablespoons olive oil

2 garlic cloves, minced

1 jalapeño pepper, seeded and chopped finely
4 medium zucchinis, spiralized with Blade C and chopped
4 medium carrots, peeled, spiralized with Blade C and chopped
¼ teaspoon red pepper flakes, crushed

Salt and freshly ground black pepper, to taste
¼ cup coconut flour
½ teaspoon baking powder
6 large eggs
¼ cup unsweetened coconut milk
2 tablespoons fresh cilantro leaves, chopped

Directions:

Preheat the oven to 350 degrees F. Line a loaf pan with parchment paper. In a skillet, heat oil on medium heat. Add garlic and jalapeño pepper and sauté for about 1 minute. Add zucchini, carrot, red pepper flakes, salt and black pepper and cook for about 8-9 minutes. Remove from heat and keep aside to cool. In a bowl, mix together flour, baking powder and pinch of salt. In another bowl, add eggs and coconut milk and beat till well combined. Mix egg mixture into flour mixture. Fold in zucchini mixture and cilantro. Transfer the mixture into prepared loaf pan evenly. Bake for about 40-45 minutes or till a toothpick inserted in the center comes out clean.

SWEET POTATO WAFFLES

Time: 25 minutes   Servings: 2

Ingredients:

1 tablespoon olive oil
2 medium sweet potatoes, peeled and spiralized with Blade C

2 teaspoons pumpkin pie spice
2 eggs, beaten
2 tablespoons pure maple syrup

Directions:

Preheat the waffle iron and then grease it. In a large skillet, heat oil on medium heat. Add sweet potato and cook for about 8-10 minutes. Transfer the sweet potato mixture into a large bowl. Sprinkle with pumpkin pie spice and mix well. Add eggs and stir to combine. Place the mixture in waffle iron and cook for about 5 minutes. Serve with the drizzling of maple syrup.

PARSNIP WAFFLES

Time: 25 minutes   Servings: 2

Ingredients:

1 tablespoon olive oil
1 garlic clove, minced
4 large parsnips, peeled and spiralized with Blade C

Salt and freshly ground black pepper, to taste
1/3 cup scallions, chopped finely
2 large eggs, beaten

Directions:

Preheat the waffle iron and then grease it. In a large skillet, heat oil on medium heat. Add garlic and sauté for about 1 minute. Add parsnip noodles, salt and black pepper and cook for about 4-5 minutes. Transfer the parsnip mixture into a large bowl. Add scallions and eggs and stir to combine. Pour the mixture in waffle iron and cook for about 5 minutes.

POTATO PANCAKES

Time: 30 minutes

Servings: 4

Ingredients:

2 tablespoons olive oil, divided
1 garlic clove, minced
1 tablespoon fresh rosemary, chopped
¼ teaspoon red pepper flakes, crushed

4 medium potatoes, peeled and spiralized with Blade C
Salt and freshly ground black pepper, to taste
4 eggs, beaten
1 cup cheddar cheese, grated

Directions:

In a large skillet, heat one tablespoon of oil on medium heat. Add garlic, rosemary and red pepper flakes and sauté for about 1 minute. Stir in potatoes, salt and black pepper and cook, covered for about 8-10 minutes. Transfer the potato mixture into a large bowl. Add eggs and cheese and stir to combine. In another large skillet, heat remaining oil on medium heat. Add 1 cup of potato mixture and flatten with the back of a spoon. Cook for about 2-3 minutes per side. Repeat with the remaining mixture. Serve immediately.

ZUCCHINI PANCAKES

Time: 25 minutes

Servings: 4

Ingredients:

½ cup almond flour
1 tablespoon flax meal
1/3 teaspoon baking soda
Pinch of salt
1 egg, separated

½ tablespoon honey
1 tablespoon coconut oil, melted
½ cup unsweetened almond milk
½ cup zucchini, spiralized with Blade C and chopped

Directions:

Preheat a greased griddle. In a large bowl, mix together flour, flax meal, baking soda and salt. In another bowl, add egg yolk, honey, oil and milk and beat till well combined. Add honey mixture into flour mixture and mix well. In a small bowl, add egg white and beat till soft peaks form. Fold egg white into flour mixture. Now fold in zucchini. Place ¼ cup of mixture into griddle and cook for about 1-2 minutes per side. Repeat with remaining mixture.

SWEET POTATO & CHICKEN ROLLS

Time: 30 minutes

Servings: 2

Ingredients:

1 medium ripe avocado, peeled, pitted and mashed
1½ tablespoons olive oil, divided
1 large sweet potato, peeled and spiralized with Blade C

4 eggs, beaten
Salt and freshly ground black pepper, to taste
2 large lettuce leaves, pat dried
¼ cup grilled chicken, shredded

Directions:

In a large skillet, heat 1 tablespoon of oil on medium heat. Add sweet potato noodles and cook for about 6-8 minutes. Transfer the sweet potato noodles into a plate. In the same skillet, heat remaining oil on medium heat. Add eggs and sprinkle with salt and black pepper and cook for about 2-3 minutes or till eggs are done completely. Remove from heat. Arrange the both lettuce leaves in 2 serving plates. Place mashed avocado over both leaves evenly and top with sweet potato noodles, followed by scrambled eggs and shredded chicken. Carefully roll the lettuce leaves and serve.

ZUCCHINI & CHICKEN PIZZA

Time: 50 minutes   Servings: 4

Ingredients:

For Crust:

1½ cups almond meal
1 cup coconut flour
1 cup tapioca flour
1½ teaspoons baking powder
Pinch of sea salt
5 eggs
5 tablespoons olive oil
1 cup water
2 garlic cloves, minced
1 tablespoon fresh rosemary, minced

For Tomato Sauce:

2 cups fresh tomatoes, chopped
1 tablespoon fresh basil leaves, chopped
1 tablespoon olive oil
1 tablespoon fresh lemon juice
Salt and freshly ground black pepper, to taste

For Topping:

1 cup cooked chicken, cubed
1 medium zucchini, spiralized with Blade C
   and chopped
8-10 black olives, pitted and sliced
Pinch of red pepper flakes, crushed
Pinch of salt

Directions:

Preheat the oven to 350 degrees F. Grease a pizza pan and then line with a parchment paper. For crust in a bowl, mix together almond meal, flours, baking powder and salt. In another bowl, add eggs, oil and water and beat till well combined. Mix egg mixture into flour mixture. Fold in garlic and rosemary and mix till a dough form. Place the dough into prepared pan evenly. Bake for about 15 minutes. Remove from oven and keep aside to cool slightly. Carefully remove parchment paper from underneath the crust. Meanwhile for tomato sauce in a blender, add all ingredients and pulse till smooth. Spread tomato sauce over crust evenly. Place chicken and zucchini over tomato sauce and top with olives. Sprinkle with red pepper flakes and salt. Bake for about 10-12 minutes.

CREAMY ZUCCHINI & EGG BAKE

Time: 70 minutes   Servings: 4

Ingredients:

4 large eggs
2 tablespoons heavy cream
1 tablespoon coconut oil, melted
¼ cup almond meal, divided

Salt and freshly ground black pepper, to taste
4 cups zucchini, spiralized with Blade C
1 scallion, sliced thinly

Directions:

Preheat the oven to 300 degrees F. Grease an 8x8-inch baking dish. In a large bowl, add eggs, cream, oil, 3 tablespoons of almond meal, salt and black pepper and beat till well combined. Stir in zucchini. Place 1/3 of zucchini noodles into prepared baking dish and top with 1/3 of scallion. Repeat the layers twice. Pour the any remaining egg mixture from bowl over the layers. Sprinkle with remaining almond meal evenly. Bake for about 50 minutes or till done completely.

SPICY ZUCCHINI WITH CHICKEN

Time: 40 minutes   Servings: 4

Ingredients:

2 tablespoons olive oil, divided
1½ pound skinless, boneless chicken
    breast, trimmed and cubed
½ teaspoon ground cumin
Salt and freshly ground black pepper, to taste

2 garlic cloves, minced
2 jalapeño pepper, seeded and minced
3 large zucchinis, spiralized with Blade C
½ cup fresh cilantro, chopped

Directions:

In a large skillet, heat 1 tablespoon of oil on medium heat. Add chicken, cumin, salt and black pepper and cook for about 5-7 minutes. Transfer the chicken into a bowl. In the same skillet, heat remaining oil on medium heat. Add garlic and jalapeño pepper and sauté for about1 minute. Add zucchini noodles, salt and black pepper and cook for about 2-3 minutes. Stir in chicken and cilantro and coo k for about 2 minutes. Serve hot.

SWEET & SOUR ZUCCHINI WITH CHICKEN

Time: 30 minutes   Servings: 4

Ingredients:

1 tablespoon coconut oil
3 garlic cloves, minced
1 pound boneless chicken thighs, cut into
    thin strips
1 tablespoon tamari
½ tablespoon fresh lime juice

½ tablespoon balsamic vinegar
½ tablespoon honey
2 large zucchinis, spiralized with Blade C
Salt and freshly ground black pepper, to taste
¼ cup fresh parsley leaves, chopped
1 tablespoon black sesame seeds, toasted

Directions:

In a large skillet, melt coconut oil on medium heat. Add garlic and sauté for about 1 minute. Add chicken and stir fry for about 3-4 minutes. Add tamari, lime juice, vinegar and honey and cook for about 4-5 minutes. Stir in zucchini, salt and black pepper and cook for about 3-4 minutes. Stir in parsley and immediately remove from heat. Garnish with sesame seeds and serve hot.

ZUCCHINI WITH EGGPLANT & CHICKEN

Time: 40 minutes   Servings: 2

Ingredients:

1½ cups eggplant, diced into ¾-inch pieces
2 tablespoons olive oil, divided
Salt and freshly ground black pepper, to taste
3 small garlic cloves, minced

½ pound skinless boneless chicken, cut into
    bite size pieces
1½ cups fresh tomatoes, chopped finely
2 medium zucchinis, spiralized with Blade C
2 tablespoons fresh basil, chopped

Directions:

Preheat the oven to 475 degrees F. Line a baking sheet with parchment paper. Arrange eggplant pieces in prepared baking sheet in a single layer. Drizzle with 1 tablespoon of oil and sprinkle with salt and black pepper. Roast for about 25 minutes, flipping occasionally. Meanwhile in a large skillet, heat remaining oil on medium heat. Add garlic and sauté for about 1 minute. Add chicken and cook for about 8-10 minutes. Add tomatoes and cook for about 8-10 minutes. Stir in zucchini, basil and seasoning and cook for about 3-4 minutes. Stir in roasted eggplant and serve hot.

ZUCCHINI WITH BROCCOLI & CHICKEN

Time: 35 minutes   Servings: 2

Ingredients:

2 tablespoons olive oil
1 large garlic clove, minced
2 (6-ounce) skinless, boneless chicken
    breasts, cubed
¼ teaspoon red chili powder

Salt and freshly ground black pepper, to taste
1 broccoli head, cut into florets
¾ cup chicken broth
2 large zucchinis, spiralized with Blade C
1 tablespoon fresh parsley, chopped

Directions:

In a large skillet, heat oil on medium heat. Add garlic and sauté for about 1 minute. Add chicken and sprinkle with chili powder, salt and black pepper and cook for about 6-8 minutes or till golden brown from all sides. Add broccoli and cook for 2-3 minutes. Add broth and cook for about 2-3 minutes. Stir in zucchini noodles and parsley and cook for about 2-3 minutes. Serve hot.

ZUCCHINI WITH BROCCOLI, TOMATOES & CHICKEN

Time: 40 minutes

Servings: 4

Ingredients:

2 tablespoons coconut oil, divided
1 garlic clove, minced
1 pound boneless chicken thighs, cubed
Salt and freshly ground black pepper, to taste
1 medium yellow onion, chopped

3 cups broccoli florets, chopped
2 cups cherry tomatoes, halved
2 large zucchinis, spiralized with Blade C
½ teaspoon red pepper flakes, crushed
2 tablespoons fresh lime juice

Directions:

In a large skillet, melt 1 tablespoon of coconut oil on medium heat. Add garlic and sauté for about 1 minute. Add chicken and sprinkle with salt and black pepper and cook for about 6-8 minutes. Transfer the chicken into a plate. In the same skillet, melt remaining coconut oil on medium heat. Add onion and sauté for 6-7 minutes. Add broccoli and tomatoes and cook for about 4-5 minutes. Stir in zucchini, red pepper flakes, salt and black pepper and cook for about 3-4 minutes. Stir in chicken and lime juice and remove from heat. Serve hot.

ZUCCHINI WITH KALE & CHICKEN

Time: 45 minutes

Servings: 2

Ingredients:

2 (4-ounce) skinless, boneless chicken
   breasts, sliced into thin strips
1½ tablespoons fresh lemon juice, divided
2 teaspoons dried rosemary, crushed
½ teaspoon cayenne pepper, divided
Salt and freshly ground black pepper, to taste

1 tablespoon olive oil, divided
1 garlic clove, minced
2 cups fresh kale, trimmed and chopped
2 large zucchinis, spiralized with Blade C
1 teaspoon fresh lemon zest, grated finely

Directions:

Preheat the oven to 350 degrees F. Grease a baking dish. Place chicken strips in prepared baking dish. Drizzle with 1 tablespoon of lemon juice and sprinkle with rosemary, ¼ teaspoon of cayenne pepper, salt and black pepper. Bake for about 15-20 minutes. Remove from oven and keep aside. Meanwhile in a large skillet, heat oil on medium heat. Add garlic and sauté for about 1 minute. Add kale and cook for about 3 minutes. Stir in zucchini noodles, remaining cayenne pepper and lemon juice and cook for about 2-3 minutes, stirring occasionally. Stir in chicken and immediately, remove from heat. Garnish with lemon zest and serve hot.

ZUCCHINI WITH GREENS, TOMATOES & CHICKEN

Time: 45 minutes

Servings: 2

Ingredients:

2 cups grape tomatoes
1 tablespoon olive oil

Salt and freshly ground black pepper, to taste
2 garlic cloves, minced

2 cups mixed fresh greens (kale, spinach, arugula), torn
2 large zucchinis, spiralized with Blade C

1 cup cooked skinless, boneless chicken breast, cubed

Directions:

Preheat the oven to 400 degrees F. Arrange the grape tomatoes in a baking dish. Drizzle with oil evenly and sprinkle with salt and black pepper. Roast for about 20 minutes. Remove from oven and keep aside. Meanwhile in a large skillet, heat oil on medium heat. Add garlic and sauté for about 1 minute. Add greens and cook for about 2-3 minutes. Add zucchini noodles, chicken and roasted tomatoes and cook for about 2-3 minutes, stirring occasionally. Serve hot.

ZUCCHINI WITH TOMATOES & CHICKEN

Time: 45 minutes

Servings: 2

Ingredients:

1 tablespoon olive oil
2 (4-ounce) skinless, boneless chicken breasts
Salt and freshly ground black pepper, to taste
¼ cup white onion, chopped
2 cups tomatoes, chopped
½ teaspoon ground cumin

¼ teaspoon ground coriander
¼ teaspoon cayenne pepper
½ cup chicken broth
2 medium zucchinis, spiralized with Blade C
2 tablespoons fresh thyme, chopped

Directions:

In a large skillet, heat oil on medium heat. Add chicken and sprinkle with salt and black pepper and cook for about 3-4 minutes. Flip the side and cook for about 4-5 minutes. Add onion and sauté for about 4-5 minutes. Add tomatoes and spices and cook for 1-2 minutes, crushing with the back of spoon. Add broth and bring to a boil. Reduce the heat to low and simmer for bout about 10 minutes. Add zucchini, salt and black pepper and cook for about 3-4 minutes. Stir in thyme and remove from heat. Serve hot.

ZUCCHINI & RADISH WITH PESTO & CHICKEN

Time: 25 minutes

Servings: 2

Ingredients:

For Zucchini & Radish:

2 tablespoons olive oil
5 radishes, peeled and spiralized with Blade C
1 large zucchini, spiralized with Blade C
Salt and freshly ground black pepper, to taste
1 cup grilled skinless, boneless chicken thighs, cubed

For Pesto:

2 cups fresh baby spinach
½ cup fresh basil, chopped
1 garlic clove, minced
½ cup pecans, chopped and divided
1 tablespoon fresh lemon juice
½ cup water
Salt and freshly ground black pepper, to taste

Directions:

In a large skillet, heat oil on medium heat. Add radish and zucchini noodles and cook for about 2-3 minutes. Stir in salt and black pepper and remove from heat. Transfer the noodles into a large bowl. In a food processor, add spinach, basil, garlic, ½ cup of pecans, lemon juice, water, salt and black pepper and pulse till smooth. Place the pesto mixture over vegetables and gently toss to coat. Top with grilled chicken and serve.

ZUCCHINI WITH SPINACH & CHICKEN

Time: 35 minutes   Servings: 2

Ingredients:

1 (6-ounce) skinless, boneless chicken
  breast, sliced into thin strips
1 tablespoon fresh rosemary, minced
Salt and freshly ground black pepper, to taste
1 tablespoon olive oil

1 garlic clove, minced
2 cups fresh spinach, chopped
2 medium zucchinis, spiralized with Blade C
½ tablespoon fresh lime juice

Directions:

Preheat the oven to 350 degrees F. Grease a baking dish. Arrange the chicken strips into prepared baking dish. Sprinkle with rosemary, salt and black pepper. Bake for about 15-20 minutes. Remove from oven and keep aside. Meanwhile in a skillet, heat oil on medium heat. Add garlic and sauté for about 1 minute. Add spinach and cook for about 2-3 minutes. Add zucchini, salt and black pepper and cook for about 34 minutes. Stir in chicken and lime juice and remove from heat. Serve hot.

CHEESY ZUCCHINI WITH SPINACH & CHICKEN

Time: 25 minutes   Servings: 2

Ingredients:

1 tablespoons olive oil
2 garlic cloves, minced
2 skinless, boneless chicken breasts,
  trimmed and cut into thin strips

Salt and freshly ground black pepper, to taste
2 large zucchinis, spiralized with Blade C
2 cups fresh spinach, chopped
¼ cup feta cheese, crumbled

Directions:

In a large skillet, heat oil on medium heat. Add garlic and sauté for about 1 minute. Add chicken and sprinkle with salt and black pepper and stir fry for about 6-8 minutes or till browned from all sides. Add zucchini and spinach and cook f or about 3-4 minutes. Stir in salt and black pepper and remove from heat. Top with feta cheese and serve.

ZUCCHINI, MUSHROOMS & CHICKEN BAKE

Time: 65 minutes   Servings: 4

Ingredients:

¼ cup coconut oil, divided
1½ pound boneless chicken breasts, cut
  into thin strips

Salt and freshly ground black pepper, to taste
½ cup white onion, chopped
2 cups fresh mushrooms, sliced

3 garlic cloves, minced
1 tablespoon fresh rosemary, chopped
½ cup coconut cream
½ cup chicken broth
2 tablespoons fresh lemon juice

6 medium zucchinis, spiralized with Blade C
1 cup almond meal
¼ cup fresh basil leave, chopped
2 tablespoons almonds, chopped

Directions:

Preheat the oven to 375 degrees F.

Lightly, grease a casserole dish.

In a large skillet, melt 2 tablespoons of coconut oil on medium heat.

Add chicken and sprinkle with salt and black pepper and cook for about 4-5 minutes.

Transfer the chicken into a plate.

Now, add onion and mushroom and sauté for about 3-4 minutes.

Add garlic and rosemary and sauté for about 1 minute.

Add coconut cream, broth and lemon juice and bring to a boil.

Reduce the heat to medium-low and simmer for about 5 minutes or till sauce becomes thick.

Remove from heat and stir in chicken, zucchinis, salt and black pepper.

Transfer the mixture into prepared casserole dish.

In a bowl, add almond meal, remaining oil and some salt and with your hands mix till crumbly.

Spread the crumbly mixture over zucchini mixture evenly.

Bake for about 25-30 minutes.

Garnish with basil and chopped almonds before serving.

YELLOW SQUASH WITH KALE & CHICKEN

Time: 30 minutes   Servings: 2

Ingredients:

1½ tablespoons olive oil
1 garlic clove, minced
2 (6-ounce) skinless, boneless chicken
    breasts, cubed

Salt and freshly ground black pepper, to taste
2 cups fresh kale, trimmed and chopped
2 large yellow squash, spiralized with Blade C
1 tablespoon fresh lime juice

Directions:

In a large skillet, heat oil on medium heat. Add garlic and sauté for about 1 minute. Add chicken and sprinkle with salt and black pepper and cook for about 6- 8 minutes or till golden brown from all sides. Add kale and cook for about 2-3 minutes. Stir in squash noodles and lime juice and cook for about 23 minutes. Serve hot.

YELLOW SQUASH WITH TOMATOES & CHICKEN

Time: 65 minutes   Servings: 4

Ingredients:

4-6 medium yellow squash, spiralized with
    Blade C

3 tablespoons olive oil, divided
Salt and freshly ground black pepper, to taste

1 pound skinless, boneless chicken breasts, cut into thin strips
1 white onion, chopped
3-4 garlic cloves, minced
¾ pound grape tomatoes, halved
1¼ cups chicken broth
½ cup fresh baby spinach
1 tablespoon fresh oregano
1 tablespoon fresh thyme, chopped

Directions:

Preheat the oven to 400 degrees F. Grease a large baking sheet. Place squash noodles into prepared baking sheet. Drizzle with 1 tablespoon of oil and sprinkle with salt and black pepper. Bake for about 25 minutes, tossing once after 10 minutes. Remove from oven and toss the squash. Bake for 15 minutes more. Remove from oven and keep aside. In a large skillet, heat 1 tablespoon of oil on medium heat. Add chicken and sprinkle with salt and black pepper and cook for about 8-10 minutes or till golden brown from all sides. Transfer the chicken into a plate. In the same skillet, heat remaining oil on medium heat. Add onion and sauté for about 3-4 minutes. Add garlic and sauté for about 1 minute. Add tomatoes and broth and cook for about 2-3 minutes. Add chicken, squash, spinach and herbs and cook for about 2 minutes. Serve hot.

Yellow Squash with Tomatoes, Pesto & Chicken

Time: 25 minutes

Servings: 4

Ingredients:

For Pesto:

2 cups fresh basil leaves
4 garlic cloves, chopped
3 tablespoons olive oil
1/3 cup mozzarella cheese
¼ cup pine nuts, chopped
Salt and freshly ground black pepper, to taste

For Chicken & Squash:

2 tablespoons olive oil, divided
1 pound skinless, boneless chicken breasts, trimmed and cubed
Salt and freshly ground black pepper, to taste
3 large yellow squash, spiralized with Blade C
2 cups grape tomatoes, halved
1 teaspoon lemon zest, grated freshly

Directions:

For pesto in a food processor, add all ingredients and pulse till smooth. Keep aside. In a large skillet, heat 1 tablespoon of oil on medium heat. Add chicken and sprinkle with salt and black pepper and cook for about 5-6 minutes or till browned from all sides. Add 1 tablespoon of pesto and cook for about 2-3 minutes. Transfer chicken into a plate. In the same skillet, heat remaining oil on medium heat. Add squash, salt and black pepper and cook for about 2-3 minutes. Add tomatoes and remaining pesto and cook for about 1-2 minutes. Stir in cooked chicken and remove from heat. Garnish with lemon zest and serve.

Yellow Squash with Pumpkin & Chicken

Time: 40 minutes

Servings: 4

Ingredients:

2 tablespoons extra virgin olive oil
1 small white onion, chopped
2 garlic cloves, minced
2 cups canned pumpkin puree

½ cup coconut milk
2 cups chicken broth
2 tablespoons fresh basil leaves, chopped and divided

Salt and freshly ground black pepper, to taste
4 large yellow squash, spiralized with Blade C
1 pound grilled skinless, boneless chicken breast, cubed

Directions:

In a large skillet, heat oil on medium-low heat. Add onion and sauté for about 3-4 minutes. Add garlic and sauté for 1 minute. Stir in pumpkin, coconut milk, broth, 1 tablespoon of basil and seasoning. Reduce the heat to low and simmer for about 10 minutes, stirring occasionally. Stir in squash noodles and chicken and cook for about 4-5 minutes. Top with remaining basil and serve hot.

Sweet Potato with Asparagus & Chicken

Time: 35 minutes

Servings: 4

Ingredients:

2 tablespoons olive oil
1 large garlic clove, minced
2 (4-ounce) skinless, boneless chicken breasts, cubed
Salt and freshly ground black pepper, to taste
1 large sweet potatoes, peeled and spiralized with Blade C

½ cup chicken broth
8 asparagus stalks, trimmed and cut into 2-inch pieces
2 tablespoons fresh basil, chopped
½ tablespoon fresh lemon juice

Directions:

In a large skillet, heat oil on medium heat. Add garlic and sauté for about 1 minute. Add chicken and sprinkle with salt and black pepper and cook for about 6 to 8 minutes or till golden brown from all sides. Add sweet potato noodles and broth and cook for about 2-3 minutes. Stir in asparagus and basil and cook for about 4-5 minutes. Drizzle with lemon juice and serve hot.

Sweet Potato with Scallion & Chicken

Time: 50 minutes

Servings: 4

Ingredients:

For Sauce:

4½ cups cauliflower, chopped
1 small garlic clove, minced
1½ cups coconut milk
½ cup chicken broth
Salt, to taste

For Scallions:

1 tablespoon olive oil
4 cups scallions, sliced

1 tablespoon fresh lime juice
2 tablespoons chicken broth

For Chicken & Sweet Potato:

2 large sweet potatoes, peeled and spiralized with Blade C
2 cups grilled skinless, boneless chicken breast, cubed
Salt and freshly ground black pepper, to taste
1 teaspoon lime zest, grated freshly
3 tablespoons fresh cilantro Leaves, chopped

Directions:

For sauce in a pan of boiling water, add cauliflower and cook for about 10 minutes. Drain well and keep aside to cool slightly. In a food processor, add cauliflower and remaining ingredients and pulse till creamy and smooth. Transfer into a large bowl and keep aside. In a large skillet, heat oil on low heat. Add scallions and cook for about 15 minutes. Stir in lime juice, broth and salt and cook for about 5 minutes more. Remove from heat and add into bowl with creamy sauce. In another pan of boiling water, add sweet potato noodles and cook for about 4-5 minutes. Drain well. In a large skillet, add scallion mixture, sweet potato and chicken and cook for about 2-3 minutes or till heated completely. S Season with salt and black pepper and remove from heat. Top with lime zest and cilantro and serve immediately.

SWEET POTATO WITH VEGGIES & CHICKEN

Time: 40 minutes   Servings: 4

Ingredients:

1 tablespoon olive oil
½ teaspoon fresh ginger, minced
1 teaspoon garlic, minced
½ teaspoon cayenne pepper
1 large red bell pepper, seeded and sliced thinly
1 large green bell pepper, seeded and sliced thinly

1 cup cauliflower, cut into small florets
½ cup vegetable broth
1¾ cups coconut milk
3 sweet potatoes, peeled and spiralized with Blade C
Salt and freshly ground black pepper, to taste
2 tablespoons fresh parsley, chopped

Directions:

In a large skillet, heat oil on medium heat. Add ginger, garlic and cayenne pepper and sauté for about 30 seconds. Add bell peppers and cauliflower and cook for about 1-2 minutes. Add broth and bring to a boil. Reduce the heat to medium-low and simmer for about 4-5 minutes. Stir in coconut milk and sweet potato and simmer for about 6-8 minutes. Garnish with parsley and serve.

SWEET POTATO WITH ARTICHOKES & CHICKEN

Time: 50 minutes   Servings: 2

Ingredients:

1½ cups artichoke hearts, quartered
2 tablespoons olive oil, divided
Salt and freshly ground black pepper, to taste
1 skinless, boneless chicken breast, trimmed
½ teaspoon dried rosemary, crushed
¼ cup white onion, chopped
2 garlic cloves, minced

¼ teaspoon dried oregano, crushed
¼ teaspoon red pepper flakes, crushed
2 cups fresh tomatoes, chopped finely
¼ cup vegetable broth
1 large sweet potato, spiralized with Blade C
1 tablespoon fresh cilantro leaves, chopped

Directions:

Preheat the oven to 375 degrees F. Lightly, grease 2 large baking dishes. In a large bowl, add artichoke hearts, ½ tablespoon of oil, salt and black pepper and toss to coat well. Transfer the artichoke mixture into a prepared baking dish. In another bowl, add chicken breast, rosemary, ½ tablespoon of oil, salt and black pepper and toss to coat well. Transfer the chicken mixture into another prepared baking dish. Bake artichoke for about 10 minutes. Now, place the baking dish of chicken in oven. Bake chicken and artichoke for about 20 minutes. Remove from oven and keep aside to cool slightly. Cut chicken into bite sized pieces. Meanwhile in a skillet, heat remaining oil on medium heat. Add onion and sauté for about 3-4 minutes. Add garlic, oregano and red pepper flakes and sauté for about 1 minute. Add tomatoes and broth and cook for about 2 minutes. Stir in sweet potato, salt and black pepper and cook, covered for about 3 minutes. Uncover and cook for about 4-5 minutes. Stir in cooked chicken and artichoke and remove from heat. Garnish with cilantro and serve.

Sweet Potato with Brussels Sprout & Chicken

Time: 40 minutes

Servings: 2

Ingredients:

1 cup Brussels sprouts, halved
Salt, to taste
2 tablespoons extra virgin olive oil, divided
2 medium sweet potatoes, peeled and spiralized with Blade C
1 garlic clove, minced

½ pound skinless, boneless chicken breast, cut into bite sized pieces
2 cups fresh spinach, torn
1 cup chicken broth
Freshly ground black pepper, to taste

Directions:

Preheat the oven to 375 degrees F. Lightly, grease a large baking dish. Arrange Brussels sprouts in prepared baking dish and sprinkle with salt. Roast for about 25 minutes. Meanwhile in a large skillet, heat 1 tablespoon of oil on medium heat. Add sweet potato noodles and cook for about 8-10 minutes. Transfer the sweet potato into a bowl and keep aside. In the same skillet, heat remaining oil on medium heat. Add garlic and sauté for about 1 minute. Add chicken and cook for about 10 minutes. Add spinach and cook for about1 minute. Add broth and bring to a boil on high heat. Reduce the heat to medium-low and simmer for about 4-5 minutes. Stir in Brussels sprouts and sweet potatoes and cook for about 2-3 minutes. Season with salt and black pepper and serve.

Curried Sweet Potato & Chicken

Time: 30 minutes

Servings: 4

Ingredients:

For Chicken:
1 tablespoon olive oil
1 pound skinless, boneless chicken breast, trimmed and cubed
1 tablespoon curry powder
½ teaspoon cayenne pepper
¼ cup white onion, chopped
1 cup red bell pepper, seeded and chopped
1 cup coconut milk
½ cup chicken broth

½ cup coconut cream
Salt and freshly ground black pepper, to taste
¼ cup cashews, chopped

For Sweet Potato:
1 tablespoon olive oil
1 teaspoon curry powder
2 Medium sweet potato, peeled and spiralized with Blade C
¼ cup chicken broth

Directions:

For chicken in a large skillet, heat oil on medium heat. Add chicken and stir fry for about 5-6 minutes. Add curry powder and cayenne pepper and stir fry for about 1 minute. Add onion and bell pepper and cook for about 3-4 minutes. Add coconut milk, broth and cream and bring to a boil on high heat. Reduce the heat to medium-low and simmer for about 1-2 minutes. Stir in cashews, salt and black pepper and remove from heat. Meanwhile for sweet potato in another large skillet, heat oil on medium heat. Add sweet potato and curry powder and cook for about 1 minute. Add broth and cook for about 6-7 minutes. Transfer the sweet potato mixture in serving plates and top with chicken and serve.

Sweet Potato & Chicken Parcel

Time: 45 minutes   Servings: 2

Ingredients:

2 tablespoons olive oil, divided
1 garlic clove, minced
2 skinless, boneless chicken breasts, trimmed and cut into 8 tenderloins
2 small green bell peppers, seeded and sliced thinly
1 avocado, peeled, pitted and cubed
1 medium red onion, cut into thin strips

2 tablespoons fresh lemon juice
¼ teaspoon dried thyme, crushed
¼ teaspoon ground cumin
¼ teaspoon smoked paprika
¼ teaspoon cayenne pepper
Salt and freshly ground black pepper, to taste
1 large sweet potato, peeled and spiralized with Blade C

Directions:

Preheat the oven to 375 degrees F. Lightly, grease a large piece of foil. In a large skillet, heat ½ tablespoon of oil on medium heat. Add garlic and sauté for about 1 minute. Add chicken and stir fry for about 2 minutes per side. Transfer the chicken into a large bowl. Add remaining all ingredients except sweet potato in the bowl with chicken and toss to coat well. Arrange sweet potato in the centre of prepared foil paper and top with the chicken mixture. Seal the foil paper to form a parcel, leaving a 1-inch space from the mixture. Arrange the parcel in a baking sheet. Bake for about 20-25 minutes.

Sweet Potato, Black Beans & Chicken Casserole

Time: 1 hour 50 minutes   Servings: 6

Ingredients:

4 medium vine tomatoes
4 dried guajillo chili peppers
1 pound skinless, boneless chicken breast
1 teaspoon olive oil
1 onion, quartered
4 garlic cloves
½ teaspoon ground cumin
Salt and freshly ground black pepper, to taste

1 (15-ounce) can black beans, rinsed and drained
1 cup frozen corn
2 sweet potatoes, peeled, spiralized with Blade C and cut into 6-inch lengths
5-ounce pepper jack cheese, shredded
3 scallions chopped

Directions:

In a large pan of boiling water, add tomatoes and peppers and again bring to a boil. Boil the tomatoes for about 10 minutes. With a slotted spoon, transfer the tomatoes into a plate and keep aside to cool. Then peel the skin of tomatoes. Boil the peppers for about 20 minutes. Drain the peppers well and keep aside to cool. Cut the stem and remove the seeds and the inside of peppers. Meanwhile in another large pan of boiling water, add chicken breasts and cook for about 10 minutes. Drain well and keep aside to cool. Shred the chicken and transfer into a large bowl. Preheat oven to 400 degrees F. In a medium skillet, heat oil on medium-high heat. Add onion and sauté for about 4-5 minutes. Add garlic, cumin, salt and black pepper and sauté for about 1 minute. In a blender, add tomatoes, peppers and onion mixture and pulse till smooth. Add the pureed mixture into the bowl of chicken with beans and corn and mix well. Arrange the sweet potatoes noodles into a 13x9-inch casserole dish. Place the chicken mixture over sweet potatoes noodles and gently, stir to combine. Sprinkle cheese over the noodles mixture evenly. With a piece of foil, cover the casserole dish and bake for about 1 hour. Top with scallions and serve.

Sweet Potato, Parsnip & Chicken Casserole

Time: 1 hour 20 minutes   Servings: 4

Ingredients:

2 sweet potatoes, peeled and spiralized
  with Blade C
2 parsnips, peeled and spiralized with Blade C
2 tablespoon olive oil, divided
Salt and freshly ground black pepper, to taste

2 bone-in, skin-on chicken legs
¼ cup teriyaki sauce
2 teaspoons Worcestershire sauce
2 teaspoons low-sodium soy sauce

Directions:

Preheat the oven to 400 degrees. In a bowl, add vegetable noodles, 1 tablespoon of oil, salt and pepper and toss to coat well. In a large baking dish, place the vegetable noodles and top with the chicken in a single layer. Sprinkle with salt and pepper and drizzle with the teriyaki sauce, Worcestershire sauce and soy sauce. Then with a brush, spread the sauces over the chicken pieces evenly. Bake for about 45-60 minutes or till chicken is done completely

Parsnip & Carrot with Chicken

Time: 30 minutes   Servings: 2

Ingredients:

For Chicken:
¼ cup olive oil
2 garlic cloves, minced
1 teaspoon dried rosemary, crushed
Salt and freshly ground black pepper, to taste
2 skinless, boneless chicken breast halves

For Vegetables:
½ cup chicken broth
2 large carrots, peeled and spiralized with
  Blade C
2 large parsnips, peeled and spiralized with
  Blade C
1 teaspoon dried rosemary, crushed

1 teaspoon dried thyme, crushed
1 teaspoon dried oregano, crushed

Salt and freshly ground black pepper, to taste
2 tablespoons fresh parsley, chopped

Directions:

Preheat the broiler of oven. In a large bowl, mix together all ingredients except chicken. Add chicken breasts and coat with mixture evenly. Broil chicken breasts for about 15 minutes, flipping occasionally. Remove the chicken from oven and keep aside to cool for about 10 minutes. With a sharp knife cut chicken breasts into desired size pieces. Meanwhile in a large skillet, add broth and remaining all ingredients except fresh parsley on medium heat. Cook for 5-7 minutes or till desired doneness, stirring occasionally. Top with broiled chicken. Garnish with parsley and serve.

PARSNIP WITH CAPERS & CHICKEN

Time: 40 minutes   Servings: 2

Ingredients:

For Chicken:

2 skinless, boneless chicken thighs
1 tablespoon olive oil
½ teaspoon cayenne pepper
Salt and freshly ground black pepper, to taste

For Parsnip:

1 tablespoon olive oil
1 garlic clove, minced
6 parsnips, peeled and spiralized with Blade C
1 tablespoon capers
2 tablespoons fresh cilantro leaves, chopped

Directions:

Preheat the oven to 425 degrees F. Lightly, grease a baking pan. Arrange chicken thighs in prepared baking dish. Drizzle with oil and sprinkle with spices. Bake for about 20-25 minutes. Remove the thighs from oven and keep aside for about 10 minutes. With a sharp knife cut into desired size pieces. Meanwhile in a large skillet, heat oil on medium heat. Add garlic and sauté for about 1 minute. Stir in parsnip noodles. Reduce the heat to low and simmer for about 15-20 minutes, stirring occasionally. Stir in capers and cilantro and immediately remove from heat. Top with chicken and serve.

BROCCOLI WITH CHICKEN

Time: 50 minutes   Servings: 4

Ingredients:

3 tablespoons olive oil, divided
1 pound boneless chicken, diced
Salt and freshly ground black pepper, to taste
2 large broccoli heads, cut into florets and
    stems spiralized with Blade B
½ cup white onion, chopped
2 garlic cloves, minced

½ cup chicken broth
¼ teaspoon dried parsley, crushed
¼ teaspoon dried thyme, crushed
¼ teaspoon onion powder
1 cup sharp cheddar cheese, shredded
1/2 cup Gouda cheese, shredded

Directions:

Preheat the oven to 400 degrees F. In an oven safe skillet, heat 1 tablespoon oil on medium heat. Add the chicken and season with salt and pepper and cook for about 3-5 or till browned completely. Transfer the chicken in to a plate. In the same skillet, heat the remaining oil on medium-high heat. Add onion and garlic and cook for about 5-8 minutes. Meanwhile in a pan of salted boiling water, cook the broccoli florets and the broccoli noodles for about 2-3 minutes. Drain well. In the skillet, add broth and cook for about 2 minutes. Stir in the chicken, broccoli florets, noodles, thyme, parsley and onion powder. Remove from the heat and top with the both cheeses With a piece of foil, cover the skillet and bake for about 25 minutes. Remove the foil and broil for about 1-2 minutes.

Mixed Veggies with Chicken

Time: 40 minutes

Servings: 4

Ingredients:
2 tablespoons butter
1 garlic clove, minced
1/3 tablespoon fresh ginger, minced
¾ pound skinless, boneless chicken breast, cut into thin strips
2 medium carrots, peeled and spiralized with Blade C

2 medium zucchini, spiralized with Blade C
1 large broccoli stem, spiralized with Blade C
¾ tablespoon honey
¾ tablespoon soy sauce
1/3 tablespoon Sriracha sauce
Salt and freshly ground black pepper, to taste

Directions:
In a large skillet, melt butter on medium heat. Add garlic, ginger and sauté for about 30 seconds. Add chicken and cook for about 5-7 minutes. Add carrot, zucchini and broccoli and cook for about 3-4 minutes. Add honey, soy sauce and Sriracha sauce and cook for about 1 minute. Season with salt and pepper and serve hot.

Cheesy Sweet Potato with Spinach & Turkey

Time: 25 minutes

Servings: 4

Ingredients:
2 large sweet potatoes, spiralized with Blade C
2 tablespoons olive oil, divided
Salt and freshly ground black pepper, to taste
3 garlic cloves, minced
½ teaspoon red pepper flakes, crushed

1 pound turkey tenderloin, trimmed and cubed
4 cups fresh spinach, torn
½ cup mozzarella cheese, divided
2 tablespoons fresh cilantro leaves, chopped

Directions:
Preheat the oven to 425 degrees F. Lightly, grease a large baking sheet. In a large bowl, add sweet potato, 1 tablespoon of oil, salt and black pepper and toss to coat well. Transfer the mixture into prepared baking sheet. Roast for about 6 minutes. Transfer the sweet potato into a large plate. Meanwhile in a large skillet, heat remaining oil on medium heat. Add garlic and red pepper flakes and sauté for about 1 minute. Add turkey and sprinkle with salt and black pepper and stir fry for about 4-5 minutes. Add spinach and cook for about 2-3 minutes. Stir in sweet potato and ¼ cup of cheese and remove from heat. Garnish with remaining cheese and cilantro and serve.

Zucchini with Bell Pepper & Turkey

Time: 40 minutes   Servings: 4

Ingredients:

2 tablespoons olive oil, divided
2 cups boneless turkey breast, cubed
Salt and freshly ground black pepper, to taste
½ cup yellow onion, chopped
½ cup green bell pepper, seeded and chopped
½ cup red bell pepper, seeded and chopped
½ cup yellow bell pepper, seeded and chopped

½ cup orange bell pepper, seeded and chopped
2 garlic cloves, minced
1 jalapeño pepper, seeded and chopped
½ teaspoon dried oregano, crushed
¼ teaspoon red chili powder
3 large zucchinis, spiralized with Blade C

Directions:

In a large skillet, heat 1 tablespoon of oil on medium heat. Add turkey and sprinkle with salt and black pepper and cook for about 6-8 minutes or till done completely. Transfer the turkey into a plate. In the same skillet, heat remaining oil. Add onion and bell peppers and sauté for 5-7 minutes. Add garlic, jalapeño pepper, oregano and red chili powder and sauté for about 1 minute. Stir in zucchini, salt and black pepper and cook for about 3-4 minutes. Stir in turkey and remove from heat. Serve hot.

Sweet Potato with Arugula & Turkey

Time: 35 minutes   Servings: 2

Ingredients:

1 tablespoon olive oil
½ cup yellow onion, chopped
2 garlic clove, minced
1 large sweet potatoes, peeled and spiralized with Blade C
Salt and freshly ground black pepper, to taste

1 cup cooked skinless, boneless turkey breast, cut into bite sized pieces
¼ cup chicken broth
3 cups fresh arugula, chopped
1 tablespoon fresh basil, chopped

Directions:

In a large skillet, heat oil on medium heat. Add onion and garlic and sauté for about 3 to 4 minute. Add sweet potato noodles and sprinkle with salt and black pepper and cook for about 2-3 minutes. Add cooked turkey and broth and cook for about 2-3 minutes. Add arugula and basil and cook for about 2-3 minutes. Serve hot.

Sweet Potato with Cranberries & Turkey

Time: 35 minutes   Servings: 2

Ingredients:

1 tablespoon olive oil
1 white onion, chopped
1 garlic clove, minced

1 large sweet potato, peeled and spiralized with Blade C
¼ cup fresh cranberries
1 tablespoon fresh parsley, chopped

½ tablespoon ground cinnamon
Salt and freshly ground black pepper, to taste

1 cup grilled boneless turkey breast, cut into bite size pieces

Directions:

In a large skillet, heat oil on medium heat. Add onion and sauté for 3-4 minutes. Add garlic and sauté for about 1 minute. Add remaining ingredients except turkey and cook for about 6-8 minutes. Stir in grilled turkey and cook for about 2-3 minutes. Serve hot.

Zucchini with Mushroom & Ground Turkey

Time: 50 minutes

Servings: 4

Ingredients:

2 tablespoons olive oil, divided
1 cup white onion, chopped
1 pound lean ground turkey
2 garlic cloves, minced
1 cup shiitake mushrooms, sliced
1 pound lean ground turkey

4 cups Roma tomatoes, chopped
Salt and freshly ground black pepper, to taste
1 cup chicken broth
3 large zucchinis, spiralized with Blade C
½ cup fresh parsley, chopped

Directions:

In a large skillet, heat 1 tablespoon of oil on medium heat. Add onion and sauté for about 4-5 minutes. Add garlic and sauté for about 1 minute. Add mushrooms and cook for 4-5 minutes. Add turkey and cook for about 5-6 minutes. Add tomatoes, salt and black pepper and cook for 2-3 minutes, crushing with the back of spoon. Add broth and bring to a boil. Reduce the heat to medium-low and simmer for about 10-15 minutes. Meanwhile in another skillet, heat remaining oil on medium heat. Add zucchini, salt and black pepper and cook for about 4-5 minutes. Transfer the zucchini into large serving plate and top with turkey gravy. Garnish with parsley and serve hot.

Yellow Squash with Ground Turkey

Time: 60 minutes

Servings: 2

Ingredients:

2 tablespoons olive oil, divided
½ pound lean ground turkey
1 teaspoon dried thyme, crushed
½ cup white onion, chopped
2 garlic cloves, minced
¾ cup carrots, peeled and chopped finely

½ cup celery, chopped finely
1 cup tomatoes, crushed
½ cup chicken broth
3 tablespoons fresh oregano, chopped
Salt and freshly ground black pepper, to taste
2 large yellow squash, spiralized with Blade C

Directions:

In a large skillet, heat 1 tablespoon of oil on medium heat. Add turkey and thyme and cook for about 4-5 minute or till browned. Transfer the turkey into a bowl. In the same skillet, heat remaining oil on medium heat. Add onion and sauté for about 3-4 minutes. Add garlic and sauté for about 1 minute. Add carrot and celery and sauté for about 2-3 minutes. Add tomatoes and turkey and cook for about 4-5 minutes, stirring occasionally. Add broth, oregano and seasoning and bring to a boil. Reduce the heat to low and simmer for about 15-20 minutes or till sauce thicken. Stir in squash and cook for about 2 minutes. Serve hot.

Zucchini with spinach & Turkey Meatballs

Time: 35 minutes   Servings: 2

Ingredients:

For Meatballs:

½ pound lean ground turkey
1½ tablespoons coconut milk
1 tablespoon coconut flour
¼ teaspoon dried oregano, crushed
¼ teaspoon dried thyme, crushed
Salt and freshly ground black pepper, to taste

For Zucchini:

2 large zucchinis, spiralized with Blade C
3 cups fresh spinach, chopped
1 garlic clove, minced
3 tablespoons walnuts, chopped
2 tablespoons almond butter
3 tablespoons olive oil
1½ tablespoons fresh lemon juice
3 tablespoons water
Salt and freshly ground black pepper, to taste

Directions:

Preheat the oven to 400 degrees F. Line a baking sheet with a parchment paper. For meatballs in a large bowl, add all ingredients and mix till well combined. Make desired size balls from mixture. Arrange the meatballs in prepared baking sheet in a single layer. Bake for about 12-15 minutes or till done completely. Meanwhile in a large serving bowl, place the zucchini noodles. In a food processor, add all remaining ingredients and pulse till smooth. Pour spinach mixture over the zucchini and gently toss to coat. Top with meatballs and serve.

Zucchini & Turkey Meatballs in Sauce

Time: 65 minutes   Servings: 4

Ingredients:

For Meatballs:

1 pound lean ground turkey
2 garlic cloves, minced
¼ cup fresh parsley, chopped
1 egg, beaten
2 tablespoons blanched almond flour
2 tablespoons soy sauce
Salt and freshly ground black pepper, to taste
2 tablespoons olive oil

For Sauce:

2 teaspoons extra virgin olive oil, divided
¼ of yellow onion, chopped

2 garlic cloves, minced
1 jalapeño pepper, seeded and chopped
1 tablespoon fresh rosemary, chopped
½ teaspoon red pepper flakes, crushed
3¼ cups plum tomatoes, chopped finely
¾ cup chicken broth
Salt and freshly ground black pepper, to taste

For Zucchini:

1 tablespoon olive oil
3 large zucchinis, spiralized with Blade C
Salt and freshly ground black pepper, to taste

Directions:

In a large bowl, add all meatballs ingredients except oil and mix till well combined. Make desired size balls from mixture. In a large skillet, heat oil on medium heat. Add meatballs and cook for about 2 minutes per side. Transfer the meatballs into a plate and keep aside. For sauce in the same skillet, heat oil on medium heat. Add onion and sauté for about 4-5 minutes. Add garlic, jalapeño pepper, rosemary and red pepper flakes and sauté for about 1 minute. Add tomatoes and broth and bring to a boil. Reduce the heat to low and simmer for about 15-20 minutes. Remove from heat and keep aside to cool slightly. Now, transfer the sauce mixture into a blender and pulse till smooth. Return the sauce into skillet and bring to a gentle simmer on medium heat. Reduce the heat to low. Stir in meatballs, salt and black pepper and cook for about 10-15 minutes. Meanwhile for zucchini in another skillet, heat oil on medium heat. Add zucchini, salt and black pepper and cook for about 4-5 minutes. Transfer the zucchini into large serving plate. Top with meatballs and sauce and serve hot.

Zucchini with Tomatoes & Duck

Time: 2 hours 15 minutes   Servings: 4

Ingredients:

For Duck:

1 (5-pound) whole duck
2 teaspoons cayenne pepper
Salt and freshly ground black pepper, to taste
½ cup butter, melted and divided

For Zucchini:

4 large zucchinis, spiralized with Blade C
1½ cups grape tomatoes, halved
1 tablespoons extra virgin olive oil
1 garlic clove, minced
1 cup fresh basil leaves, chopped
Salt and freshly ground black pepper, to taste

Directions:

Preheat the oven to 375 degrees F. Line a roasting pan with a parchment paper. Arrange duck in prepared roasting pan and rub with cayenne pepper, salt and black pepper generously. Roast for about 1 hour. Pour half of melted butter over duck and roast for about 45 minutes. Now, pour remaining butter over duck and roast for about 15 minutes more. Remove the duck from oven and transfer onto a cutting board. Keep aside for about 15 minutes. With a sharp knife cut into desired size pieces. Meanwhile in a large serving bowl, place zucchini noodles and remaining ingredients and mix. Top with sliced duck and serve immediately.

Spiralized Recipes with Meat

Zucchini with Beef

Time: 30 minutes   Servings: 2

Ingredients:

1½ tablespoons olive oil
½ pound boneless beef fillet, sliced thinly
Salt and freshly ground black pepper, to taste
1 small onion, chopped
1 garlic clove, minced

½ teaspoon fresh ginger, minced
1 tablespoon soy sauce
2 large zucchinis, spiralized with Blade C
1 tablespoon fresh basil leaves, chopped
1 teaspoon sesame seeds

Directions:

In a skillet, heat oil on medium-high heat. Add beef and sprinkle with salt and black pepper and stir fry for about 4-5 minutes. Transfer the beef into a plate. In the same skillet, add onion on medium heat and sauté for about 4-5 minutes. Add garlic and ginger and sauté for about 1 minute.

Stir in soy sauce and cook for about 1 minute. Stir in zucchini, salt and black pepper and stir fry for about 2 minutes. Add beef and cook for 1-2 minutes. Stir in basil leaves and remove from heat. Garnish with sesame seeds and serve.

Zucchini with Grilled Steak

Time: 25 minutes   Servings: 4

Ingredients:

For Beef:

1 tablespoon olive oil
2 garlic cloves, minced
2 teaspoons fresh thyme, minced
2 teaspoons fresh oregano, minced
1 teaspoon fresh lime zest, grated finely
Salt and freshly ground black pepper, to taste
1½ pound beef tri-tip, cut into 4 steaks
    lengthwise

For Zucchini:

1 tablespoon olive oil
1 garlic clove, minced
¼ teaspoon red pepper flakes, crushed
3 medium zucchinis, spiralized with Blade C
Salt and freshly ground black pepper, to taste
1 tablespoon fresh lime juice

Directions:

In a large bowl, Mix together all ingredients except steak. Add steaks and coat with the garlic mixture generously. Keep aside for at least 30 minutes. Preheat the grill to medium-high. Grease the grill grate. Grill the steaks for about 5 minutes per side. Transfer into a bowl. Meanwhile for zucchini in a skillet heat oil on medium heat. Add garlic and red pepper flakes and sauté for about 1 minute. Add zucchini, salt and black pepper and cook for about 3-4 minutes. Stir in lime juice and remove from heat. Transfer the zucchini into a serving plate. Top with steak and serve.

ZUCCHINI & SWEET POTATO WITH GRILLED STEAK

Time: 35 minutes   Servings: 4

Ingredients:

For Steak:

1 tablespoon fresh lemon juice
½ teaspoon ground cumin
1 teaspoon cayenne pepper
Salt and freshly ground black pepper, to taste
1 (1¼-pound) flank steak, trimmed

For Vegetables:

2 large sweet potatoes, peeled and
  spiralized with Blade C
2 medium zucchinis, spiralized with Blade C
¼ cup cashews, toasted

For Sauce:

½ teaspoon fresh ginger, minced
½ teaspoon garlic, minced
3 tablespoons fresh basil, minced
3 tablespoons peanut butter
2 tablespoons balsamic vinegar
2 tablespoons honey
2 teaspoons extra virgin olive oil
2 teaspoons soy sauce
Salt and freshly ground black pepper, to taste

Directions:

For steak preheat the grill for medium heat. Grease the grill grate. In a bowl, mix together lemon juice and spices. Add steak and coat with spice mixture generously. Place the steak over grill and grill, covered for about 12-15 minutes, turning once in the middle. Remove from grill and keep aside to cool for about 10 minutes. With a sharp knife slice the steak in desired pieces. Meanwhile in a pan of boiling water, add sweet potato and cook for about 2 minutes. Add zucchini and cook for about 2 minutes. Drain well and transfer into a bowl. Place steak pieces over vegetables. Top with sauce. Garnish with cashews and serve.

ZUCCHINI WITH SPINACH & STEAK

Time: 35 minutes   Servings: 2

Ingredients:

¼ cup soy sauce
1 tablespoon balsamic vinegar
½ teaspoon red pepper flakes, crushed
2 tablespoons olive oil, divided
½ pound beef round steak, trimmed and
  cut into thin strips
Salt and freshly ground black pepper, to taste
¼ cup onion, chopped

1 garlic clove, minced
1 teaspoon fresh ginger, minced
1 jalapeño pepper, seeded and chopped
2 cups fresh spinach, chopped
2 medium zucchinis, spiralized with Blade C
2 tablespoons scallions, chopped
1 tablespoon black sesame seeds

Directions:

In a bowl, mix together soy sauce, vinegar and red pepper flakes and keep aside. In a large skillet, heat 1 tablespoon of oil on medium heat. Add steak strips and sprinkle with cayenne pepper, salt and black pepper and stir fry for about 3-4 minutes or till browned from all sides. Transfer the steak strips into a bowl. In the same skillet, heat remaining oil on medium heat. Add onion and sauté for about 4-5 minutes. Add garlic, ginger and jalapeño pepper and sauté for about 1 minute. Add spinach and soy sauce mixture and cook for about 2 minutes. Add zucchini and cook for about 2-3 minutes. Stir in steak strips and scallion and remove from heat. Garnish with sesame seeds and serve.

CREAMY ZUCCHINI WITH STEAK

Time: 40 minutes

Servings: 4

Ingredients:

1½ tablespoons olive oil, divided
1 pound skirt steak, trimmed and sliced thinly
Salt and freshly ground black pepper, to taste
½ teaspoon arrowroot powder
¼ cup vegetable broth

1 garlic clove, minced
1 cup coconut milk
½ teaspoon coconut aminos
3-4 zucchinis, spiralized with Blade C
2 tablespoons fresh parsley leaves, chopped

Directions:

In a large skillet, heat 1 tablespoon of oil on medium-high heat. Add steak and sprinkle with salt and black pepper and cook the steak for about 5 minutes, flipping once in the middle way. Transfer the steak into a late. In the same skillet, heat remaining oil on medium heat. Meanwhile in a bowl, mix together arrowroot and broth. Add garlic in the preheated skillet and sauté for about 1 minute. Pour broth mixture, stirring continuously for about 1 minute. Add coconut milk, coconut aminos, salt and black pepper and cook for about 10 minutes, stirring occasionally. Stir in zucchini and cook for about 2 minutes. Transfer the zucchini mixture into a serving plate and top with steak slices. Garnish with parsley and serve.

ZUCCHINI WITH GREENS & STEAK

Time: 40 minutes

Servings: 4

Ingredients:

For Steak:

2 garlic cloves, minced
1 teaspoon fresh ginger, minced
¼ teaspoon red chili powder
Salt and freshly ground black pepper, to taste
2 tablespoons balsamic vinegar
1 pound flank steak, trimmed and sliced thinly
1 tablespoon olive oil

For Zucchini:

1 tablespoon olive oil

1 small white onion, chopped
1 teaspoon fresh ginger, minced
2 garlic cloves, minced
1 cup carrot, peeled and chopped very finely
¼ cup beef broth
1 tablespoon balsamic vinegar
½ tablespoon dried basil, crushed
Salt and freshly ground black pepper, to taste
4 cups mixed greens (arugula, spinach, kale)
3 large zucchinis, spiralized with Blade C
¼ cup scallions, sliced thinly

Directions:

For steak in a large bowl, mix together all ingredients except steak and oil. Add steak and coat with marinade generously. Refrigerate, covered for at least 20-24 hours. Remove beef from refrigerator and discard any excess marinade. In a large skillet, heat oil on medium heat. Cook for about 5-6 minutes. Transfer the beef into a plate and keep aside. For vegetables in the same skillet, heat oil on medium heat. Add onion and sauté for about 4-5 minutes. Add ginger and garlic and sauté for about 1 minute. Stir in carrots and cook for about 3-4 minutes. Add broth, vinegar, basil and seasoning and bring to a boil. Stir in greens and reduce the heat to low. Simmer for about 4-5 minutes. Stir in zucchini noodles and cook for about 4-5 minutes. Divide the zucchini mixture into serving plates and top with steak slices. Garnish with scallion and serve.

ZUCCHINI WITH TOMATOES & GROUND BEEF

Time: 30 minutes   Servings: 4

Ingredients:

1 tablespoon olive oil
1 medium onion, chopped
2 garlic cloves, minced
1 pound lean ground beef
¼ cup beef broth

1 cup cherry tomatoes, halved
3 medium zucchinis, spiralized with Blade C
Salt and freshly ground black pepper, to taste
3 tablespoons fresh basil, chopped

Directions:

In a large skillet heat oil on medium heat. Add garlic and sauté for about 1 minute. Add beef and cook for about 4-5 minutes. Add broth, tomatoes and cook for about 4-5 minutes. Stir in zucchini, salt and black pepper and cook for about 3-4 minutes. Stir in basil and remove from heat. Serve hot.

ZUCCHINI WITH OLIVES & GROUND BEEF

Time: 45 minutes   Servings: 2

Ingredients:

1 tablespoon olive oil
¼ cup white onion, chopped
1 garlic clove, minced
½ pound lean ground beef
1 teaspoon dried thyme, crushed
Salt and freshly ground black pepper, to taste

¼ cup beef broth
2 large tomatoes, seeded and chopped
3 zucchinis, spiralized with Blade C
1 cup black olives, pitted and halved
1 large avocado, peeled, pitted and cubed

Directions:

In a large skillet, heat oil on medium heat. Add onion and sauté for 4-5 minutes. Add garlic and sauté for about 1 minute. Add beef and sprinkle with thyme, salt and black pepper and cook for about 10 minutes, stirring occasionally. Add broth and cook for about 3-4 minutes. Add tomatoes and cook for about 1-2 minutes, stirring occasionally. Stir in remaining ingredients and cook for about 2-3 minutes. Serve hot.

Zucchini with Mushrooms & Ground Beef

Time: 25 minutes

Servings: 4

Ingredients:

For Beef Mixture:

1 tablespoon olive oil
1 large onion, chopped
2 carrots, peeled and chopped
2 cups baby Bella mushrooms, chopped
2 garlic cloves, crushed
1 pound ground beef
2 tomatoes, chopped
1 (6-ounce) can tomato paste

1/3 cup red wine
1 tablespoon Italian seasoning
1 tablespoon fresh basil
1 teaspoon garlic powder
Salt and freshly ground black pepper, to taste

For Zucchini:

2 tablespoons olive oil
4 medium zucchinis, spiralized with Blade C
Salt and freshly ground black pepper, to taste

Directions:

In a large skillet, heat oil on medium heat. Add onion, carrots and mushrooms and garlic and cook for about 3-5 minutes. Add beef and cook for about 4-5 minutes. Add tomatoes, tomato paste and cook for about 1-2 minutes. Add red wine, Italian seasoning, salt, pepper, ground garlic and red pepper flakes and bring to a boil. Reduce the heat and simmer for about 15 minutes or till desired thickness. Meanwhile in a large skillet, heat oil on medium heat. Add zucchini, salt and black pepper and cook for about 3-4 minutes. Divide zucchini noodles in serving plates and top with beef mixture. Serve hot.

Zucchini with Beans & Ground Beef

Time: 45 minutes

Servings: 2

Ingredients:

1 tablespoon olive oil
1/3 cup onion, chopped
2 garlic cloves, minced
1 teaspoon dried rosemary, crushed
1/8 teaspoon red pepper flakes, crushed
½ pound lean ground beef
2 medium tomatoes, chopped finely

Salt and freshly ground black pepper, to taste
¼ cup beef broth
2 medium zucchinis, spiralized with Blade C
½ cup canned red kidney beans, rinsed and drained
½ cup black olives, pitted and sliced
2 tablespoons fresh parsley leaves, chopped

Directions:

In a large skillet, heat oil on medium heat. Add onion and sauté for about 4-5 minutes. Add garlic, rosemary and red pepper flakes and sauté for about 1 minute. Add beef and cook for about 5-7 minutes. Add tomatoes, salt and black pepper and cook for about 3-4 minutes. Add broth and bring to a boil. Cook for about 2-3 minutes. Add zucchini, beans and olives and cook for about 3-4 minutes. Garnish with parsley and serve.

Zucchini with Beef Meatballs

Time: 30 minutes   Servings: 4

Ingredients:

For Meatballs:

1 pound extra lean ground beef
¼ cup fresh rosemary, chopped
¼ teaspoon cayenne pepper
Salt and freshly ground black pepper, to taste

For Zucchini:

1 tablespoon olive oil
4 garlic cloves, minced
1 cup red bell pepper, seeded and chopped
1 cup black olives, pitted and sliced
3-4 large zucchinis, spiralized with Blade C
½ cup fresh cilantro leaves, chopped

Directions:

Preheat the oven to 400 degrees F. Line a cookie sheet with a parchment paper. For meatballs in a large bowl, mix together all ingredients. Make desired size balls from mixture. Arrange he balls in prepared cookie sheet in a single layer. Bake for about 12-15 minutes. Meanwhile in a large skillet, heat oil on medium heat. Add garlic and bell pepper and sauté for about 4-5 minutes. Add olives and cook for about 2 minutes. Stir in zucchini and cilantro and cook for 2-3 minutes. In a serving plate, place zucchini mixture and top with meatballs and sauce. Serve immediately.

Zucchini & Beef Meatballs Bake

Time: 40 minutes   Servings: 4

Ingredients:

For Meatballs:

1 pound lean ground beef
1 garlic clove, minced
2 tablespoons fresh cilantro leaves, chopped
½ teaspoon ground coriander
1 teaspoon ground cumin
1 teaspoon cayenne pepper
Salt and freshly ground black pepper, to taste

For Zucchini:

2 tablespoons extra-virgin olive oil
1 white onion, chopped
2 garlic cloves, minced
½ teaspoon ground coriander
½ teaspoon ground cumin
1 teaspoon cayenne pepper
Salt and freshly ground black pepper, to taste
2 cups tomatoes, chopped finely
4 small zucchinis, spiralized with Blade C

Directions:

Preheat the oven to 350 degrees F. In a large bowl, add all meatballs ingredients and mix till well combined. Make desired size balls from mixture. In a large oven proof skillet, heat oil on medium heat. Add onion and sauté for about 4-5 minutes. Add garlic and spices and sauté for about 1 minute. Add tomatoes and zucchini and cook for about 2-3 minutes. Remove from heat and add in meatballs and gently press into zucchini mixture. Transfer the skillet into oven. Bake for about 25-30 minutes.

Zucchini & Yellow Squash Curry with Beef

Time: 40 minutes

Servings: 4

Ingredients:

2 tablespoons olive oil, divided
1 pound boneless beef, trimmed and cut into thin strips
Salt and freshly ground black pepper, to taste
1 medium white onion, chopped
1 red bell pepper, seeded and chopped
1 garlic clove, minced
1 teaspoon fresh ginger, minced

1 teaspoon curry powder
1 cup coconut milk
2 medium zucchini, spiralized with Blade C
2 medium yellow squash, spiralized with Blade C
2 tablespoons fresh lime juice
2 tablespoon fresh cilantro leaves, chopped
1 teaspoon lime zest, grated freshly

Directions:

In a large pan, heat 1 tablespoon of oil on medium heat. Add beef and sprinkle with salt and black pepper and cook for about 4-5 minutes or till browned. Transfer the beef into a bowl. In the same pan, heat remaining oil on medium heat. Add onion and bell pepper and sauté for about 3-4 minutes. Add garlic and curry powder and sauté for about 1 minute. Slowly, add coconut milk and bring to a boil. Stir in beef and cook for about 4-5 minutes. Add zucchini and squash and cook for about 4-5 minutes. Stir in lime juice, salt and black pepper and remove from heat. Garnish with cilantro and lime zest and serve hot.

Yellow Squash Curry with Kale & Steak

Time: 35 minutes

Servings: 2

Ingredients:

For Beef

¼ cup soy sauce
1 tablespoon fresh lime juice
1 tablespoon olive oil
Salt and freshly ground black pepper, to taste
½ pound sirloin steak, trimmed and sliced thinly

For Yellow Squash:

1 tablespoon olive oil
½ small onion, chopped

1 celery rib, chopped
1 garlic clove, minced
1 teaspoon fresh ginger, minced
1 jalapeño pepper, chopped
¼ cup soy sauce
Salt and freshly ground black pepper, to taste
2 medium yellow squash, spiralized with Blade C
1 cup fresh kale, trimmed and chopped
1 tablespoon black sesame seeds

Directions:

For steak in a large bowl, mix together all ingredients except steak. Add steak slices and coat with marinade generously. Refrigerate, covered for at least 2-3 hours. Heat a large nonstick skillet on medium heat. Add beef with marinade and cook for about 5-6 minutes. Remove from heat and keep aside. In another large skillet, heat oil on medium heat. Add onion and celery and sauté for about 3-4 minutes. Add garlic, ginger and jalapeño pepper and sauté for about 1 minute. Add soy sauce and cook for about 1-2 minutes. Stir in squash noodles, salt and black pepper and cook for about 3-4 minutes. Divide squash noodles in serving plates and top with beef. Garnish with sesame seeds and serve.

YELLOW SQUASH WITH TOMATOES & STEAK

Time: 40 minutes   Servings: 4

Ingredients:

For Steak:
2 garlic cloves, minced
2 tablespoons fresh oregano, minced
2 tablespoons fresh parsley, minced
½ cup balsamic vinegar
¼ cup extra-virgin olive oil
1 teaspoon red pepper flakes, crushed
Salt and freshly ground black pepper, to taste
1 pound flank steak

For Yellow Squash:
2 tablespoons olive oil
1 yellow onion, sliced finely
4 garlic cloves, chopped finely
1 teaspoon red pepper flakes, crushed
4 large yellow squash, spiralized with Blade C
¼ cup cherry tomatoes, quartered
Salt and freshly ground black pepper, to taste
2 tablespoons fresh basil, chopped

Directions:

Preheat the grill to medium-high heat. Grease the grill grate. For steak in a large bowl, mix together all ingredients except steak. Add steak and coat with marinade generously. Grill the steak for about 4-6 minutes per side. Remove from grill and place onto cutting board for about 10 minutes. Meanwhile in a large skillet, heat oil on medium heat. Add onion and sauté for about 3-4 minutes. Add garlic and red pepper flakes and sauté for about 1 minute. Stir in squash noodles and cook for about 1-2 minutes. Stir in tomatoes, salt and black pepper and cook for about 2 minutes. Cut the steak into desired sized slices and serve. Divide squash noodles in serving plates and top with steak slices. Serve immediately with the garnishing of basil.

YELLOW SQUASH WITH BEEF MEATBALLS

Time: 60 minutes   Servings: 4

Ingredients:

For Meatballs:
1 pound lean ground beef
2 tablespoons chia seeds
2 garlic cloves, minced
2 tablespoons tomato puree
1 tablespoon fresh thyme, minced
Salt and freshly ground black pepper, to taste
2 teaspoons olive oil

For Squash:
½ tablespoon olive oil
1 medium onion, chopped
1 garlic clove, minced
2 tablespoons fresh thyme, chopped
½ cup beef broth
2 tablespoons fresh lemon juice
1½ cups fresh tomatoes, chopped finely
1½ cups tomato puree
Salt and freshly ground black pepper, to taste
3 large yellow squash, spiralized with Blade C

Directions:

For meatballs in a large bowl, mix together all ingredients except oil. Keep aside for at least 10 minutes. Make desired sized balls from mixture. In a large skillet, heat oil on medium heat. Add meatballs and cook for about 3-4 minutes. Transfer into a plate and keep aside. For Sauce in the same skillet, heat oil on medium heat. Add onion and sauté for about 4-5 minutes. Add garlic and thyme and sauté for about 1 minute. Add broth and lemon juice and cook for about 1 minute. Add remaining ingredients except squash noodles and cook for about 10-15 minutes. Stir in meatballs and immediately, reduce the heat to medium-low. Simmer for about 10-15 minutes. Add squash noodles and cook for about 2-3 minutes. Serve immediately.

Sweet Potato with Asparagus & Steak

Time: 50 minutes   Servings: 2

Ingredients:

2 tablespoons olive oil
¾ pound sirloin steak, trimmed and cut
   into thin strips
Salt and freshly ground black pepper, to taste
¼ cup onion, chopped
1 garlic clove, minced
10 asparagus spears, trimmed and cut into
   1-inch pieces

1 small red bell pepper, seeded and sliced
   thinly
1½ cups fresh tomatoes, chopped finely
¼ cup beef broth
1 large sweet potato, peeled and spiralized
   with Blade C
1 tablespoon fresh parsley leaves, chopped

Directions:

In a large skillet, heat 1 tablespoon of oil on medium heat. Add beef and sprinkle with salt and black pepper and cook for about 3-4 minutes or till browned from all sides. Transfer the beef into a bowl. In the same skillet, heat remaining oil on medium heat. Add onion and sauté for about 3-4 minutes. Add garlic and sauté for about 1 minute. Add asparagus and bell pepper and cook for about 8-10 minutes. Add tomatoes, salt and black pepper and cook for about 2 minutes, mashing with the back of spoon. Add broth and cook for about 2 minutes. Stir in sweet potato and cook for about 5 minutes. Stir in beef and cook for about 2-3 minutes. Garnish with parsley and serve.

Sweet Potato with Veggies & Beef

Time: 60 minutes   Servings: 4

Ingredients:

1½ tablespoons extra virgin coconut oil
1 large onion, chopped
1 cup celery, chopped
2 carrots, peeled and chopped
1 cup green bell pepper, seeded and chopped
1 pound beef stew meat, trimmed and cubed
3-4 fresh tomatoes, chopped finely
1½ cups tomato puree

½ cup beef broth
1 tablespoon dried basil, crushed
Salt and freshly ground black pepper, to taste
2 large sweet potatoes, peeled and
   spiralized with Blade C
2 tablespoons fresh scallions, chopped

Directions:

In a large skillet, heat oil on medium heat. Add onion, celery, carrots and bell peppers and sauté for about 4-5 minutes. Add beef and cook for about 10 minutes, stirring occasionally. Add tomatoes and cook for 1-2 minutes, crushing them. Add remaining ingredients except sweet potato and bring to a boil. Reduce the heat to low and simmer, covered for about 10-15 minutes. Stir in sweet potato noodles and cook for about 8-10 minutes. Garnish with scallion and serve.

Sweet Potato with Ground Beef

Time: 45 minutes

Servings: 4

Ingredients:

2 large sweet potatoes, peeled and spiralized with Blade C
1 tablespoon olive oil
1 white onion, chopped
2 garlic cloves, minced
1 pound lean ground beef
¼ teaspoon red chili powder

Salt and freshly ground black pepper, to taste
½ cup beef broth
3 cups fresh tomatoes, crushed
2 red bell peppers, seeded and chopped
1 tablespoon mixed dried herbs (thyme, oregano, marjoram, basil), crushed
¼ cup fresh cilantro leaves, chopped

Directions:

In a large pan of boiling water, add sweet potato noodles and cook for about 4-5 minutes. Drain well and keep aside. In a large skillet, heat oil on medium heat. Add onion and sauté for about 8-9 minutes. Add garlic and sauté for about 1 minute. Add beef and sprinkle with chili powder, salt and black pepper and cook for about 10 minutes, stirring occasionally. Add broth, tomatoes, bell pepper and herbs and cook for about 5-10 minutes, stirring occasionally. In a serving plate place sweet potato and top with beef mixture. Garnish with cilantro and serve.

Sweet Potato with Mushrooms & Ground Beef

Time: 50 minutes

Servings: 4

Ingredients:

For Beef & Mushroom Sauce:

1 tablespoon olive oil
1 cup white onion, chopped
3 garlic cloves, minced
1 cup fresh button mushrooms, sliced
1 pound lean ground beef
3¼ cups plum tomatoes, chopped finely
Salt and freshly ground black pepper, to taste
¼ cup beef broth
¼ cup tomato paste
1 cup fresh basil leaves, chopped

For Sweet Potato:

1 tablespoon olive oil
1 jalapeño pepper, seeded and chopped
3 large sweet potatoes, peeled and spiralized with Blade C
Salt and freshly ground black pepper, to taste

Directions:

In a large skillet, heat oil on medium heat. Add onion and sauté for about 4-5 minutes. Add garlic and sauté for about 1 minute. Add mushrooms and cook for about 4-5 minutes. Add beef and cook for about 4-5 minutes. Add tomatoes, salt and black pepper and cook for about 2 minutes, mashing with the back of spoon. Stir in the broth and tomato paste and bring to a boil. Reduce the heat to medium-low and simmer for about 8-10 minutes. Stir in basil and remove from heat. Meanwhile for sweet potato in another skillet, heat oil on medium heat. Add jalapeño pepper and sauté for about 1 minute. Add sweet potato noodles, salt and black pepper and cook for about 6-8 minutes. Transfer the sweet potato noodles in serving plates and top with beef and mushroom sauce. Serve immediately.

Sweet Potato with Beef Meatballs

Time: 55 minutes   Servings: 4

Ingredients:

For Meatballs:

2 tablespoons olive oil, divided
1 small white onion, chopped finely
1 teaspoon fresh ginger, minced
2 garlic cloves, minced
1 pound lean ground beef
1 tablespoon fresh basil, chopped
Salt and freshly ground black pepper, to taste
½ cup fresh orange juice
¼ cup soy sauce

For Sweet Potato:

1½ tablespoons olive oil
2 garlic cloves, minced
½ teaspoon red pepper flakes, crushed
2 large sweet potatoes, peeled and spiralized with Blade C
Salt and freshly ground black pepper, to taste

Directions:

For meatballs in a large skillet heat 1 tablespoon of oil on medium heat. Add onion and sauté for about 7-8 minutes. Add ginger and garlic and sauté for about 1 minute. Transfer the onion mixture into a bowl and keep aside to cool completely. Add beef, basil, salt and black pepper in bowl with onion mixture and mix till well combined. Make small sized balls from mixture. In the same skillet, heat remaining oil on medium heat. Add meatballs and cook for about 2-3 minutes per side or till browned. Add orange juice and soy sauce and cook, covered for about 8-10 minutes. Transfer the balls into a bowl. Increase the heat to medium-high and cook for about 5-10 minutes or till desired thickness. Remove from heat and stir in meatballs. For sweet potato in another large skillet, heat oil on medium heat. Add garlic and red pepper flakes and sauté for about 1 minute. Add sweet potato, salt and black pepper and cook for about 6-8 minutes. Transfer the sweet potato mixture in large serving bowls. Top with meatball sauce and serve.

Sweet Potato & Beef Meatballs Curry

Time: 55 minutes

Servings: 4

Ingredients:

For Meatballs:

1 pound lean ground beef
1 tablespoon garlic, minced
1 tablespoon fresh ginger, minced
¼ cup yellow onion, chopped finely
1 cup brown mushrooms, chopped finely
1 jalapeño pepper, minced
1 teaspoon Sriracha
½ teaspoon fish sauce
Salt and freshly ground black pepper, to taste
1 large egg
1 tablespoon cornstarch

For Curry Sauce:

1 (13½-ounce) can coconut milk
2 tablespoons red curry paste
2 teaspoons honey
½ teaspoon fish sauce

For Sweet Potatoes:

1 tablespoon olive oil
2 large sweet potatoes, peeled and spiralized with Blade C
Salt and freshly ground black pepper, to taste

Directions:

Preheat the oven to 400 degrees F. Line a large baking sheet with a greased piece of foil. In a large bowl, add all ingredients and mix till well combined. Make small sized balls from the mixture. Arrange the meatballs onto prepared baking sheet in a single layer. Bake for about 13 minutes. Flip and cook for about 2-3 minutes. Remove from oven and keep aside. For curry sauce in a large pan, add coconut milk on medium-high heat and bring to a boil. Add the red curry paste and beat till well combined. Stir in honey and fish sauce. Carefully, add the meatballs and reduce the heat to medium-low. Simmer for about 10 minutes. Meanwhile in a large skillet, heat oil on medium-high heat. Add sweet potatoes and cook for about 6-8 minutes. Season with salt and pepper and remove from heat. Divide sweet potato noodles into serving bowls and top with meatballs and curry sauce.
Serve hot.

Cabbage with Ground Beef

Time: 45 minutes

Servings: 4

Ingredients:

1 tablespoon Extra Virgin Olive Oil
1 Yellow Onion, chopped
2 Large Red Bell Peppers, seeded and chopped
1 Pound Lean Ground Beef
1 teaspoon Dried thyme, crushed

1 Medium Head Cabbage, spiralized with Blade C
3 cups Fresh Roma Tomatoes, pureed
Salt and freshly ground black pepper, to taste
1/3 cup Fresh Parsley, chopped

Directions:

In a large skillet, heat oil on medium heat. Add onion and bell peppers and sauté for about 4-5 minutes. Add beef and thyme and cook for about 8-10 minutes. Stir in cabbage noodles, tomato puree and seasoning. Reduce the heat to low and simmer for about 10-15 minutes. Garnish with parsley and serve.

Sweet & Sour Cabbage with Ground Beef

Time: 30 minutes   Servings: 4

Ingredients:

1 teaspoon olive oil
1 pound lean ground beef
1 medium head cabbage, spiralized with
   Blade C
1/3 cup almond butter

1 tablespoon coconut oil, melted
3 tablespoons tamari
2 tablespoons balsamic vinegar
1 tablespoon honey
1 tablespoon sesame seeds, toasted

Directions:

In a large nonstick skillet, heat oil on medium-high heat. Add beef and cook for about 4-5 minutes. Spread cabbage noodles over beef evenly and cook, covered for about 10 minutes. Uncover and cook for about 5 minutes more. In a small bowl, add remaining ingredients except sesame seeds and beat till well combined. Pour butter mixture over cabbage noodles and cook for about 2 minutes or till heated completely. Garnish with sesame seeds and serve.

Carrot with Steak

Time: 30 minutes   Servings: 2

Ingredients:

2 tablespoon olive oil, divided
8-ounce sirloin steak, trimmed and cut into
   thin strips
½ teaspoon cayenne pepper
Salt and freshly ground black pepper, to taste

1 garlic clove, minced
1 Serrano pepper, seeded and minced
2 cups carrot, peeled and spiralized with
   Blade C
¼ cup Parmesan cheese, shredded

Directions:

In a large skillet, heat 1 tablespoon of oil on medium heat. Add beef and sprinkle with cayenne pepper, salt and black pepper and sear for about 5 minutes or till browned from all sides. Transfer the beef into a large bowl. In the same skillet, heat remaining oil on medium heat. Add garlic and Serrano pepper and sauté for about 30 seconds. Add carrot noodles and cook for about 3-4 minutes. Stir in steak slices, salt and black pepper and cook for about 1-2 minutes. Serve hot with the sprinkling of cheese.

BROCCOLI WITH STEAK

Time: 35 minutes   Servings: 2

Ingredients:

For Steak:

¼ cup hoisin sauce
¼ cup fresh orange juice
2 tablespoons soy sauce
1/8 teaspoon red pepper flakes, crushed
2 (5-ounce) (1-inch thick) sirloin steaks
1 tablespoon olive oil

For Broccoli:

2 cups broccoli florets
1 teaspoon olive oil
1 small white onion, chopped finely
1 tablespoon fresh ginger, minced
1 tablespoon garlic, minced
2 broccoli stems, spiralized with Blade C
Salt and freshly ground black pepper, to taste

Directions:

For steak in a bowl, mix together all ingredients except steaks and oil. Add sirloin steaks and coat with marinade generously. Refrigerate for at least 2 hours. Remove the steak from refrigerator and keep in room temperature for about 5 minutes before cooking. Remove the steaks from bowl, reserving the marinade for later. In a nonstick skillet, heat olive oil on high heat. Add steaks and cook for about 3 minutes per side. Transfer the steaks onto a cutting board and cut into thin strips. In the same skillet, add the reserved marinade on medium-low heat and bring to a gentle boil. Simmer for about 2-3 minutes. Meanwhile in a large pan of boiling water, cook the broccoli florets for about 3-4 minutes. Drain well and immediately, place in ice water till chilled, and then drain well. In a large nonstick skillet, heat oil on medium-high heat. Add onions, ginger and garlic and sauté for about 1-2 minutes. Add broccoli noodles, salt and black pepper and cook for about 3 minutes. Add broccoli florets and cook for about 1-2 minutes. Divide broccoli mixture into 2 serving plates and top with beef strops. Pour marinade sauce on top and serve.

CELERIAC WITH GROUND LAMB

Time: 55 minutes   Servings: 4

Ingredients:

½ tablespoon olive oil
1 onion, chopped
1 garlic clove, minced
1 pound ground lamb
1 teaspoon ground cumin
1 tablespoon fresh rosemary, chopped
Salt and freshly ground black pepper, to taste

1 celeriac, peeled and spiralized with Blade C
½ cup celery rib, chopped
1 cup tomatoes, chopped finely
1 tablespoon tomato paste
¼ teaspoon red pepper flakes, crushed
½ cup low sodium chicken broth

Directions:

In a large skillet, heat oil on medium heat. Add onion and garlic and sauté for about 2-3 minutes. Add lamb and cook for about 8-10 minutes or till browned. Add cumin, rosemary, salt and pepper and cook for about 1 minute. Add Celeriac, celery rib, tomato, tomato paste and red pepper flakes and cook for about 2-3 minutes until vegetable are tender. Add broth and bring to a boil on high heat. Reduced heat to medium and cook, covered for about 10-15 minutes or till desired doneness.

Sweet Potato with Lamb Cutlets

Time: 40 minutes   Servings: 4

Ingredients:

For Lamb Cutlets:
8 lamb cutlets, trimmed
½ tablespoon olive oil
2 tablespoons fresh rosemary, chopped
2 tablespoons fresh basil Leaves, chopped
Salt and freshly ground black pepper, to taste

For Sweet Potato:
2 tablespoons olive oil
1 garlic clove, minced
2 sweet potatoes, peeled and spiralized
    with Blade C
Salt and freshly ground black pepper, to taste
3 tablespoons fresh cilantro leaves, chopped

Directions:

Preheat the oven to 425 degrees F. Grease a baking dish. Arrange lamb cutlets in prepared baking dish. Drizzle with oil and sprinkle with herbs and seasoning generously. Bake for about 20 minutes, flipping once in the middle way. Meanwhile in a large skillet, heat oil on medium heat. Add garlic and sauté for about 1 minute. Add sweet potato noodles, salt and black pepper and cook for about 8-10 minutes. Divide the sweet potato noodles in serving plates and top with lamb cutlets. Serve with the garnishing of cilantro.

Zucchini with Lamb Cutlets

Time: 30 minutes   Servings: 6

Ingredients:

For Lamb Cutlets:
2 garlic cloves, minced
2 tablespoons olive oil
2 teaspoons dried oregano, crushed
2 teaspoons sweet paprika
Salt and freshly ground black pepper, to taste

12 lamb cutlets, trimmed

For Zucchini:
3 tablespoons olive oil
6 large zucchinis, spiralized with Blade C
Salt and freshly ground black pepper, to taste

Directions:

Preheat the grill to high heat. Grease the grill grate. For lamb in a bowl mix together all ingredients except lamb cutlets. Add cutlets and coat with garlic mixture evenly. Keep aside for at least 10 minutes. Grill the cutlets for about 2-3 minutes per side or till desired doneness. Meanwhile in a large skillet, heat oil on medium heat. Add zucchini, salt and black pepper and cook for about 3-4 minutes. Divide the zucchini noodles in serving plates and top with lamb cutlets. Serve immediately.

ZUCCHINI WITH LAMB CHOPS

Time: 30 minutes   Servings: 4

Ingredients:
2 tablespoons olive oil, divided
1 garlic clove, minced
8 lamb chops, trimmed
Salt and freshly ground black pepper, to taste

3 large zucchinis, spiralized with Blade C
1 tablespoon fresh lime Juice
½ cup fresh basil, chopped

Directions:
In a large skillet, heat 1tablespoon of oil on medium-high heat. Add garlic and sauté for about 30 seconds. Add lamb chops and sprinkle with salt and black pepper and cook for about 6 minutes, flipping once in the middle way. Transfer the lamb chops into a plate In the same skillet, heat remaining oil on medium-high heat. Add zucchini noodles and sprinkle with a little salt and black pepper and cook for about 1-2 minutes. Stir in lime juice and basil and remove from heat. Divide the zucchini noodles in a serving plates and top with chops and serve.

ZUCCHINI WITH GROUND LAMB

Time: 40 minutes   Servings: 4

Ingredients:
2 tablespoons coconut oil
1 medium onion, chopped
2 garlic cloves, minced
1 teaspoon fresh ginger, minced
1 jalapeño pepper, seeded and chopped
½ teaspoon dried rosemary, crushed
½ teaspoon dried thyme, crushed
1 teaspoons ground cumin
½ teaspoon ground coriander

½ teaspoon cayenne pepper
¼ teaspoon ground turmeric
1 pound lean ground lamb
1 large, tomato, chopped finely
3 large zucchinis, spiralized with Blade C
Salt and freshly ground black pepper, to taste
2 tablespoons fresh lime juice
¼ cup fresh cilantro leaves, chopped

Directions:
In a large skillet, heat oil on medium heat. Add onion and sauté for about 4-5 minutes. Add garlic, ginger, jalapeño pepper, herbs and spices and sauté for about 1 minute. Add lamb and cook, stirring occasionally for about 10-12 minutes. Stir in tomato and cook for about 2-3 minutes. Stir in zucchini, salt and black pepper and cook for about 2-3 minutes. Stir in lime juice and cilantro and cook for about 1-2 minutes more. Serve hot.

Zucchini with Lamb Meatballs

Time: 25 minutes   Servings: 4

Ingredients:

For Meatballs:

1 pound lean ground lamb
1 egg, beaten
2 garlic cloves, minced
1 medium white onion, chopped finely
¼ teaspoon ground cumin
Salt and freshly ground black pepper, to taste
1 tablespoon olive oil

For Sauce:

1 cup fresh parsley leaves
1 cup fresh mint leaves
2 garlic cloves, minced
¼ cup extra-virgin olive oil
1 tablespoon fresh lime juice
Pinch of cayenne pepper
Salt and freshly ground black pepper, to taste

For Zucchini:

1 tablespoon Extra Virgin Olive Oil
4 medium zucchinis, spiralized with Blade C
Salt and freshly ground black pepper, to taste
2 scallions, chopped

Directions:

Preheat the grill to high heat. Grease the grill grate. In a bowl, add all meatballs ingredients except oil and mix till well combined. Make desired size balls from mixture. Coat the balls with oil evenly. Grill the balls for about 8 minutes, flipping once after 4 minutes. Transfer the balls into a bowl. Meanwhile for zucchini in a skillet, heat oil on medium heat. Add zucchini, salt and black pepper and cook for about 3-4 minutes. Transfer the zucchini into a large serving plate. Meanwhile in a food processor, add all sauce ingredients and pulse till smooth. Pour sauce over zucchini and gently, stir to combine. Top with grilled meatballs and serve with the garnishing of cilantro.

Zucchini with Lamb Muffins

Time: 40 minutes   Servings: 4

Ingredients:

For Lamb Muffins:

1 pound lean ground lamb
¼ cup onion, chopped
1 garlic clove, minced
1 large egg, beaten
3 tablespoons almond flour
¼ teaspoon cayenne pepper
Salt and freshly ground black pepper, to taste

For Zucchini:

4 large zucchinis, spiralized with Blade C
Salt and freshly ground black pepper, to taste
2 cups fresh spinach
½ cup fresh basil, chopped
1 garlic clove, minced
½ cup walnuts, chopped
1 tablespoon fresh lime juice
¼-½ cup vegetable broth

Directions:

Preheat the oven to 375 degrees F. Line a 12 cups muffin pan with paper liners. In a large bowl, mix together all ingredients. Make 12 even sized balls from mixture Transfer the mixture into prepared muffin cups evenly. Bake for about 20 minutes. Meanwhile in a micro wave safe bowl, place ½ of the zucchini noodles and sprinkle with salt and black pepper. Microwave on high for about 2 minutes. Repeat with remaining zucchini noodles. Transfer the zucchini in a large serving plate. In a food processor, add remaining ingredients and pulse till smooth. Pour spinach sauce over zucchini noodles and gently stir to combine. Top with lamb muffins and serve.

YELLOW SQUASH WITH LAMB CHOPS

Time: 40 minutes   Servings: 4

Ingredients:

For Lamb Chops:
2 tablespoons olive oil, divided
1 tablespoon fresh rosemary, minced
2 garlic cloves, minced
Salt and freshly ground black pepper, to taste
4 lamb loin chops

For Yellow Squash:
2 tablespoons olive oil
1 garlic clove, minced
1 Serrano pepper, seeded and chopped finely
3 Large yellow squashes, spiralized with Blade C
Salt and freshly ground black pepper, to taste
1 tablespoon Fresh Lemon Juice
2 scallions, chopped

Directions:

For chops in a bowl, mix together 1 tablespoon of oil, rosemary, garlic, salt and black pepper. Add chops and coat with marinade generously. Refrigerate, covered for about 1-2 hours. Preheat the oven to 400 degrees F. In an ovenproof skillet, heat remaining oil on high heat. Add chops and cook for about 3 minutes per side. Now, transfer the skillet in oven and roast for about 10 minutes. Meanwhile for squash in a skillet, heat oil on medium-high heat. Add garlic and Serrano pepper and sauté for about 1 minute. Add squash and sprinkle with a little salt and black pepper and cook for about 2-3 minutes. Stir in lemon juice and remove from heat. Divide squash noodles in serving plates and top with chops Garnish with scallion and serve.

MIXED VEGGIES WITH LAMB CHOPS

Time: 45 minutes   Servings: 4

Ingredients:

For Lamb Chops:
1 onion, chopped finely
4 garlic cloves, minced
2 tablespoons fresh lemon juice
Salt and freshly ground black pepper, to taste
8 lamb chops, trimmed

For Vegetables:
1 medium sweet potato, peeled and spiralized with Blade C
1 medium carrot, peeled and spiralized with Blade C

1 medium yellow Squash, spiralized with Blade C
2 small red bell Peppers, seeded and sliced thinly
1 medium zucchini, spiralized with Blade C
3 tablespoons olive oil
1 tablespoon dried thyme, crushed
Salt and freshly ground black pepper, to taste

Directions:

For chops in a bowl, mix together all ingredients except chops. Add chops and coat with marinade generously. Refrigerate for at least 3-4 hours. Preheat the oven to 400 degrees F. Grease 2 large baking sheets. In a large bowl, add all vegetables, oil, thyme and seasoning and toss to combine. Arrange all vegetables onto prepared baking sheets in a thin layer. Roast for about 20 minutes, tossing once after 10 minutes. Meanwhile preheat the grill to medium-high heat. Remove the chops from marinade and shake off any excess marinade. Grill for about 3-4 minutes per side. In a serving plate, place roasted vegetables. Top with grilled chops and serve.

Turnip with Lamb Shoulder Chops

Time: 25 minutes   Servings: 2

Ingredients:

For Lamb Chops:

1 garlic clove, minced
1 teaspoon fresh rosemary, minced
½ tablespoon fresh lemon juice
½ tablespoon olive oil
Salt and freshly ground black pepper, to taste
2 lamb shoulder chops, trimmed

For Turnip:

1 tablespoon olive oil
2 large turnips, trimmed, peeled and spiralized with Blade C
Salt and freshly ground black pepper, to taste

Directions:

For chops in a bowl, mix together all ingredients except lamb chops Add lamb chops and coat with marinade mixture generously. Keep aside in the room temperature for about 15-20 minutes. Preheat the broiler of oven. Arrange an oven rack 4-5-inches from heating element. Line a broiler pan with a piece of foil. Remove the chops from bowl and shake off excess marinade. Broil for about 5 minutes per side. Meanwhile in a skillet, heat oil on medium heat. Add onion and sauté for about 4 to 5 minutes. Add turnip, salt and black pepper and cook for about 3-4 minutes. Transfer the turnip mixture in serving plate and top with lamb chops. Serve hot.

Turnip with Pork Tenderloin

Time: 45 minutes   Servings: 2

Ingredients:

For Pork:

½ teaspoon fresh ginger, minced
2 garlic cloves, minced
1 tablespoon fresh rosemary, minced
2 tablespoons soy sauce

1 tablespoon fresh lemon juice
½ tablespoon honey
Salt and freshly ground black pepper, to taste
½ pound pork tenderloin, trimmed

For Turnip:
1 tablespoon olive oil
½ small white onion, chopped
2 garlic cloves, minced

1 Serrano pepper, seeded and minced
2 large turnips, trimmed, peeled and
  spiralized with Blade C
Salt and freshly ground black pepper, to taste
1 scallion, chopped

Directions:

In a large bowl, add all pork ingredients and toss to coat well. Refrigerate for about 2-3 hours, tossing occasionally. Preheat the oven to 450 degrees F. Heat an oven proof skillet in oven for about 15 minutes. Place pork with marinade in heated skillet and bake for about 10 minutes. Remove from oven and toss well. Bake for about 10-15 minutes. Remove from oven and keep aside to cool for about 10 minutes. With a sharp knife slice the pork tenderloin in desired pieces. In a skillet, heat oil on medium heat. Add onion and sauté for about 4-5 minutes. Add garlic and Serrano pepper and sauté for about 1 minute. Add turnip, salt and black pepper and cook for about 3-4 minutes. Divide the turnip noodles in serving plates and top with pork pieces. Garnish with scallion and serve.

CABBAGE WITH GROUND PORK

Time: 35 minutes   Servings: 4

Ingredients:

1 tablespoon fresh ginger, minced
1 teaspoon garlic, minced
3 tablespoons tamari
1 tablespoon dried oregano, crushed
1½ tablespoons extra virgin olive oil, divided
1 onion, chopped

1 medium head cabbage, spiralized with
  Blade C
1 pound lean ground pork
4 scallions, chopped
½ cup fresh parsley leaves, chopped
Salt and freshly ground black pepper, to taste
1 tablespoon fresh lemon juice

Directions:

In a bowl, mix together, ginger, garlic, tamari and oregano and keep aside. In a large skillet, heat 1 tablespoon of oil on medium heat. Add onion and sauté for about 4-5 minutes. Add cabbage and half of ginger mixture and cook for about 2-3 minutes. Transfer the cabbage mixture into a large serving bowl. In the same skillet, heat remaining oil on medium heat. Add pork and remaining ginger mixture and cook for about 8-10 minutes. Stir in scallions, parsley and seasoning and cook for about 2 minutes. Transfer the pork mixture into bowl with cabbage and gently too to mix. Drizzle with lemon juice and serve.

ZUCCHINI WITH PORK CHOPS

Time: 30 minutes   Servings: 2

Ingredients:

For Pork Chops:
2 tablespoons olive oil
2 boneless pork chops, trimmed

1 teaspoon dried rosemary, crushed
¼ teaspoon cayenne pepper
Salt and freshly ground black pepper, to taste

For Zucchini:
2 large zucchinis, spiralized with Blade C
1 cup fresh basil leaves, chopped
1 garlic clove minced

½ cup unsalted cashews, roasted
¼ cup extra-virgin olive oil
¼ cup coconut milk
Salt and freshly ground black pepper, to taste

Directions:

Preheat the oven to 400 degrees F. In a large oven proof skillet, heat oil on medium heat. Add chops and sprinkle with rosemary and seasoning and cook for about 3 minutes per side. Transfer the skillet into oven and bake for about 8 minutes. Remove the chops from oven and transfer onto a cutting board for about 10 minutes. With a sharp knife cut into desired size pieces. Meanwhile in a large pan of boiling water, cook the zucchini noodles for about 2-3 minutes. Drain well and transfer into a serving bowl. In a food processor, add all remaining ingredients and pulse till smooth. Pour basil mixture over zucchini and gently stir to combine. Top with sliced pork chops and serve.

ZUCCHINI WITH GROUND PORK

Time: 25 minutes

Servings: 2

Ingredients:

4-ounce pork tenderloin, sliced
1 tablespoon rice wine
Salt, to taste
1 tablespoon cornstarch
1 teaspoon fresh ginger, minced

2 tablespoons vegetable oil
3 garlic cloves, minced
2 dried chili peppers, torn
2 zucchinis, spiralized with Blade C
2 teaspoons tamari

Directions:

In a bowl, add pork, wine, salt, cornstarch and ginger and mix till well combined. Refrigerate for about 30 minutes. In a large skillet, heat 1 tablespoon of oil on medium-high heat. Add pork and stir fry for about 2-3 minutes. Transfer pork into a plate and keep aside. In the same skillet, heat remaining oil on medium heat. Add garlic and chili peppers and sauté for about 30 seconds. Add zucchini noodles and increase the heat to medium-high heat. Stir fry for about 1 minute. Stir in pork, tamari and salt and cook for about 2-3 minutes. Serve hot.

ZUCCHINI WITH BELL PEPPER & GROUND PORK

Time: 25 minutes

Servings: 2

Ingredients:

2 tablespoons tamari
1 teaspoon rice vinegar
2 teaspoons oyster sauce
½ teaspoon sugar
1 tablespoon olive oil
½ medium onion, chopped
3 garlic cloves, minced

½ pound ground pork
2 medium red bell peppers, seeded and
  sliced thinly
2 medium zucchinis, spiralized with Blade C
Salt and freshly ground black pepper, to taste
¼ cup fresh cilantro, chopped

Directions:

In a bowl mix together tamari, vinegar, oyster sauce and sugar. In a large skillet, heat olive oil on medium high heat. Add onion and garlic and sauté for about 4-5 minutes. Add pork and cook for about 3-5 minutes. Add bell peppers and cook for about 2 minutes. Stir in zucchini noodles and sauce and cook for about 2-3 minutes. Garnish with cilantro and serve.

ZUCCHINI & CARROT WITH GROUND PORK

Time: 30 minutes   Servings: 4

Ingredients:

1 tablespoon virgin coconut oil
2-3 garlic cloves, minced
1 pound lean ground pork
1 Serrano Pepper, seeded and chopped
1 tablespoon fresh ginger, grated
1 tablespoon fresh thyme, chopped
1 tablespoon balsamic vinegar

2 tablespoons soy sauce
2 small carrots, peeled and spiralized with Blade C
4 medium zucchinis, spiralized with Blade C
1 cup black olives, pitted and chopped
Salt and freshly ground black pepper, to taste
¼ cup fresh parsley, chopped

Directions:

In a large skillet, heat oil on medium-high heat. Add garlic and sauté for about 1 minute. Add pork and cook for about 5-6 minutes. Add Serrano pepper, ginger and thyme and cook for about 1 minute. Add vinegar and soy sauce and cook for about 2 minutes. Stir in carrot and cook for about 2 minutes. Stir in zucchini, olives, salt and black pepper and cook for about 2-3 minutes. Garnish with parsley and serve.

SWEET POTATO WITH GROUND PORK

Time: 35 minutes   Servings: 6

Ingredients:

2 tablespoons olive oil
5 garlic cloves garlic, minced
1 pound ground pork
4 large sweet potatoes, peeled and spiralized with Blade C
2 teaspoons ground cumin

2 teaspoons ancho chili powder
Salt, to taste
1 cup milk
½ cup fresh cilantro, chopped
½ cup scallion, chopped
1½ cups Mozzarella cheese, shredded

Directions:

In a large skillet, heat oil on medium heat. Add garlic and sauté for about 30 seconds. Add pork and cook for about 6-7 minutes. Add sweet potato, spices and milk and cook for about 6-8 minutes. Stir in cilantro, scallion and cheese and remove from heat. Serve hot.

MIXED VEGGIES WITH PORK LOIN ROAST

Time: 1 hour 45 minutes

Servings: 4

Ingredients:

For Pork:

2 large garlic cloves, crushed
2 teaspoons fresh rosemary, chopped
Salt and freshly ground black pepper, to taste
1¼ pound boneless pork loin roast, trimmed

For Veggies:

1 large sweet potato, peeled and spiralized with Blade C

1 large carrot, peeled and spiralized with Blade C
2 large parsnips, peeled and spiralized with Blade C
2 large red onions, spiralized with Blade A
2 tablespoons olive oil
2 teaspoons fresh thyme, chopped
Salt and freshly ground black pepper, to taste

Directions:

Preheat the oven to 400 degrees F. Line a 13x9-inch roasting pan with a piece of foil. For pork in a bowl, mix together garlic, rosemary, salt and pepper. Rub the garlic mixture over the pork evenly. Arrange the pork roast onto prepared roasting pan, fat side down. Roast for about 30 minutes. Flip and roast for about 20-30 minutes. Remove from the oven and transfer onto a cutting board for about 10 minutes. Line 2 large baking sheets with parchment papers. Place the veggies onto prepared baking sheets. Drizzle with oil and sprinkle with thyme, salt and pepper. Roast for 15 minutes. Cut the pork roast into 1/3-inch thick slices. Divide the veggie noodles into serving plates and top with pork slices. Serve hot.

Spiralized Recipes with Seafood

Zucchini with Tilapia

Time: 30 minutes

Servings: 2

Ingredients:

For Tilapia:

2 (4-ounce) tilapia fillets
1 tablespoon fresh lemon juice
Salt and freshly ground black pepper, to taste
1 jalapeño pepper, sliced thinly

For Zucchini:

1 tablespoon olive oil
1 garlic clove, minced
2 large zucchinis, spiralized with Blade C
2 tablespoons fresh basil leaves, chopped
Salt and freshly ground black pepper, to taste
2 tablespoons pumpkin seeds

Directions:

Preheat the oven to 400 degrees F. Lightly, grease a baking dish. Arrange fish fillets in prepared baking dish in a single layer. Drizzle with lemon juice and sprinkle with salt and black pepper. Bake for about 6-7 minutes. Remove baking dish from oven. Arrange jalapeño pepper slices over fillets evenly. Bake for about 4-5 minutes. Meanwhile in a skillet, heat oil on medium heat. Add zucchini and cook for about 3-4 minutes. Stir in basil, salt and black pepper and remove from the heat. Divide the zucchini noodles in serving plates and top with fish fillets. Serve with the topping of pumpkin seeds.

Zucchini with Mahi Mahi

Time: 25 minutes

Servings: 2

Ingredients:

For Mahi Mahi:

1 tablespoon olive oil
2 (6-inch) mahi mahi fillets
¼ teaspoon dried rosemary, crushed
¼ teaspoon red pepper flakes, crushed
Salt and freshly ground black pepper, to taste

For Zucchini:

1 tablespoon olive oil

1 tablespoon shallots, minced
2 garlic cloves, minced
3 tablespoons vegetable broth
1 tablespoon fresh basil leaves, chopped
1medium zucchini, spiralized with Blade C
1 tablespoon plain yogurt
2 tablespoons Dijon mustard
Salt and freshly ground black pepper, to taste

Directions:

For fish in a large skillet, heat oil on medium heat. Add fillets and sprinkle with rosemary, red pepper flakes, salt and black pepper and cook for about 3-4 minutes per side. Remove from heat and keep aside. Meanwhile for zucchini in another large skillet, heat oil on medium heat. Add shallots and garlic and sauté for about

2 minutes. Add broth, basil and zucchini and cook for about 2-3 minutes. Stir in yogurt, mustard, salt and black pepper and cook for about 1 minute. Divide the zucchini mixture into serving plates and top with mahi mahi fillets. Serve hot.

CARROT WITH GROUPER

Time: 25 minutes   Servings: 4

Ingredients:

For Grouper:
2 tablespoons olive oil
1 tablespoon minced garlic
1 tablespoon minced ginger
Salt and freshly ground black pepper, to taste
4 grouper fillets

For Carrot:
2 tablespoons oil
4 large carrots, peeled and spiralized with Blade C
½ teaspoon red pepper flakes, crushed
Salt and Freshly Ground Black Pepper, to taste

Directions:

For grouper fillets in a large bowl, mix together all ingredients. Refrigerate for about 2-3 hours. Preheat the grill to high heat. Grease the grill grate. Place the grouper fillets on the hot grill with the flesh side down and cook for about 3-4 minutes per side. Meanwhile in a skillet, heat oil on medium heat. Add carrot and seasoning and cook for about 4-5 minutes. Divide the carrot noodles in serving plates and top with fish fillets.

ZUCCHINI WITH SPINACH & COD

Time: 25 minutes   Servings: 2

Ingredients:

For Cod:
1 (8-ounce) black cod fillet
Salt and freshly ground black pepper, to taste

For Spinach & Zucchini:
1 tablespoon sunflower oil
1 teaspoon fresh ginger, minced

1 garlic clove, minced
2 cups fresh spinach, torn
¾ cup vegetable broth
1 tablespoon soy sauce
Salt and freshly ground black pepper, to taste
2 medium zucchinis, spiralized with Blade C
¼ cup scallions, chopped

Directions:

Preheat the grill to medium-high heat. Grease the grill grate. Season the cod fillet with salt and black pepper. Grill for about 4-5 minutes per side. Slice the cod in 2 pieces and keep aside. Meanwhile in a large skillet, heat oil on medium heat. Add ginger and garlic and sauté for about 1 minute. Add spinach and cook for about 1 minute. Add broth, soy sauce, salt and black pepper and cook for about 1-2 minutes. Stir in zucchini and cook for about 3-4 minutes. Transfer the zucchini mixture into 2 serving plates and top with cod pieces. Garnish with scallion and serve.

Zucchini, Chard & Cod Parcel

Time: 35 minutes

Servings: 2

Ingredients:

12-ounce wild cod
1 tomato, chopped
2 zucchini, spiralized with Blade C
4 scallions, chopped
6-8 baby chard leaves
1 tablespoon fresh lime juice

2 tablespoons fresh parsley leaves, chopped
¼-ounce chilled butter, chopped
1/8 teaspoon smoked paprika
Salt and freshly ground black pepper, to taste

Directions:

Preheat the oven to 350 degrees F. Arrange a large parchment paper onto a smooth surface. Place the cod in the center of parchment paper. Top the cod with remaining ingredients and fold into a pouch to seal the filling. Bake for about 20 minutes.

Zucchini with Mushrooms & Haddock

Time: 45 minutes

Servings: 4

Ingredients:

2 tablespoons olive oil
1 medium white onion, sliced
½ teaspoon dried rosemary, crushed
2 cups portabella mushrooms, sliced

Salt and freshly ground black pepper, to taste
2 large zucchinis, spiralized with Blade C
4 (4-ounce) haddock fillets

Directions:

Preheat the oven to 450 degrees F. Grease a baking dish. In a large skillet, heat oil on medium heat. Add onion and sauté for about 2-3 minutes. Add rosemary and mushrooms and sauté for about 3-4 minute. Add zucchini, salt and black pepper and sauté for about 3 minutes. Sprinkle fish fillets with salt and black pepper from both sides. Arrange fish fillets in prepared baking dish in a single layer. Top with zucchini mixture. Cover the baking dish with a piece of foil and bake for about 15-20 minutes or till desired doneness.

Butternut Squash with Broccoli & Herring

Time: 40 minutes

Servings: 4

Ingredients:

For Herring:

2 tablespoons olive oil
¼ cup tamari
1 tablespoon fresh lime juice

2 teaspoons white sesame seeds
Salt and freshly ground black pepper, to taste
4 (3-ounce) herring fillets

For Vegetables:

2 large butternut squash, peeled and spiralized with Blade C
2 cups broccoli florets
3 tablespoons extra virgin olive oil
2 teaspoons fresh ginger, minced
2 teaspoons garlic, minced

3 tablespoons honey
¼ cup tamari
2 teaspoons white sesame seeds
Salt and freshly ground black pepper, to taste
1 teaspoon black sesame seeds

Directions:

Preheat the oven to 400 degrees F. Lightly, grease a baking dish. For fish in a large bowl, add all ingredients and toss to coat well. Refrigerate to marinade for at least 10 minutes. Arrange fish fillets in prepared baking dish in a single layer. Bake for about 10 minutes. Remove baking dish from oven. Place the squash noodles in baking dish and bake for about 6-7 minutes. Meanwhile in a pan of boiling water, add broccoli and cook for about 3-4 minutes. Drain well and keep aside. In a large skillet, heat oil on medium heat. Add ginger and garlic and sauté for about 1 minute. Stir in broccoli noodles and remaining ingredients except black sesame seeds. Transfer the squash noodles in skillet and cook for about 1-2 minutes. In a serving dish, place squash mixture and top with fish fillets. Garnish with black sesame seeds and serve.

ZUCCHINI WITH SALMON

Time: 35 minutes   Servings: 4

Ingredients:

For Salmon:

1 tablespoon fresh ginger, minced
3 garlic cloves, minced
1 tablespoon fresh thyme, minced
2 tablespoons olive oil
2 tablespoons fresh lemon juice
Salt and freshly ground black pepper, to taste
4 (4-ounce) salmon fillets

For Zucchini:

1 tablespoon olive oil
2 garlic cloves, minced
4 medium zucchinis, spiralized with Blade C
Salt and freshly ground black pepper, to taste
2 tablespoons fresh lemon juice
¼ cup fresh parsley leaves, chopped

Directions:

For salmon in a large bowl, add all ingredients and mix well. Refrigerate for at least 1-2 hours. Preheat the grill to medium heat. Grease the grill grate. Grill the salmon for about 6-8 minutes per side. Remove from grill and keep aside. Meanwhile for zucchini in another large skillet, heat oil on medium heat. Add garlic and sauté for about 1 minute. Add zucchini, salt and black pepper and cook for about 2-3 minutes. Stir in lemon juice and parsley and remove from heat. Divide the zucchini mixture into serving plates and top with salmon fillets. Serve hot.

Zucchini with Spinach & Salmon

Time: 35 minutes   Servings: 2

Ingredients:

For Salmon:

2 (4-ounce) salmon fillets
2 tablespoons extra virgin olive oil
1 tablespoon fresh lime juice
½ teaspoon garlic powder
Salt and freshly ground black pepper, to taste

For Vegetables:

1 tablespoon olive oil
2 teaspoons fresh ginger, minced
2 garlic cloves, minced
2 cups fresh spinach, torn
1½ cups vegetable broth
3 zucchinis, spiralized with Blade C
½ cup scallions, chopped
Salt and freshly ground black pepper, to taste

Directions:

Preheat the grill to medium heat. Grease the grill grate. Drizzle the salmon fillets with oil and lime juice and sprinkle with seasoning. Grill the salmon fillets for about 6-8 minutes per side. Meanwhile in a skillet, heat oil on medium heat. Add ginger and garlic and sauté for about 1 minute. Add spinach and cook for about 1-2 minutes. Add broth and cook for 2-3 minutes. Stir in zucchini noodles and cook for about 3-5 minutes. Stir in scallion and remove from heat. In a serving plate place zucchini mixture. Top with salmon and serve.

Zucchini with Mushrooms & Salmon

Time: 35 minutes   Servings: 2

Ingredients:

For Salmon:

1 (8-ounce) salmon fillet, cubed
1 tablespoon olive oil
2 tablespoons soy sauce
Salt and freshly ground black pepper, to taste

For Vegetables:

1 tablespoon olive oil
1 teaspoon garlic, minced
¼ teaspoon fresh ginger, minced
1 cup shiitake mushrooms, stemmed and sliced
3 medium zucchinis, spiralized with Blade C
Salt and freshly ground black pepper, to taste

Directions:

Preheat the oven to 400 degrees F. Lightly, grease a baking dish. In a bowl, add salmon and all ingredients and toss to coat well. Transfer the salmon in prepared baking dish. Bake for about 15 minutes. Remove from oven and cut the salmon into small pieces. Meanwhile in a large skillet, heat oil on medium heat. Add garlic and ginger and sauté for about 1 minute. Add mushrooms and cook for about 5 minutes. Add zucchini, salt and black pepper and cook for about 3-4 minutes. Stir in salmon and remove from heat. Serve hot.

Zucchini & Salmon Casserole

Time: 1 hour 25 minutes   Servings: 4

Ingredients:

3 tablespoons olive oil, divided
1 small onion, chopped
1 celery stalk, chopped
3 garlic cloves, minced
Salt and freshly ground black pepper, to taste

2 medium zucchinis, spiralized with Blade C
1¼ cups cooked salmon, chopped very finely
1 tablespoon arrowroot powder
1½ cups unsweetened almond milk

Directions:

Preheat the oven to 350 degrees F. Lightly, grease a casserole dish. In a skillet, heat 1 tablespoon of oil on medium heat. Add onion and celery and sauté for about 3-4 minutes. Add garlic and sauté for about 1 minute. Stir in zucchini, salmon, salt and black pepper. Transfer the zucchini mixture in a casserole dish. In another pan, heat oil on medium-low heat. Add arrowroot powder, beating continuously for about 1 minute. Slowly, add almond milk, beating continuously and cook for about 2-3 minutes or till thick. Pour sauce over zucchini mixture evenly. Bake for about 45-60 minutes.

Yellow Squash with Salmon

Time: 30 minutes   Servings: 8

Ingredients:

For Salmon:

4 (6-ounce) fresh salmon fillets
1 teaspoon red pepper flakes, crushed
Freshly ground black pepper, to taste
Pinch of salt
2 tablespoons fresh lemon juice
4 teaspoons olive oil, divided
2 tablespoons pure maple syrup
2 tablespoons tamari
2 tablespoons scallion, chopped

For Yellow Squash:

1 tablespoon olive oil
1 garlic clove, minced
1 Serrano pepper, seeded and chopped
3 large yellow squashes, spiralized with Blade C
Salt and freshly ground black pepper, to taste

Directions:

In a large bowl, add salmon fillets, seasoning, lemon juice and 2 teaspoons of oil and toss to coat well. Cover and refrigerate for at least 2 hours. In a small pan, mix together maple syrup and tamari on medium heat. Cook for about 7-10 minutes, stirring occasionally. Meanwhile in a large skillet, heat remaining oil on high heat. Add salmon fillets, flesh side down and cook for about 4 minutes. Carefully, flip the side and add maple syrup glaze and cook for about 4 minutes more. Transfer the fillets in serving plates. Meanwhile for squash in another skillet, heat oil on medium heat. Add garlic and Serrano pepper and sauté for about 1 minute. Add squash noodles, salt and black pepper and cook for about 3-4 minutes. Transfer the squash noodles in a serving plate. Top with salmon mixture and serve.

Sweet Potato with Salmon

Time: 60 minutes   Servings: 2

Ingredients:

For Salmon:

2 garlic cloves, minced
1 tablespoon fresh basil, minced
1 tablespoon fresh parsley, minced
¼ cup extra virgin olive oil
1 tablespoon fresh lime juice
Salt and freshly ground black pepper, to taste
2 (6-ounce) salmon fillets

For Sweet Potato:

2 tablespoons olive oil
2 sweet potatoes, peeled and spiralized
  with Blade C
½ cup coconut milk
1 tablespoon fresh basil, minced
Salt and freshly ground black pepper, to taste

Directions:

For fish in a large bowl, add all ingredients and toss to coat well. Refrigerate for at least 1-2 hours. Preheat the oven to 375 degrees F. Arrange fish fillets over a piece of foil. Top with excess marinade. Fold the foil to seal the fish and place the parcel in a baking dish. Bake for about 35-45 minutes. Meanwhile in a skillet, heat oil on medium heat. Add sweet potato noodles and cook for about 1-2 minutes. Add coconut milk, salt and black pepper and cook for about 2-3 minutes or till desired consistency. In a serving plate place sweet potato mixture. Top with salmon and serve.

Mixed Veggies with Salmon

Time: 40 minutes   Servings: 6

Ingredients:

For Salmon:

4 (6-ounce) salmon fillets
3 tablespoons coconut oil, melted
Sea salt and freshly ground black pepper,
  to taste

For Vegetables:

4¼ cups chicken broth
1 can chopped tomatoes, drained
2 tablespoons fresh cilantro, chopped

3 tablespoons fresh lime juice
1 teaspoon balsamic vinegar
1/8 teaspoon red pepper flakes, crushed
Salt and freshly ground black pepper, to taste
1 medium butternut squash, peeled and
spiralized with Blade C
4 large carrots, peeled and spiralized with
  Blade C
3 large zucchinis, spiralized with Blade C
3 scallions, chopped

Directions:

Preheat the broiler of oven. Line a baking sheet with a piece of foil. Coat the salmon fillets with melted coconut oil and sprinkle with salt and black pepper. Broil the salmon fillets for about 15 minutes. Remove from oven and keep aside for about 5 minutes. With a sharp knife, cut the salmon in bite sized pieces. Meanwhile in a large pan, add broth and bring to a boil. In a bowl, mix together canned tomatoes, cilantro, lime juice, vinegar, red pepper flakes, salt and black pepper. Add about ½ cup of boiling broth in the bowl of tomato mixture and gently, stir to combine. Keep aside. Add veggie noodles in the pan of boiling broth and cook for about 2-3 minutes. Stir in a little salt and black pepper and remove from the heat. Divide the veggie noodles into serving bowls and top with tomato mixture and salmon pieces. Garnish with scallion and serve.

BUTTERNUT SQUASH WITH BROCCOLI & SALMON

Time: 30 minutes   Servings: 4

Ingredients:

For Salmon:

¼ cup soy sauce
2 tablespoons honey
2 tablespoons sunflower oil
2 teaspoons sesame seeds
Salt and freshly ground black pepper, to taste
4 (3-ounce) skinless salmon fillets

For Butternut Squash:

2 butternut squashes, peeled and spiralized
   with Blade C
1 tablespoon sunflower oil
Salt and freshly ground black pepper, to taste

For Broccoli:

2 cups broccoli florets
2 tablespoons sunflower oil
2 teaspoons fresh ginger, minced
2 teaspoons garlic, minced
¼ cup soy sauce
2 tablespoons honey
Salt and freshly ground black pepper, to taste
1 teaspoon black sesame seeds

Directions:

Preheat the oven to 400 degrees F. For salmon in a bowl, mix together all ingredients except salmon. Add salmon fillets and toss to coat well. Keep aside in room temperature for about 10-15 minutes. Arrange fillets in a baking dish in a single layer. Bake for about 10 minutes. Meanwhile in another baking dish, place squash noodles. Drizzle with oil and sprinkle with salt and black pepper. Now place the baking dish of squash noodles in oven alongside the baking dish of salmon. Bake salmon and squash for about 5 minutes. Remove from oven and keep aside. Meanwhile in a pan of boiling water, add broccoli and cook for about 2-3 minutes. Drain well. In a large skillet, heat oil on medium heat. Add ginger and garlic and sauté for 1 minute. Add broccoli, soy sauce, honey, salt and black pepper and cook for about 2 minutes. Stir in baked squash and remove from heat. Transfer the squash mixture in 4 serving plates and top with salmon fillets. Garnish with sesame seeds and serve.

TURNIP & SALMON CURRY

Time: 25 minutes   Servings: 4

Ingredients:

1 tablespoon coconut oil
2 garlic cloves, minced
2 teaspoons fresh ginger, minced
3 scallions, chopped (white and green parts
   separated)

3 teaspoons Thai red curry paste
1 (13½-ounce) can coconut milk (chilled)
1¼ cups vegetable broth
2 medium turnips, trimmed, peeled and
   spiralized with Blade D

5-ounce fresh green beans, trimmed and cut into ½-inch pieces

6-ounce skinless salmon fillet, cut into chunks
¼ cup fresh basil leaves, chopped

Directions:

In a large skillet, heat oil on medium-high heat. Add garlic, ginger, and white part of the scallions and sauté for about 1 minute. Add curry paste and sauté for about 1 minute. Carefully, scoop the coconut cream from the top of the can of coconut milk. Add the coconut cream into the skillet and stir to combine. Cook for about 1 minute, stirring continuously. Add the remaining coconut milk and broth and bring to a boil. Stir in the turnip noodles, green beans and salmon chunks. Reduce heat to low and simmer, covered for about 5-7 minutes or till desired doneness. Serve hot with the garnishing of basil.

ZUCCHINI WITH SARDINES

Time: 30 minutes

Servings: 4

Ingredients:

For Sardines:

4 medium whole fresh sardines, gutted, rinsed and patted dry
1½ tablespoons olive oil
2 tablespoons fresh lemon juice
Salt and freshly ground black pepper, to taste

For Zucchini:

1 tablespoon olive oil
1 garlic clove, minced
1 jalapeño pepper, seeded and chopped
3 large zucchinis, spiralized with Blade C
Salt and freshly ground black pepper, to taste
1 tablespoon fresh lemon juice
1 teaspoon lemon zest, grated freshly

Directions:

Preheat the grill to medium-high heat. Grease the grill grate. In a large baking dish, place sardines. Drizzle with oil and lemon juice and sprinkle with salt and black pepper. Grill for about 5 minutes, flipping once in the middle way. Transfer the sardines into a large dish and cover with a piece of foil to keep warm. For zucchini in a large skillet, heat oil on medium heat. Add garlic and jalapeño pepper and sauté for about 1 minute. Add zucchini, salt and black pepper and cook for about 3-4 minutes. Stir in lemon juice and remove from heat. Transfer the zucchini mixture into serving plates evenly. Place sardines alongside the zucchini evenly. Garnish with lemon zest and serve.

CHAYOTE WITH SOLE

Time: 30 minutes

Servings: 4

Ingredients:

2 eggs
¼ cup almond meal
½ teaspoon garlic powder
½ pound lemon sole fillets
2 tablespoons olive oil, divided

2 chayote, peeled and spiralized with Blade C
1 can tomato basil sauce
2 large lemon wedges
Salt and freshly ground black pepper, to taste

Directions:

In a small bowl, add egg and beat well. In another bowl, mix together almond meal, garlic powder, salt and black pepper. Dip the sole fillets in egg and then coat with almond meal mixture evenly. In a skillet, heat 1 tablespoon oil on medium heat. Add sole fillets and cook for about 2-3 minutes per side. Transfer the fillets into a plate and cover with a piece of foil to keep warm. In the same skillet, heat remaining oil on medium heat. Add chayote noodles and cook for about 3-4 minutes. Add tomato basil sauce, salt and black pepper and cook for about 2-3 minutes. Divide the chayote noodles into serving plates and top with sole fillets. Garnish with lemon wedges and serve.

Zucchini with Asparagus & Tuna

Time: 25 minutes   Servings: 2

Ingredients:

For Tuna:

1 small garlic clove, minced
1 teaspoon fresh ginger, minced
1 teaspoon dried rosemary, crushed
1 tablespoon olive oil
1 tablespoon soy sauce
½ tablespoon fresh lime juice
2 (1-inch thick) tuna steaks

For Zucchini & Asparagus:

4 garlic cloves, minced and divided
3 cups fresh basil leaves, chopped
½ cup plus 1 tablespoon olive oil
½ cup walnuts, chopped
Salt and freshly ground black pepper, to taste
½ pound asparagus, trimmed and cut into
1½-inch pieces
3 medium zucchinis, spiralized with Blade C

Directions:

For tuna in a large bowl, add all ingredients and toss to coat well. Refrigerate, covered for at least 1 hour. Preheat the broiler of oven. Arrange the rack 4-inch from heating element. Broil the tuna steaks for about 3 minutes per side. In a food processor, add 3 garlic cloves, basil, ½ cup of oil, walnuts, salt and black pepper and pulse till smooth. Keep aside. In a skillet, heat remaining oil on medium heat. Add remaining garlic and sauté for about 1 minute. Add asparagus and cook for about 4-5 minutes. Meanwhile in a pan of boiling water, add zucchini noodles and cook for about 2-3 minutes. Drain well and pat dry with paper towel. In a serving plate mix together zucchini, asparagus and basil mixture. Top with tuna and serve.

Cabbage with Tuna

Time: 25 minutes   Servings: 2

Ingredients:

1 tablespoon olive oil
2 garlic cloves, minced
1/8 teaspoon red pepper flakes, crushed
½ cup red onion, chopped
1 head cabbage, spiralized with Blade C

Salt and freshly ground black pepper, to taste
1/3 cup chicken broth
2 cans chunky light tuna, drained (packed in water)
2 tablespoons almonds, chopped

Directions:

In a skillet, heat oil on medium heat. Add garlic and red pepper flakes and sauté for 30 seconds. Add onion and sauté for about 2 minutes. Add cabbage, salt and black pepper and cook for about 2-3 minutes. Add broth and cook for about 2-3 minutes. Add tuna and cook for about 1 minute. Top with almonds and serve.

Zucchini with Shrimp

Time: 20 minutes   Servings: 2

Ingredients:

1½ tablespoons extra virgin coconut oil, divided
2 garlic cloves, minced
¼ cup shallots, minced
Pinch of red pepper flakes, crushed
1 pound shrimp, peeled and deveined

3 tablespoons fresh lime juice
Salt and freshly ground black pepper, to taste
3 medium zucchinis, spiralized with Blade C
2 tablespoons fresh cilantro leaves, chopped
1 teaspoon lime zest, grated freshly

Directions:

In a skillet, heat 1 tablespoon of oil on medium heat. Add garlic and sauté for about 1 minute. Add shallot and red pepper flakes and sauté for about 1 minute. Add shrimp and sprinkle with salt and black pepper and cook for about 4 minutes, flipping once after 2 minutes. Stir in lime juice and immediately transfer shrimp into a bowl. In the same skillet, heat remaining oil on medium heat. Add zucchini and cook for about 2-3 minutes. Stir in shrimp and remove from heat. Transfer the zucchini mixture into serving plates. Garnish with cilantro and lime zest and serve hot.

Zucchini with Tomatoes & Shrimp

Time: 25 minutes   Servings: 2

Ingredients:

1 tablespoon coconut oil, divided
3 garlic cloves, minced and divided
½ pound shrimp, peeled and deveined
2 large zucchinis, spiralized with Blade C

1/8 teaspoon chili powder
Salt and freshly ground black pepper, to taste
½ cup cherry tomatoes, halved
1 tablespoon fresh lime juice

Directions:

In a large skillet, heat ½ tablespoon of oil on medium-high heat. Add 2 garlic cloves and sauté for about 30 seconds. Add shrimp and sprinkle with seasoning and cook for about 3-4 minutes. Transfer the shrimp into a plate and keep aside. In the same skillet, heat remaining oil on medium heat. Add remaining garlic and sauté for about 30 seconds. Add zucchini and cook for 1-2 minutes. Stir in tomatoes, shrimp and lime juice and cook for about 1 minute. Remove from heat and serve immediately.

Zucchini with Broccoli & Shrimp

Time: 30 minutes

Servings: 2

Ingredients:

3 tablespoons soy sauce
1 teaspoon balsamic vinegar
1 teaspoon honey
1½ tablespoons olive oil
¼ cup onion, chopped
2 garlic cloves, minced

½ teaspoon fresh ginger, minced
1 cup broccoli florets
4 jumbo shrimp, peeled and deveined
1 large zucchini, spiralized with Blade C
Salt and freshly ground black pepper, to taste
¼ teaspoon black sesame seeds

Directions:

In a bowl, mix together soy sauce, vinegar and honey. Keep aside. In a large skillet, heat oil on medium heat. Add onion and sauté for about 4-5 minutes. Add garlic and ginger and sauté for about 1 minute. Add broccoli and cook for about 3-4 minutes. Add shrimp and cook for about 2 minutes. Flip the side of shrimp and stir in zucchini, salt, black pepper and soy sauce mixture and cook for about 2-3 minutes. Garnish with sesame seeds and serve.

Zucchini with Asparagus & Shrimp

Time: 25 minutes

Servings: 4

Ingredients:

2 tablespoons olive oil
2 garlic cloves, minced
1 cup asparagus, trimmed and cut into
1-inch pieces
4 medium zucchinis, spiralized with Blade C

1 teaspoon soy sauce
1 pound shrimp, peeled and deveined
Salt and freshly ground black pepper, to taste
3 tablespoons fresh parsley, chopped
1 tablespoon black sesame seeds

Directions:

In a skillet, heat oil on medium heat. Add garlic and sauté for about 1 minute. Add asparagus and zucchini and cook for about 2-3 minutes. Add soy sauce and shrimp and cook for about 4 minutes. Stir in parsley and immediately remove from heat. Garnish with sesame seeds and serve hot.

Zucchini with Asparagus, Pesto & Shrimp

Time: 25 minutes

Servings: 2

Ingredients:

For Pesto:

2 cups fresh basil leaves
3 garlic cloves, chopped
1/3 cup pine nuts
½ cup olive oil'

Salt and freshly ground black pepper, to taste

For Zucchini:

2 medium zucchinis, spiralized with Blade C
Salt, as required

For Asparagus:
½ tablespoons olive oil
1 garlic clove, minced
6 asparagus stalks, trimmed and chopped
Salt and freshly ground black pepper, to taste

For Shrimp:
½ tablespoons olive oil
1 garlic clove, minced
8 medium shrimp, peeled and deveined
Salt and freshly ground black pepper, to taste

Directions:

For pesto in a food processor, add all ingredients and pulse till smooth. Keep aside. In a pan of lightly salted boiling water, add zucchini and cook for about 3-4 minutes. Drain well and keep aside. For asparagus in a large skillet, heat oil on medium heat. Add garlic and sauté for about 1 minute. Add asparagus, salt and black pepper and cook for about 4 minutes. Meanwhile for shrimp in another skillet, heat oil on medium heat. Add garlic and sauté for about 1 minute. Add shrimp, salt and black pepper and cook for 2 minutes per side. In a large serving bowl, add pesto, zucchini, asparagus and shrimp and mix well. Serve immediately.

ZUCCHINI & YELLOW SQUASH WITH SHRIMP

Time: 25 minutes   Servings: 4

Ingredients:

For Shrimp:
2 garlic cloves, minced
1 teaspoon fresh rosemary, minced
1 teaspoon fresh oregano, minced
2 teaspoons lemon zest, grated freshly
2 tablespoons olive oil
1 tablespoon fresh lemon juice
Salt and freshly ground black pepper, to taste
1 pound shrimp, peeled and deveined

For Vegetables:
1 tablespoon olive oil
1 garlic clove, minced
2 medium zucchinis, spiralized with Blade C
2 medium yellow squash, spiralized with
   Blade C
Salt and freshly ground black pepper, to taste
½ tablespoon fresh lemon juice

Directions:

For shrimp in a large bowl, add all ingredients except shrimp and mix well. Add shrimp and coat with marinade generously. Cover and refrigerate for about 2-3 hours. Remove shrimp from refrigerator and keep aside in room temperature for about 20-30 minutes. Preheat the grill to medium-high. Grease the grill grate. Grill the shrimp for about 2 minutes per side. Transfer the shrimp into a bowl and cover loosely with a piece of foil to keep warm. In a skillet, heat oil on medium heat. Add garlic and sauté for about 1 minute. Add zucchini and squash and cook for about 3-4 minutes. Stir in lemon juice and immediately remove from heat. Transfer zucchini mixture into a serving plate. Top with shrimp and serve.

YELLOW SQUASH WITH SHRIMP

Time: 20 minutes   Servings: 2

Ingredients:
1 tablespoon olive oil
1 garlic clove, minced

Pinch of red pepper flakes, crushed
6 large shrimp, peeled and deveined

Salt and freshly ground black pepper, to taste
1/3 cup chicken broth

3 medium yellow squash, spiralized with Blade C
1 tablespoon fresh parsley, chopped

Directions:

In a large skillet, heat oil on medium heat.

Add garlic and red pepper flakes and sauté for about 1 minute.

Add shrimp, salt and black pepper and cook for about 1 minute per side.

Add broth and squash and cook for about 3-4 minutes.

Garnish with parsley and serve.

YELLOW SQUASH WITH TOMATO & SHRIMP

Time: 30 minutes   Servings: 4

Ingredients:

2 tablespoons coconut oil
2 tablespoons coconut flour
1½ cups coconut milk
1/8 teaspoon red chili powder
Salt and freshly ground black pepper, to taste
1 teaspoon dried thyme, crushed

1 teaspoon dried oregano, crushed1 pound shrimp, peeled and deveined
1 cup grape tomatoes, chopped
1 pound yellow squash, spiralized with Blade C

Directions:

In a skillet, melt coconut oil on medium heat. Add coconut flour and cook for about 1 minute, stirring continuously. Stir in coconut milk. Cook for about 4-5 minutes, stirring continuously. Add seasoning and herbs and cook for about 1 minute. Stir in shrimp and tomatoes. Reduce the heat to low and simmer, covered for 1-2 minutes. Stir in squash noodles and cook for about 2-3 minutes. Serve hot. Yellow Squash with Asparagus & Shrimp

Time: 35 minutes   Servings: 4

Ingredients:

1 cup asparagus, trimmed and cut into 1½-inch pieces
4 medium yellow squash, spiralized with Blade C
1½ pound shrimp, peeled and deveined
¼ teaspoon fresh ginger, minced

½ teaspoon garlic, minced
½ cup tamari
½ cup almond butter
Salt and freshly ground black pepper, to taste
¼ cup scallions, sliced thinly

Directions:

Arrange a steamer basket over a pan of boiling water. Place asparagus in steamer basket and steam, covered for about 4-5 minutes or till done. Transfer the asparagus into a colander. Place the squash noodles in steamer basket and steam for about 3 minutes. Transfer the squash into a colander and keep aside to drain completely. Now, place the shrimp in the same steamer basket and steam for about 4-5 minutes. Transfer the shrimp, squash and asparagus into a serving plate. Meanwhile in a bowl, add ginger, garlic, tamari and almond butter and beat till well combined. Pour almond butter sauce over squash mixture and gently, stir to combine. Top with scallion and serve.

SWEET POTATO WITH OLIVES & SHRIMP

Time: 40 minutes   Servings: 4

Ingredients:

1 tablespoon coconut oil
3 garlic cloves, minced
3 cups fresh tomatoes, chopped finely
¼ cup vegetable broth
¼ cup green olives, pitted and halved
¼ cup capers

¼ cup fresh cilantro, chopped and divided
¼ teaspoon cayenne pepper
Salt and freshly ground black pepper, to taste
2 large sweet potatoes, peeled and spiralized with Blade C
14-16 medium shrimp, peeled and deveined

Directions:

In a large skillet, melt coconut oil on medium-low heat. Add garlic and sauté for about 1 minute. Add tomatoes and cook for about 1-2 minutes, crushing them. Add broth, olives, capers, 2 tablespoons of cilantro, cayenne pepper, salt and black pepper and cook for about 4-5 minutes, stirring occasionally. Stir in sweet potato noodles and cook, covered for about 3-4 minutes, tossing once after 2 minutes. Gently, stir in shrimp and cook, covered for about 4-5 minutes. Garnish with remaining cilantro and serve.

SWEET POTATO WITH SPINACH & SHRIMP

Time: 40 minutes   Servings: 4

Ingredients:

For Shrimp:

2 garlic cloves, minced
2 tablespoons olive oil
2 tablespoons fresh lemon juice
1 teaspoon fresh lemon zest, grated finely
Salt and freshly ground black pepper, to taste
1 pound large shrimp, peeled and deveined

For Sweet Potato:

2 tablespoons olive oil
½ cup yellow onion, chopped

2 garlic cloves, minced
¼ teaspoon red pepper flakes, crushed
2 large sweet potatoes, peeled and spiralized with Blade C
Salt and freshly ground black pepper, to taste
½ cup vegetable broth
¼ cup fresh rosemary, chopped
4 cups fresh spinach, torn

Directions:

For shrimp in a large bowl, add all ingredients and refrigerate for at least 1 hour. Preheat the grill to high heat. Grease the grill grate. Grill the shrimp for about 3-4 minutes per side. Remove from grill and keep aside. For sweet potato in a large skillet, heat oil on medium heat. Add onion and sauté for about 4-5 minutes. Add garlic and red pepper flakes and sauté for about 1 minute. Add sweet potato, salt and black pepper and cook for about 2-3 minutes. Add broth and rosemary and cook for about 3-4 minutes. Stir in spinach and cook for about 3 minutes. Stir in shrimp and remove from heat. Serve hot.

POTATO WITH SHRIMP

Time: 30 minutes   Servings: 2

Ingredients:

1½ tablespoons olive oil, divided
2 garlic cloves, minced
½ pound shrimp, peeled and deveined
Salt and freshly ground black pepper, to taste
2 tablespoons fresh lemon juice

3 potatoes, peeled and spiralized with
    Blade C
1 cup chicken broth
1 tablespoon fresh parsley, chopped

Directions:

In a large skillet, heat ½ tablespoon of oil on medium heat. Add garlic and sauté for about 1 minute. Add shrimp, salt and black pepper and cook for about 2 minutes per side. Stir in lemon juice and remove from heat and keep aside. In another skillet, heat remaining oil on medium heat. Add potatoes and cook for about 1-2 minutes. Add broth, salt and black pepper and cook for about 4-5 minutes. Stir in shrimp mixture and remove from heat. Garnish with parsley and serve.

POTATO WITH SHRIMP IN SAUCE

Time: 40 minutes   Servings: 2

Ingredients:

For Sauce:

1 tablespoon honey
1 tablespoon soy sauce
1 tablespoon chili garlic sauce
2 tablespoons fresh orange juice
½ tablespoon rice vinegar

For Shrimp:

¾ pound shrimp, peeled and deveined
½ tablespoons arrowroot powder

1 tablespoon olive oil
2 garlic cloves, minced
1 tablespoon fresh ginger, minced

For Potato:

1 tablespoon olive oil
2 small potatoes, peeled and spiralized with
Blade C with Blade C

Directions:

In a bowl, mix together all sauce ingredients. Keep aside. In a bowl, add shrimp and sprinkle with arrowroot powder and toss to coat well. In a large skillet, heat oil on medium-high heat. Add garlic and ginger and sauté for about 30 seconds. Add shrimp and cook for about 3 minutes. Add sauce and cook for about 2 minutes, stirring continuously. With a slotted spoon, transfer the shrimp into a bowl. Cook for about 2-4 minutes, stirring continuously. In a large skillet, heat oil on medium heat. Add potatoes and cook for about 8-10 minutes, tossing occasionally. Divide potato noodles in serving plates and top with shrimp. Pour orange sauce on top and serve.

PARSNIPS WITH CARROTS & SHRIMP

Time: 30 minutes

Servings: 4

Ingredients:

3 tablespoons olive oil
2 large carrots, peeled and sliced thinly
1 large onion, sliced thinly
1 garlic clove, minced
1 pound parsnip, peeled and spiralized with
  Blade C

2 tablespoons soy sauce
Salt and freshly ground black pepper, to taste
1 pound shrimp, peeled and deveined
2 tablespoons white sesame seeds

Directions:

In a large skillet, heat oil on medium heat. Add carrots and onion and sauté for about 3-4 minutes. Add garlic and sauté for about 1 minute more. Add parsnip noodles and cook for about 6-7 minutes. Stir in soy sauce, salt and black pepper. Meanwhile, arrange a steamer basket over a pan of boiling water. Place the shrimp in the steamer basket and steam for about 3-4 minutes. Transfer the shrimp into skillet with parsnip mixture and cook for about 2-3 minutes. Top with sesame seeds and serve.

CARROTS WITH SHRIMP

Time: 25 minutes

Servings: 2

Ingredients:

¼ cup fresh lime juice
3 tablespoons soy sauce
2 tablespoons fish sauce
2 tablespoons tamarind pulp
3 tablespoons palm sugar
1 tablespoon olive oil
2 chopped shallots
2 minced garlic cloves

½ pound shrimps, peeled and deveined
2 large carrots, peeled and spiralized with
  Blade C
2 tablespoons roasted peanuts
¼ cup scallions, chopped (green part)
¼ cup fresh cilantro, chopped
1 lime, cut into wedges

Directions:

In a pan, mix together lime juice, soy sauce, fish sauce, tamarind and sugar and cook for about 5 minutes, stirring continuously. Remove from the heat and keep aside. In a skillet, heat oil on medium heat. Add onion and garlic and sauté for about 5 minutes. Add shrimp and cook for about 3-4 minutes. Meanwhile in a pan of boiling water, cook the carrot noodles for about 2-3 minutes. Drain well. Add carrot noodles and sauce mixture in skillet with shrimp and mix till well combined. Add peanuts and cook for about 1 minutes. Stir in scallions and cilantro and remove from heat. Serve hot with lime wedges.

Zucchini with Prawns

Time: 30 minutes   Servings: 2

Ingredients:

3 garlic cloves, minced and divided
¼ teaspoon fresh ginger, minced
1 teaspoon soy sauce
1 teaspoon honey
½ teaspoon red pepper flakes, crushed
12 fresh king prawns, peeled and deveined

3 tablespoons coconut oil, divided
2 large zucchinis, spiralized with Blade C
Salt and freshly ground black pepper, to taste
1 tablespoon fresh lemon juice
2 tablespoons fresh parsley, chopped

Directions:

In a large bowl, mix together 2 garlic cloves, ginger, soy sauce, honey and ¼ teaspoon of red pepper flakes. Add prawns and coat with marinade generously. Refrigerate, covered to marinate for at least 2-3 hours. In a large skillet, heat 2 tablespoons of oil on medium heat. Add prawns with marinade and stir fry for about 2-4 minutes. Remove from heat and keep warm. In another large skillet, heat remaining oil on medium heat. Add remaining garlic and sauté for about 1 minute. Add zucchini, remaining red pepper flakes, salt and black pepper and cook for about 2-3 minutes. Stir in lemon juice and remove from the heat. Transfer the zucchini mixture into a serving plate and top with prawns. Garnish with parsley and serve hot.

Sweet Potato with Calms

Time: 30 minutes   Servings: 2

Ingredients:

1 tablespoon olive oil
1 small white onion, chopped
1 celery stalk, chopped
2 small garlic cloves, minced
¼ cup fish broth
1 tablespoon fresh lime juice

10 little neck clams
3 teaspoons fresh thyme, chopped
¼ teaspoon chili powder
Salt and freshly ground black pepper, to taste
1 large sweet potato, peeled and spiralized with Blade C

Directions:

In a skillet, heat oil on medium heat. Add onion and celery and sauté for about 3-4 minutes. Add garlic and sauté for about 1 minute. Add broth and lime juice and bring to a boil. Stir in clams and reduce the heat to medium-low. Simmer, covered for about 6-7 minutes. Stir in thyme and seasoning and immediately, remove from heat. Meanwhile, place sweet potato noodles in a steamer basket. Arrange the basket over a pan of boiling water and steam for about 6-8 minutes. Transfer the sweet potato into a serving bowl. Top with clam mixture and serve.

Zucchini with Calms & Shrimp

Time: 30 minutes   Servings: 4

Ingredients:

2 tablespoons extra virgin olive oil
2-3 garlic cloves, minced
12 clams, scrubbed
¼ cup fish broth
1 pound shrimp, peeled and deveined

Salt and freshly ground black pepper, to taste
1 tablespoon fresh lime juice
4 large zucchinis, spiralized with Blade C
3 tablespoons fresh parsley, chopped

Directions:

In a skillet, heat oil on medium heat. Add garlic and sauté for about 1 minute. Add clams and broth and cook for about 4 minutes. Add shrimp and sprinkle with salt and black pepper and cook for about 2 minutes. Stir in lime juice and zucchini and cook for about 2-3 minutes. Garnish with parsley and serve.

Zucchini with Scallops

Time: 25 minutes   Servings: 4

Ingredients:

3 tablespoons olive oil, divided
2 garlic cloves, minced
6medium zucchini, spiralized with Blade C
Salt and freshly ground black pepper, to taste
1 tablespoon fresh lemon juice

4 scallions, chopped (white and green part, separated)
1 pound bay scallops, cleaned, rinsed and pat dried

Directions:

In a large skillet, heat 2 tablespoons of oil on medium-high heat. Add garlic and sauté for about 1 minute. Add zucchini noodles, and sprinkle with salt and black pepper and cook for about 4-5 minutes. Transfer the zucchini into a plate. Add lime juice and white part of scallions and gently, stir t combine. In the same skillet, heat remaining oil on medium-high heat. Add scallops and cook for about 4 minutes, tossing once after 2 minutes. Transfer the scallops into the plate with zucchini. Top with green part of scallions and serve.

Zucchini with Spinach & Scallops

Time: 20 minutes   Servings: 4

Ingredients:

For Scallops:

3 tablespoons bacon fat
3 garlic cloves, minced
1½ pounds large scallops
2 tablespoons fresh lemon juice

For Zucchini & Spinach:

3 tablespoons bacon fat
2 garlic cloves, minced
1 pound fresh spinach, chopped
3 large zucchinis, spiralized with Blade C

Directions:

For scallops in a large skillet, heat bacon fat on medium heat. Add garlic and sauté for about 1 minute. Add scallops and cook for about 1½ minutes per side. Stir in lemon juice and cook for about 1 minute. Transfer the scallops into a plate. Meanwhile in another large skillet, heat bacon fat on medium heat. Add garlic and sauté for about 1 minute. Add zucchini noodles and spinach and cook for about 3-4 minutes. Transfer the zucchini mixture into serving plate. Place scallops over spinach with the sauce in pan and serve.

APPLE WITH SPINACH & SCALLOPS

Time: 25 minutes   Servings: 2

Ingredients:

2 tablespoon olive oil, divided
6 large scallops
1 green apple, peeled and spiralized with
    Blade C

1 cup fresh baby spinach
Salt and freshly ground black pepper, to taste
2 tablespoons freshly squeezed lemon juice

Directions:

In a large skillet, heat 2 tablespoon of oil on medium heat. Add scallops and cook for 3-4 minutes. Transfer the scallops into a plate. In the same skillet, heat remaining oil on medium heat. Add apple, spinach, salt and black pepper and cook for about 2-3 minutes. Stir in lemon juice and remove from heat. Transfer the apple mixture into serving plate. Place scallops over spinach with the sauce in pan and serve.

ZUCCHINI WITH LOBSTER

Time: 45 minutes   Servings: 2

Ingredients:

2 tablespoons coconut oil, divided
2 (4-ounce) lobster tails, shelled and cut
into bite size pieces
½ small onion, chopped
2 garlic cloves, minced
2 cups fresh tomatoes, chopped finely

½ cup vegetable broth
¼ teaspoon chili powder
Salt and freshly ground black pepper, to taste
3 medium zucchinis, spiralized with Blade C
1 tablespoon fresh cilantro, chopped

Directions:

In a large skillet, heat 1 tablespoon of oil on medium heat. Add lobster tails and cook for about 6-7 minutes. Transfer the lobster into a serving plate. In the same skillet, heat remaining oil on medium heat. Add onion and sauté for 4-5 minutes. Add garlic and sauté for about 1 minute. Add tomatoes and cook for about 3-4 minutes, crushing them. Add broth and seasoning and bring to a boil. Reduce the heat to low and simmer for about 10-15 minutes. Stir in zucchini and lobster meat and cook for about 5 minutes. Garnish with cilantro and serve.

SWEET POTATO WITH LOBSTER

Time: 35 minutes

Servings: 2

Ingredients:

For Lobster:

2 tablespoons olive oil
2 tablespoons butter, melted
2 cloves garlic, minced
1 tablespoon fresh ginger, minced
¼ cup fresh chives, chopped
2 tablespoons Sriracha
Salt, to taste
8-ounce lobster tails

For Sweet Potato:

1 tablespoon olive oil
2 garlic cloves, minced
2 medium sweet potatoes, peeled and spiralized with Blade C
¼ cup chicken broth
Salt and freshly ground black pepper, to taste
2 tablespoons fresh cilantro
2 fresh lemon wedges

Directions:

In a large bowl, add olive oil, butter, garlic, ginger, chives, Sriracha, salt and lobster and mix till well combined. Refrigerate, covered for about 3-4 hours. Preheat the grill on high heat. Grease the grill grate. Place the lobster tails on the hot grill, flesh side down. Grill for about 4-5 minutes. Top with fresh cilantro and serve with lemon wedges. Meanwhile in a skillet, heat oil on medium heat. Add garlic and sauté for about 30 seconds. Add sweet potato noodles and cook for about 3-4 minutes. Add broth, salt and black pepper and cook for about 3-4 minutes. Stir in cilantro and remove from the heat. Divide sweet potato noodles in serving plates and top with lobster tails. Serve with lemon wedges.

ZUCCHINI WITH MUSSELS

Time: 35 minutes

Servings: 4

Ingredients:

1 tablespoon coconut oil
1 cup yellow onion, chopped
2 celery stalks, chopped
2 garlic cloves, minced
2 cups grape tomatoes, halved

¼ teaspoon cayenne pepper
Salt and freshly ground black pepper, to taste
20-24 mussels, scrubbed and debearded
2 tablespoons fresh parsley, chopped
4 zucchinis, spiralized with Blade C

Directions:

In a skillet, melt coconut oil on medium heat. Add onion and celery and sauté for about 3-4 minutes. Add garlic and sauté for about 1 minute. Stir in tomatoes and seasoning and cook, covered for about 4-5 minutes. Reduce the heat to low and stir in mussels and parsley. Cook, covered for about 2 minutes. Meanwhile in a pan of boiling water, cook the zucchini noodles for about 2-3 minutes. Drain well. In a large serving bowl, place zucchini noodles. Add mussel mixture and gently stir to combne.

BUTTERNUT SQUASH WITH CRAB

Time: 25 minutes   Servings: 2

Ingredients:

1 butternut squash, peeled and spiralized with Blade C

3 tablespoons olive oil, divided

Salt and freshly ground black pepper, to taste

1 garlic clove, minced

¾ cup fresh crab meat

¼ teaspoon red pepper flakes, crushed

1 tablespoon fresh cilantro leaves, chopped

Directions:

Preheat the oven to 400 degrees F. Lightly, grease a baking sheet. In a large bowl, add butternut squash, 1 tablespoon of oil, salt and black pepper and toss to coat well. Transfer the squash mixture in prepared baking sheet. Bake for about 10 minutes, tossing once after 5 minutes. Transfer the baked butternut squash in serving bowl Meanwhile in a large skillet, heat remaining oil on medium heat. Add garlic and sauté for about 1 minute. Add crab meat and red pepper flakes and cook for about 3 minutes. Place crabmeat mixture over butternut squash. Garnish with cilantro and serve.

Spiralized Vegetarian Recipes

Potato Waffles

Time: 25 minutes   Servings: 2

Ingredients:
1 russet potato, peeled and spiralized with   ½ teaspoon fresh rosemary, chopped
  Blade C   Salt and freshly ground black pepper, to taste
½ teaspoon fresh thyme, chopped

Directions:
Preheat the waffle iron and grease it before cooking. Squeeze the potato noodles well. Transfer the squeezed
potato noodles in a large bowl. Add remaining ingredients and mix well. Place the desired amount of the
potato mixture into preheated waffle iron and cook for 8-10 minutes or till golden brown. Repeat with the
remaining mixture.

Sweet Potato & Zucchini Waffles

Time: 25 minutes   Servings: 2

Ingredients:
2 small zucchinis, spiralized with Blade C,   2 garlic cloves, minced
  chopped and squeezed   1 tablespoon fresh parsley, minced
½ pound sweet potato, peeled, spiralized   ¼ teaspoon cayenne pepper
  with Blade C, chopped and squeezed   Salt and freshly ground black pepper, to taste
½ small red onion, chopped finely

Directions:
Preheat the waffle iron and grease it before cooking. In a large bowl, add all ingredients and mix till well
combined. Place the desired amount of the sweet potato mixture into preheated waffle iron and cook for 8-10
minutes or till golden brown. Repeat with the remaining mixture.

Sweet Potato Pancakes

Time: 20 minutes   Servings: 4

Ingredients:
2 tablespoons ground flax feeds   ½ tablespoon olive oil
6 tablespoons water   ¼ teaspoon red pepper flakes, crushed
2 medium sweet potatoes, peeled and   Salt and freshly ground black pepper, to taste
  spiralized with Blade C   3 tablespoons honey

Directions:

In a bowl, mix together flax seeds and water and keep aside. In a large nonstick skillet, heat oil on medium heat. Add sweet potato, salt and black pepper and cook for about 8-10 minutes, stirring occasionally. Transfer the sweet potatoes into a large bowl and keep aside to cool slightly. Stir in flax seed mixture. Meanwhile preheat a greased griddle. Place the desired amount of the sweet potato mixture in the griddle and cook for about 2-3 minutes. Carefully flip the side and cook for about 1-2 minutes. Repeat with the remaining mixture. Serve the pancakes with the topping of honey.

Apple Pancakes

Time: 20 minutes   Servings: 2

Ingredients:

¾ cup whole wheat flour
¼ cup oats
1 teaspoons baking powder
½ teaspoon ground cinnamon
1/8 teaspoon ground nutmeg

¼ teaspoon sea salt
1 cup unsweetened almond milk
1 medium apple, peeled and spiralized with Blade C
¼ cup raisins

Directions:

Preheat the griddle and grease it before cooking. In a large bowl, mix together flour, oats, baking powder, cinnamon, nutmeg and salt. Add milk and mix till well combined. Stir in apple and raisins. Place the desired amount of the sweet potato mixture in the griddle and cook for about 2-3 minutes. Carefully flip the side and cook for about 1-2 minutes. Repeat with the remaining mixture.

Zucchini & Sweet Potato Hash

Time: 30 minutes   Servings: 4

Ingredients:

2 small zucchinis, Spiralized with Blade C and chopped
1 medium sweet potato, peeled, spiralized with Blade C and chopped

Salt, to taste
½ cup white onion, minced
Freshly ground black pepper, to taste
1 tablespoon extra-virgin coconut oil

Directions:

In a colander, place zucchini and salt. Arrange colander over a large bowl and keep aside for about 10 minutes. Then squeeze the extra moisture from zucchini and transfer into a large bowl. Add the sweet potato, onion, salt and black pepper and mix well. In a large skillet, heat oil on medium heat. add vegetable hash browns and cook for about 4 to 6 minutes. Carefully flip the side and cook for about 4 to 6 minutes. Serve immediately.

POTATO HASH

Time: 25 minutes   Servings: 2

Ingredients:

1 pound red potatoes, peeled and spiralized   1 teaspoon fresh parsley, chopped
   with Blade C   Freshly ground black pepper, to taste
Salt, to taste   1 tablespoon olive oil

Directions:

In a colander, place the potatoes and sprinkle with salt. Arrange colander over a large bowl and keep aside for about 10 minutes. Then squeeze the extra moisture from potatoes and transfer into a large bowl. Add parsley, salt and black pepper and mix well. In a large skillet, heat oil on medium heat. In batches, add hash browns and cook for about 4-5 minutes per sid. Serve immediately.

SWEET POTATO, VEGGIES & CHICKEN HASH

Time: 30 minutes   Servings: 2

Ingredients:

2½ tablespoons olive oil, divided   ½ teaspoon dried thyme, crushed
½ pound skinless, boneless chicken breast,   ¼ teaspoon red pepper flakes, crushed
trimmed and cut into bite sized pieces   ¼ cup onion, chopped
Salt and freshly ground black pepper, to taste   1 red bell pepper, seeded and chopped
2 garlic cloves, minced and divided   1½ cups button mushrooms, chopped
2 small sweet potatoes, peeled and   2 tablespoons fresh cilantro leaves, chopped
   spiralized with Blade C

Directions:

In a large skillet, heat ½ tablespoon of oil on medium heat. Add chicken and sprinkle with salt and black pepper and cook for about 4-5 minutes. Transfer the chicken into a plate. In the same skillet, heat 1 tablespoon of oil on medium heat. Add 1 garlic clove and sauté for about 1 minute. Add the sweet potato, salt and black pepper and cook for about 6-8 minutes. Transfer the sweet potato in serving plates. Meanwhile in another large skillet, heat on medium heat. Add remaining garlic, thyme and red pepper flakes and sauté for about 1 minute. Add onion and sauté for about 4-5 minutes. Add bell pepper and mushrooms and cook for about 3-4 minutes. Stir in chicken and cook for about 2 minutes and remove from heat. Place the hash over sweet potato. Garnish with cilantro and serve.

BROCCOLI & TOFU SCRAMBLE

Time: 30 minutes

Servings: 2

Ingredients:

2 broccoli stems, spiralized with Blade C
2 tablespoons olive oil
½ onion, chopped
1 small red bell pepper, seeded and chopped
2 garlic cloves, minced
1 teaspoon ground turmeric

1 teaspoon ground cumin
1 (14-ounce) block extra firm tofu,
   crumbled and pressed
1 tablespoon nutritional yeast flakes
Salt and freshly ground black pepper, to taste

Directions:

In a pan of boiling water, add broccoli noodles and cook for about 2-3 minutes. Remove from heat and drain well. In a large skillet, heat oil on medium heat. Add onion and bell pepper and sauté for about 4-5 minutes. Add garlic, turmeric and cumin and sauté for about 1 minute more. Add remaining ingredients and cook for about 2-3 minutes. Serve hot.

SPICED CARROTS

Time: 35 minutes

Servings: 2

Ingredients:

5½ cups carrots, peeled and spiralized with
   Blade C
1 teaspoon ground ginger
1 teaspoon sweet paprika

½ teaspoon ground cumin
1 teaspoon ground cinnamon
Salt and freshly ground black pepper, to taste

Directions:

In a large skillet, heat oil on medium heat. Add carrot and sauté for about 5-6 minutes. Stir in ginger, paprika, cumin and cinnamon and cook for about 1-2 minutes. Season with salt and black pepper and serve.

CARROTS & POTATOES WITH HERBS

Time: 45 minutes

Servings: 4

Ingredients:

1 large white potato, peeled and spiralized
   with Blade C
1 large carrot, peeled and spiralized with
Blade C

2 tablespoons olive oil
1 teaspoon salt
1 teaspoon chopped rosemary
1 teaspoon chopped thyme

Directions:

Preheat the oven to 400 degrees F. In a bowl, add all ingredients and Transfer the veggie mixture into 2 baking dishes. Bake for about 20-25 minutes.

Carrots with Tofu

Time: 35 minutes   Servings: 2

Ingredients:

For Tofu:

6 ounces extra-firm tofu, drained and cubed
1 teaspoon sesame oil
¼ cup low-sodium soy sauce

For Carrots:

2 tablespoon olive oil

½ teaspoon fresh ginger, grated
2 large carrots, peeled and spiralized with Blade C
3 cups fresh baby spinach
1 tablespoon rice vinegar
Salt and freshly ground black pepper, to taste

Directions:

Preheat the oven to 350 degrees F. Line a baking sheet with a parchment paper. In a bowl, add tofu, sesame oil and soy sauce and mix till well combined. Transfer the tofu mixture onto the prepared baking sheet. Bake for about 30 minutes or till browned. Meanwhile in a large skillet, heat olive oil on medium heat. Add ginger and sauté for about 30 seconds. Add carrots and cook for about 2-3 minutes. Add spinach and cook for about 2-3 minutes. Stir in the vinegar, salt and black pepper and remove from the heat. Divide the carrot mixture into serving plates evenly. Top with the baked tofu evenly and serve.

Butternut Squash with Tomatoes

Time: 50 minutes   Servings: 2

Ingredients:

¼ cup whole cherry tomatoes
¼ cup cherry tomatoes, halved
2 tablespoons extra virgin olive oil, divided
2 teaspoons cayenne pepper
Salt and freshly ground black pepper, to taste
2 cups butternut squash, peeled and spiralized with Blade C

1 garlic clove, minced
1 jalapeño pepper, seeded and chopped
3 cups fresh spinach, torn
1 small avocado, peeled, pitted and cubed
¼ teaspoon red pepper flakes, crushed
2 tablespoons fresh cilantro, chopped

Directions:

Preheat the oven to 375 degrees F. Line a baking dish with a piece of foil. In a bowl, add tomatoes, 1 tablespoon of oil, cayenne pepper, salt and black pepper and toss to coat well. Transfer the tomato mixture into prepared baking dish. Roast for about 25 minutes. In a large skillet, heat remaining oil on medium heat. Add squash noodles and cook for about 4-5 minutes. Transfer the squash in a large bowl. In the same skillet, add garlic and jalapeño pepper and sauté for about 1 minute. Add spinach and avocado and cook for about 2 minutes. Stir in cooked squash, roasted tomatoes and red pepper flakes and cook for about 2 minutes. Garnish with cilantro and serve hot.

BUTTERNUT SQUASH WITH BRUSSELS SPROUT

Time: 25 minutes   Servings: 4

Ingredients:

1 medium butternut squash, peeled and spiralized with Blade C
2 tablespoons olive oil, divided
Salt and freshly ground black pepper, to taste
1 medium onion, chopped

2 garlic cloves, minced
1 Serrano pepper, seeded and chopped
1 cup Brussels sprouts, trimmed and sliced thinly
¼ cup pecans, toasted and chopped

Directions:

Preheat the oven to 400 degrees F. Lightly, grease a baking sheet. In a large bowl, add butternut squash, 1 tablespoon of oil, salt and black pepper and toss to coat well. Transfer the squash mixture in prepared baking sheet. Bake for about 10 minutes, tossing once after 5 minutes. Meanwhile in a large skillet, heat remaining oil on medium heat. Add onion and sauté for about 3-4 minutes. Add garlic and Serrano pepper and sauté for about 1 minute. Stir in Brussels sprouts, salt and black pepper and cover the skillet. Cook, stirring occasionally for about 4 to 5 minutes. In a large serving bowl, mix together cooked butternut squash and Brussels sprout mixture. Top with pecans and serve.

BEETS WITH TOMATOES

Time: 35 minutes   Servings: 2

Ingredients:

10-12 cherry tomatoes
2 tablespoon olive oil, divided
Salt and freshly ground black pepper, to taste

2 large beets, peeled and spiralized with Blade C
2 tablespoons fresh cilantro leaves, chopped

Directions:

Preheat the oven to 400 degrees F. Arrange the tomatoes in a large baking sheet. Drizzle with 1 tablespoon of oil and sprinkle with salt and black pepper. Roast for about 10 minutes. Remove baking sheet from oven. Now, arrange the beets in the baking dish. Drizzle with remaining oil and sprinkle with salt and black pepper. Roast for about 8-10 minutes. Top with cilantro and serve.

BEETS WITH TOMATOES & CHEESE

Time: 25 minutes   Servings: 4

Ingredients:

1 tablespoon olive oil
1 garlic clove, minced
4 medium beets, peeled and spiralized with Blade C
Salt and freshly ground black pepper, to taste

1 cup cherry tomatoes, halved
½ cup feta cheese, crumbled
¼ teaspoon fresh lemon juice
2 Tbsp. fresh basil, chopped

Directions:

In a large skillet, heat olive oil on medium-high heat. Add garlic and sauté for about 30 seconds. Add beet noodles, salt and black pepper and cook for about 1-2 minutes. Add tomatoes and cook, covered for about 4-5 minutes, stirring occasionally. Stir in lemon juice and remove from heat. Top with feta and basil and serve.

BEETS IN SWEET & SOUR SAUCE

Time: 25 minutes   Servings: 4

Ingredients:

4 medium beets, peeled and spiralized with Blade C
2½ tablespoons extra virgin olive oil, divided
Salt and freshly ground black pepper, to taste
1 tablespoons onion, minced

1 garlic clove, minced
2 tablespoons almond butter
2½ tablespoons honey
2½ tablespoons fresh lemon juice
¼ cup almonds, chopped

Directions:

Preheat the oven to 400 degrees F. Grease a baking sheet. Place beets noodles onto prepared baking sheet. Drizzle with ½ tablespoon of oil and sprinkle with salt and black pepper. Roast for about 5 minutes. Remove the baking sheet from oven and transfer the beets into a serving bowl. In a food processor, add remaining ingredients except almonds and pulse till smooth. Pour honey mixture over beets and toss to coat well. Top with almonds and serve immediately.

CHEESY POTATOES

Time: 35 minutes   Servings: 4

Ingredients:

1½ pound potatoes, scrubbed and spiralized with Blade C
1 garlic clove, minced
1 tablespoon olive oil

Salt and freshly ground black pepper, to taste
2 tablespoons feta cheese, crumbled
2 tablespoon mozzarella cheese, grated
2 tablespoons fresh basil leaves, chopped

Directions:

Preheat the oven to 425 degrees F. Lightly, grease a baking dish. In a large bowl, add all ingredients and toss to coat well. Transfer the potato mixture into prepared baking dish. Bake for about 12-15 minutes. Remove baking dish from oven and sprinkle with cheese. Now, set the oven to broil. Broil for about 3-5 minutes. Garnish with basil and serve.

Buttered Sweet Potatoes

Time: 20 minutes   Servings: 4

Ingredients:

2 large sweet potatoes, peeled and
    spiralized with Blade C
1 tablespoon almond butter

1 teaspoon coconut palm sugar
½ teaspoon ground cinnamon

Directions:

Arrange a steamer basket over a pan of boiling water. Place sweet potato noodles in the steamer basket. Steam for about 6-8 minutes or till tender. Transfer the sweet potato into a serving bowl. Stir in butter. Sprinkle with sugar and cinnamon and serve.

Sweet Potato in Creamy Sauce

Time: 30 minutes   Servings: 4

Ingredients:

1 cup marinara sauce
2 cups cream
3 tablespoons olive oil
2 teaspoons garlic powder
3 tablespoons arrowroot powder

Salt and freshly ground black pepper, to taste
2 large sweet potatoes, peeled and
spiralized with Blade C
2 tablespoons fresh basil leaves, chopped

Directions:

In a large pan, add all ingredients except sweet potato and basil on medium heat and cook for about 2-3 minutes, stirring continuously. Add sweet potato and cook for about 6-8 minutes, stirring occasionally. Garnish with basil and serve.

Sweet Potato with Spinach

Time: 25 minutes   Servings: 2

Ingredients:

For Dressing:

¼ cup raw cashews, soaked for 2 hours
    and drained
1 small garlic clove, chopped
¼ cup unsweetened almond milk
½ tablespoon fresh lime juice
Salt and freshly ground black pepper, to taste

For Veggies:

1½ tablespoons olive oil, divided
1 large sweet potato, peeled and spiralized
    with Blade C
Salt and freshly ground black pepper, to taste
1 garlic clove, minced
3 cups fresh spinach, chopped
½ teaspoon lime zest, grated freshly

Directions:

For dressing in a blender, add all ingredients and pulse till smooth. Keep aside. In a skillet, heat 1 tablespoon of oil on medium heat. Add sweet potato and sprinkle with salt and black pepper and cook for about 6-8 minutes. Meanwhile in another skillet, heat remaining oil on medium heat. Add garlic and sauté for about 1 minute. Add spinach and cook for about 3 minutes. Season with salt and black pepper and remove from heat. In a large bowl, place sweet potato and spinach. Pour dressing over veggies and gently, mix. Garnish with lime zest and serve immediately.

Zucchini with Tomatoes

Time: 40 minutes

Servings: 2

Ingredients:

2 cups cherry tomatoes
3 tablespoons extra virgin olive oil, divided
2 tablespoons fresh lemon juice
Salt and freshly ground black pepper, to taste

2 garlic cloves, minced
1 jalapeño pepper, seeded and chopped
2 large zucchinis, spiralized with Blade C
2 tablespoons fresh basil, chopped

Directions:

Preheat the oven to 400 degrees F. Grease a roasting pan. In a large bowl, add tomatoes, 1 tablespoon of oil, lemon juice, salt and black pepper and toss well. Transfer the tomato mixture into a roasting pan. Roast for about 20 minutes. Meanwhile in a large skillet, heat remaining oil on medium heat. Add garlic and jalapeño pepper and sauté for about 1 minute. Add zucchini, salt and black pepper and cook for about 3-4 minutes. Transfer the zucchini mixture into a serving plate. Top with roasted tomatoes. Garnish with basil and serve hot.

Zucchini with Tomatoes & Cheese

Time: 25 minutes

Servings: 4

Ingredients:

½ tablespoon olive oil
3 tablespoons butter
1 onion, peeled and spiralized with Blade C
3 large zucchini, peeled and spiralized with Blade C
1 cup cherry tomatoes, halved

1 garlic clove, minced
½ tablespoon red pepper flakes, crushed
1 teaspoon dried oregano, crushed
2 tablespoons wine
2 tablespoons Parmesan cheese
Salt and freshly ground black pepper, to taste

Directions:

In a large skillet, heat oil and butter on medium heat. Add onion and zucchini and cook for about 1 minute. Add tomatoes, garlic, red pepper, oregano, wine and cheese and cook for about 3-4 minutes. Season with salt and pepper and serve.

Zucchini with Broccoli

Time: 25 minutes   Servings: 2

Ingredients:

1½ tablespoons olive oil
1 garlic clove, minced
1 jalapeño pepper, seeded and chopped
1 cup broccoli florets

¼ cup soy sauce
2 medium zucchinis, spiralized with Blade C
Freshly ground black pepper, to taste
1 tablespoon black sesame seeds, toasted

Directions:

In a large skillet, heat oil on medium heat. Add garlic and jalapeño pepper and sauté for about 1 minute. Add broccoli and stir fry for about 2 minutes. Stir in soy sauce and zucchini and cook for about 4-5 minutes. Garnish with sesame seeds and serve.

Zucchini with Pears

Time: 35 minutes   Servings: 2

Ingredients:

1 large pear, cored and cut into 8 slices
2 tablespoons olive oil, divided
Salt and freshly ground black pepper, to taste

2 garlic cloves, minced
2 large zucchinis, spiralized with Blade C
¼ cup pecans, chopped

Directions:

Preheat the oven to 425 degrees F. Lightly, grease a baking dish. In a bowl, add pear slices. Drizzle with 1 tablespoon of oil and sprinkle with salt and black pepper. Arrange the slices in prepared baking dish in a single row. Bake for about 20-25 minutes. Remove from oven and keep aside. Meanwhile in a large skillet, heat remaining oil on medium heat. Add garlic and sauté for about 1 minute. Add zucchini and sprinkle with salt and black pepper and cook for about 3-4 minutes. Transfer the zucchini in 2 serving plates and top with pear slices. Garnish with pecans and serve.

Zucchini in Wine Sauce

Time: 35 minutes   Servings: 2

Ingredients:

2 tablespoons olive oil
1 garlic clove, minced
3 cups cherry tomatoes
2 large onions, peeled and spiralized with
   Blade C

1 zucchini, peeled and spiralized with Blade C
2 tablespoons fresh lemon juice
½ teaspoon red pepper flakes, crushed
¼ cup dry white wine
Salt and freshly ground black pepper, to taste

Directions:

In a large skillet, heat oil on medium heat. Add garlic and tomatoes and cook for about 3-4 minutes. Add zucchini, onion, lemon juice, red pepper flakes and white wine and cook for 3-4 minutes. Season with salt and pepper and serve.

Zucchini in Creamy Sauce

Time: 25 minutes   Servings: 2

Ingredients:

3-4 medium zucchinis, spiralized with Blade C
1 teaspoon extra virgin coconut oil
1 cup white onion, chopped
2 garlic cloves, minced

1/3 cup unsweetened coconut milk
Pinch of red pepper flakes, crushed
Salt and freshly ground black pepper, to taste
1 scallion, chopped

Directions:

Arrange a steamer basket over a pan of boiling water. Place zucchini noodles in the steamer basket. Steam, covered for about 2 minutes. Drain well and transfer into a serving bowl. In a skillet, heat oil on medium heat. Add onion and sauté for about 4-5 minute. Add garlic and sauté for about 1 minute. Remove from heat and keep aside to cool slightly. In a blender, add onion mixture, coconut milk and seasoning and pulse till smooth. Pour sauce over steamed zucchini and gently toss to coat well. Garnish with scallions and serve immediately.

Zucchini in Avocado Sauce

Time: 25 minutes   Servings: 2

Ingredients:

2 tablespoons extra virgin olive oil, divided
2 garlic clove, minced and divided
1 large zucchini, spiralized with Blade C

2 avocados, peeled, pitted and chopped
½ tablespoon fresh lemon juice
Salt and freshly ground black pepper, to taste

Directions:

In a large skillet, heat oil on medium-high heat. Add garlic and sauté for about 1 minute. Add zucchini and sauté for about 4-5 minutes. Transfer the mixture into a large serving bowl. In another bowl, add remaining oil, garlic clove, avocados, lemon juice and seasoning and mash till creamy. Place avocado sauce over zucchini and serve.

Zucchini in Tomato Sauce

Time: 40 minutes   Servings: 2

Ingredients:

1 tablespoon olive oil
½ cup white onion, chopped
1 tablespoon garlic, minced
1½ cups fresh tomatoes, chopped finely
1 cup filtered water

¼ teaspoon ground cumin
1/8 teaspoon cayenne pepper
Salt and freshly ground black pepper, to taste
2 tablespoons fresh thyme, chopped
3 medium zucchinis, spiralized with Blade C

Directions:

In a large skillet, heat oil on medium-high heat. Add onion and sauté for about 4-5 minute. Add garlic and sauté for about 1 minute. Add tomatoes and cook for about 3-4 minutes, stirring occasionally. Add water and spices and bring to a boil. Reduce the heat to medium-low and simmer for about 10-15 minutes, stirring occasionally. Stir in thyme and zucchini and cook for about 2-3 minutes. Serve hot.

Zucchini in Pumpkin Sauce

Time: 30 minutes   Servings: 4

Ingredients:

2 large zucchinis, spiralized with Blade C
1 tablespoon canola oil
¼ cup white onion, chopped
1 large carrot, peeled and chopped finely
2 garlic cloves, minced
½ teaspoon red pepper flakes, crushed

½ cup canned pumpkin puree
½ cup vegetable broth
¼ cup coconut milk
Pinch of ground cinnamon
Salt and freshly ground black pepper, to taste
2 tablespoons fresh basil leaves, chopped

Directions:

In a large pan of boiling water, add zucchini and cook for about 2-3 minutes. Drain well and keep aside. In a large skillet, heat oil on medium heat. Add onion and carrot and sauté for about 8-10 minutes. Add garlic and red pepper flakes and sauté for about 1 minute. Add pumpkin puree, broth and coconut milk and cook for about 1 minute, stirring continuously. Remove from heat and keep aside to cool slightly. Transfer the mixture in a blender and pulse till smooth. Return the mixture into pan and cook for about 2-3 minutes or till heated completely. Stir in zucchini and remove from heat. Garnish with basil and serve.

Zucchini & Carrot Wraps

Time: 20 minutes   Servings: 4

Ingredients:

For Pesto:

2 cups fresh basil leaves
2 large garlic cloves, chopped finely
1/3 cup cashews
½ cup olive oil
Salt and freshly ground black pepper, to taste

For Wraps:

1 medium zucchini, spiralized with Blade C and chopped
1 small carrot, peeled and spiralized with Blade C and chopped
1 orange bell pepper, seeded and sliced thinly
1 red bell pepper, seeded and sliced thinly
½ medium avocado, peeled, pitted and sliced thinly
4 large fresh kale leaves, trimmed

Directions:

For pesto in a blender, add all ingredients and pulse till smooth. Transfer the pesto into a bowl and refrigerate before serving. In a bowl, mix together, zucchini, carrot and bell peppers. In a large plate place a kale leaf. Arrange ¼ of zucchini mixture over leaf. Top with ¼ of pesto. Roll the leaves around zucchini mixture. Repeat with the remaining leaves, zucchini mixture and pesto.

ZUCCHINI WITH ROASTED VEGGIES

Time: 55 minutes   Servings: 4

Ingredients:

For Vegetables:

2 sweet potatoes, peeled and cubed
1 bunch asparagus, trimmed and cut into
 bite size pieces
1 tablespoon olive oil
Salt and freshly ground black pepper, to taste

For Zucchini:

2 tablespoons extra virgin olive oil
1 garlic clove, minced
3 medium zucchinis, spiralized with Blade C
Salt and freshly ground black pepper, to taste
¼ cup fresh basil, chopped

Directions:

Preheat the oven to 350 degrees F. Arrange sweet potato and asparagus in prepared baking sheet. Drizzle with oil and sprinkle with salt and black pepper. Roast for about 30-35 minutes. Meanwhile in a large skillet, heat oil on medium heat. Add garlic and sauté for about 1 minute. Add zucchini, salt and black pepper and cook for about 2-3 minutes. Divide the zucchini in serving plates and top with roasted sweet potato and asparagus. Drizzle with lemon juice and serve with the garnishing of basil.

ZUCCHINI & VEGGIES IN CASHEW SAUCE

Time: 35 minutes   Servings: 4

Ingredients:

For Sauce:

4 cups water
1 cup raw cashews
2 tablespoons fresh basil leaves, chopped
1 garlic clove, minced
1 tablespoon fresh lemon juice
Salt and freshly ground black pepper, to taste

For Veggies:

4 medium zucchinis, spiralized with Blade C
1 large bunch asparagus, trimmed and cut
 into 2-inch pieces
2 tablespoons olive oil
1½ cups fresh cremini mushrooms, chopped
½ cup cherry tomatoes, halved
¼ cup pine nuts, chopped

Directions:

In a bowl of hot water, soak cashews for about 30 minutes. Drain the cashews, reserving 1 cup of soaking water. In a blender, add soaked cashews, reserved water and remaining sauce ingredients and pulse till smooth. Keep aside. In a pan of boiling water, add zucchini and cook for about 2 minutes. With a slotted spoon, transfer zucchini into a colander and immediately run under cold water. Drain well and transfer the zucchini in a large plate lined with paper towel. In the same pan of boiling water, add asparagus and cook for about 2-3 minutes. Drain well and keep aside. In a large skillet, heat oil on medium heat. Add mushrooms and sauté for about 4-5 minutes. Add cashew sauce and cook for about 6-8 minutes. Add asparagus and cook for about 2 minutes. Stir in tomatoes and remove from heat. Transfer zucchini in serving plate and top with veggie mixture. Garnish with pine nuts and serve.

Summer Squash with Tomato Balls

Time: 40 minutes   Servings: 2

Ingredients:

For Sauce:

1 small cucumber, peeled, seeded and chopped
1 garlic clove, minced
1 tablespoon fresh basil, chopped
¼ cup coconut milk
½ tablespoon olive oil
1 tablespoon fresh lemon juice
salt and freshly ground black pepper, to taste

For Tomato Balls:

1 cup fresh tomatoes, chopped

1 tablespoon fresh mint leaves, chopped
¼ cup scallion, chopped
Pinch of dried thyme, crushed
1 small egg, beaten
¼ cup almond flour
Salt and freshly ground black pepper, to taste

For Summer Squash:

1 tablespoon olive oil
1 large summer squash, spiralized with Blade C
Salt and freshly ground black pepper, to taste

Directions:

Preheat the oven to 400 degrees F. Grease a baking sheet. Keep aside. For sauce in a food processor, add all ingredients and pulse till smooth. Refrigerate, covered to chill before serving. For tomato balls in a large bowl, add all ingredients and mix till well combined. Make desired size balls from mixture. Arrange balls in prepared baking dish in a single layer. Bake for about 10 minutes. Flip the side and bake for about 10-15 minutes. Meanwhile in a large skillet, heat oil on medium heat. Add squash noodles, salt and black pepper and cook for about 2-3 minutes. In a serving plate, place the cooked squash noodles. Pour sauce over squash and gently stir to combine. Top with tomato balls and serve.

Kohlrabi Bulb with Nuts & Raisins

Time: 20 minutes   Servings: 2

Ingredients:

1½ tablespoons olive oil
2 garlic cloves, minced
2 kohlrabi bulbs, peeled and spiralized with Blade C
1 teaspoon dried oregano, crushed

¼ cup golden raisins
Salt and freshly ground black pepper, to taste
2 tablespoons walnuts, chopped
2 tablespoons pine nuts, chopped

Directions:

In a large skillet, heat oil on medium-high heat. Add garlic and sauté for about 1 minute. Add kohlrabi bulbs and cook for about 2-3 minutes. Stir in oregano and golden raisins and cook for about 1-2 minutes. Season with salt and pepper and remove from heat. Top with nuts and serve immediately.

Spicy Jicama

Time: 40 minutes   Servings: 4

Ingredients:

1 large jicama, peeled and spiralized with   ½ teaspoon chili powder
  Blade C   ½ teaspoon cayenne pepper
2 tablespoons olive oil   Salt and freshly ground black pepper, to taste

Directions:

Preheat the oven to 400 degrees F. Grease a baking dish. Arrange jicama noodles in prepared baking dish. Drizzle with oil and sprinkle with seasoning. Roast for about 30 minutes, flipping once in the middle way.

Turnip with tomatoes & Green Beans

Time: 35 minutes   Servings: 4

Ingredients:

1 cup fresh green beans, trimmed and cut   ¼ teaspoon red pepper flakes, crushed
  into 2-inch pieces   1 teaspoon dried thyme, crushed
2 tablespoons olive oil, divided   3 cups fresh tomatoes, chopped finely
Salt and freshly ground black pepper, to taste   ½ cup vegetable broth
1 fennel bulb, chopped   3 large turnips, peeled and spiralized with
1 cup white onion, chopped2 garlic cloves,   Blade C
  minced   2 tablespoons fresh cilantro leaves, chopped

Directions:

Preheat the oven to 400 degrees F. Lightly, grease a baking dish. In a large bowl, add green beans, 1 tablespoon of oil, salt and black pepper and toss to coat well. Transfer the beans mixture into prepared baking dish. Roast for about 15-20 minutes. Remove from oven and keep aside. Meanwhile in a large skillet, heat remaining oil on medium heat. Add fennel bulb and onion and sauté for about 4-5 minutes. Add garlic, red pepper flakes and thyme and sauté for about 1 minute. Add tomatoes and cook for about 2 minutes, crushing with back of spoon. Stir in turnip and broth and cook, covered for about 6-8 minutes, stirring occasionally. Stir in salt and black pepper and remove from heat. Divide the turnip noodles in serving plates and top with roasted green beans. Garnish with cilantro and serve.

Apples with Spinach

Time: 25 minutes   Servings: 2

Ingredients:

¼ cup whole walnuts   2 cups fresh baby spinach
½ tablespoon honey   ½ teaspoon Dijon mustard
1/8 teaspoon cinnamon   2 tablespoons freshly squeezed lemon juice
1 tablespoon olive oil   Salt and freshly ground black pepper, to taste
1 large green apple peeled and spiralized
  with Blade C

Directions:

Preheat the oven to 425 degrees F. Line a baking sheet with a parchment paper. In a medium bowl, mix together walnuts, honey, cinnamon and cayenne. Transfer the walnuts mixture onto the prepared baking sheet. Roast for about 5 minutes. Remove from the oven and keep aside. In a large skillet, heat oil on medium heat. Add remaining ingredients and cook for about 2-3 minutes. Serve immediately with the topping of roasted walnuts.

MIXED VEGGIES

Time: 30 minutes

Servings: 4

Ingredients:

1½ tablespoons canola oil
¼ cup white onion, chopped
2 garlic cloves, minced
1 Serrano pepper, seeded and chopped
1 medium carrot, peeled and spiralized with Blade C

1 large yellow squash, spiralized with Blade C
1 large zucchini, spiralized with Blade C
2 tablespoons fresh lime juice
Salt and freshly ground black pepper, to taste
½ cup scallion, chopped

Directions:

In a large skillet, heat oil on medium heat. Add onion and sauté for about 4-5 minutes. Add garlic and Serrano pepper and sauté for about 1 minute. Add carrot and sauté for about 2 minutes. Add squash and zucchini and sauté for about 3-4 minutes. Stir in lime juice, salt and black pepper and remove from heat. Garnish with scallion and serve immediately.

SWEET POTATO CURRY

Time: 55 minutes

Servings: 2

Ingredients:

1 tablespoon olive oil
½ teaspoon fresh ginger, minced
1 teaspoon garlic, minced
½ tablespoon curry powder
1 small red bell pepper, seeded and sliced thinly
1 small green bell pepper, seeded and sliced thinly

1 cup small cauliflower florets
1¾ cups coconut milk
¼ cup vegetable broth
2 medium sweet potatoes, peeled and spiralized with Blade C
Salt and freshly ground black pepper, to taste
2 tablespoons fresh parsley, chopped

Directions:

In a large pan, heat oil on medium heat. Add ginger, garlic and curry powder and sauté for about 1 minute. Add bell peppers and cauliflower and cook for about 4-5 minutes. Add coconut milk and broth and bring to a boil. Stir in sweet potato and reduce the heat to medium-low. Simmer, covered for about 6-8 minutes. Stir in salt and black pepper and remove from heat. Garnish with parsley and serve immediately.

POTATO CURRY

Time: 40 minutes

Servings: 4

Ingredients:

1 tablespoon coconut oil
½ white onion, chopped
2 carrots, peeled and chopped
2 teaspoons fresh ginger, minced
2 garlic cloves, minced
2½ cups broccoli florets
1 tablespoon curry powder
¼ teaspoon ground cumin

¼ teaspoon red pepper flakes, crushed
1 (14½-ounce) can diced tomatoes, drained
1 (14½-ounce) can lite coconut milk
1½ cups vegetable broth
Salt and freshly ground black pepper, to taste
1 large red potato, peeled and spiralized
    with Blade C
¼ cup fresh cilantro leaves, chopped

Directions:

In a large pan, heat oil on medium-high heat. Add the onion and carrot and sauté for about 3-4 minutes. Add ginger and garlic and sauté for about 1 minute. Add broccoli, curry powder, cumin, and red pepper flakes and cook for about 1-2 minutes, stirring continuously. Add tomatoes, coconut milk, broth, salt and black pepper and bring to a boil. Reduce the heat to medium-low and simmer for about 5 minutes. Stir in the potato noodles and simmer for about 7 minutes. Stir in the cilantro and serve.

RADISH & TOFU CURRY

Time: 45 minutes

Servings: 4

Ingredients:

1 (15-ounce) can coconut milk
1 tablespoon olive oil
5 scallions, sliced (whites and green parts
    separated)
1 tablespoon fresh ginger, minced
2 garlic cloves, minced
2 tablespoons red curry paste
½ tablespoon curry powder
2 cups broccoli florets

2 red bell peppers, seeded and sliced into
    ¼" strips
12-ounce extra firm tofu, drained and
    cubed into ½-inch size
1 large daikon radish, peeled and spiralized
    with Blade C
1 tablespoon Sriracha
¼ cup fresh cilantro, chopped

Directions:

In a bowl, add the can of coconut milk and with a fork, beat well. In a large pan, heat oil on medium-high heat. Add scallion whites, ginger, garlic, curry paste and curry powder and cook for about 2 minutes, stirring occasionally. Add broccoli and bell peppers and sauté for about 3-5 minutes. Add coconut milk and bring to a boil. Reduce the heat to medium-low and stir in tofu. Simmer for about 5 minutes. Stir in the daikon noodles and cook for about 5 minutes. Garnish with cilantro green scallions and serve.

SWEET POTATO WITH QUINOA

Time: 35 minutes   Servings: 4

Ingredients:

For Sauce:

3 tablespoons apple cider vinegar
2 tablespoons tahini
1 tablespoon pure maple syrup
1 tablespoon olive oil
1 tablespoon water
Salt and freshly ground black pepper, to taste

For Sweet Potato & Quinoa:

2 cups water
¾ cup uncooked quinoa
1 tablespoon olive oil
2 medium sweet potatoes, peeled and spiralized with Blade C
½ teaspoon garlic powder
Salt and freshly ground black pepper, to taste
2 tablespoons raisins
2 tablespoons almonds, toasted and chopped

Directions:

For sauce in a bowl, add all ingredients and mix till well combined. Keep aside. In a pan, add water and quinoa on medium heat and bring to a boil. Reduce the heat to low and simmer for about 15-20 minutes. Remove from heat and fluff with a fork. Meanwhile in a skillet, heat oil on medium heat. Add sweet potatoes, garlic powder, salt and black pepper and cook, covered for about 5-7 minutes. Uncover and cook for about 2 minutes. Transfer the sweet potato into a large serving bowl. Stir in quinoa and raisins. Drizzle with sauce and top with almonds and serve.

BUTTERNUT SQUASH WITH LENTILS

Time: 35 minutes   Servings: 4

Ingredients:

For Sauce:

1¼ tablespoons tahini
1 tablespoon extra-virgin olive oil
2 tablespoons apple cider vinegar
1 tablespoon maple syrup
1 tablespoon water
Salt and freshly ground black pepper, to taste

For Squash & Lentils:

1 medium butternut squash, peeled and spiralized with Blade C
1 tablespoon olive oil
¼ cup dry lentils
1 cup water
Salt and freshly ground black pepper, to taste

Directions:

For sauce in a bowl, add all ingredients and beat till well combined. Keep aside. Preheat the oven to 400 degrees F. Line a baking sheet with a parchment paper. In bowl, mix together butternut squash, olive oil, salt and pepper. Transfer the squash mixture onto the prepared baking dish. Bake for about 10-15 minutes until tender. Meanwhile in a pan, add lentils and water on high heat and bring to a boil. Reduce heat to a medium and cook for about 10-15 minutes. Drain well. Divide butternut squash and lentils in serving plates. Drizzle with sauce and serve.

Broccoli with Chickpeas

Time: 30 minutes   Servings: 4

Ingredients:

For Cheese Sauce:
¼ cup feta cheese
½ cup shallot, chopped
1 garlic clove, minced
2 tablespoons fresh basil, chopped
2 tablespoons olive oil
1 tablespoon red wine vinegar
1 tablespoon lemon juice

For Broccoli & Chickpeas:
3 broccoli stems, spiralized with Blade C
½ cup fresh green peas, shelled
2 tablespoons extra-virgin olive oil
½ cup scallion, chopped
1 garlic clove, minced
1 Serrano pepper, chopped
1 teaspoon dried oregano, crushed
1 tomato, chopped finely
1 cup canned chickpeas, rinsed and drained
Salt and freshly ground black pepper, to taste

Directions:

For sauce in a food processor, add all ingredients and pulse till smooth and creamy. Keep aside. In a large pan of boiling water, cook the broccoli noodles and green peas and cook for about 2-3 minutes. Drain well and keep aside. In a large skillet, heat oil on medium heat. Add scallion, garlic, Serrano pepper and thyme and sauté for about 2-3 minutes. Add tomatoes and cook for about 2-3 minutes, crushing with the back of spoon. Add chickpeas, salt and black pepper and cook for about 2-3 minutes. In a large bowl, add chickpeas, broccoli mixture and sauce and gently, stir to combine. Serve immediately.

Sweet Potato & Beans Chili

Time: 55 minutes   Servings: 4

Ingredients:

2 tablespoons olive oil ¾ cup red onion, chopped
1 cup celery stalk, chopped
1 cup carrots, peeled and chopped
1 cup red bell pepper, seeded and chopped
2 large garlic cloves, minced
1 teaspoon dried oregano, crushed
1 teaspoon ground cumin
½ teaspoon chili powder
Salt and freshly ground black pepper, to taste

2 (14-ounce) cans diced tomatoes
1 (14-ounce) can of red kidney beans, rinsed and drained
1 (14-ounce) can white beans, rinsed and drained
2 cups vegetable broth
2 cups water
1 large sweet potato peeled, spiralized with Blade C and chopped
2 tablespoons fresh parsley, chopped

Directions:

In a large pan, heat oil on medium heat. Add onions, carrots, celery and bell pepper and sauté for about 4-5 minutes. Add garlic, oregano, cumin, chili powder, salt and pepper and sauté for about 5 minutes. Add tomatoes, beans, broth and water and bring to a boil. Reduce the heat and simmer, uncovered for about 20 minutes. Add sweet potato noodles and parsley and simmer, uncovered for about 10 minutes. Serve hot.

Spiralized Desserts

Sweet Potato & Apple Casserole

Time: 55 minutes

Servings: 4

Ingredients:

2 cups almond flour, blanched
1 teaspoon baking soda
¼ teaspoon sea salt
2 eggs
¼ cup honey

1/3 cup fresh orange juice
2 cups sweet potato, spiralized with Blade C and cut into 2-inch pieces
1 cup apple, peeled, spiralized with Blade C and cut into 2-inch pieces

Directions:

Preheat the oven to 325 degrees F. Grease an 8x8-inch baking dish. In a large bowl, mix together flour, baking soda and salt. In another bowl, add eggs, honey and orange juice and beat till well combined. Mix egg mixture into flour mixture. Fold in sweet potato and apple. Transfer the mixture into prepared baking dish evenly. Bake for about 40 minutes. Serve warm.

Sweet Potato & Marshmallow Casserole

Time: 55 minutes

Servings: 8

Ingredients:

For Filling:
2 (1-pound) sweet potatoes, peeled and spiralized with Blade C
¼ cup unsalted butter, melted
½ teaspoon ground cinnamon
¼ teaspoon ground nutmeg
Salt, to taste
½ cup water

For Topping:
1/3 cup all-purpose flour
¼ cup brown sugar
½ cup pecans, chopped
Salt, to taste
¼ cup unsalted butter, cubed
2 cups mini marshmallows

Directions:

Preheat the oven to 375°F. Grease a 13x9-inch baking dish. In a large bowl, add the sweet potato noodles, melted butter, spices and salt and gently toss to coat. Transfer the sweet potato mixture into the prepared baking dish. Place the water over the sweet potatoes. With a piece of foil, cover the baking dish and bake for about 20-25 minutes. Meanwhile for topping in a bowl, mix together flour, sugar, pecans and salt. Slowly, add the butter and mix till a crumbly mixture forms. Remove the baking dish from the oven and top with the pecan mixture and marshmallows evenly. Bake for about 15 minutes. Serve warm.

SWEET POTATO & PEAR PIE

Time: 65 minutes   Servings: 2

Ingredients:

2 tablespoons extra virgin coconut oil
1 large sweet potato, peeled and spiralized
  with Blade C
2 medium pears, peeled, cored and
chopped
4 eggs

2/3 cup coconut milk
1 teaspoon ground ginger
1 teaspoon ground nutmeg
3 teaspoons ground cinnamon
½ cup fresh cranberries
1 tablespoon honey, melted

Directions:

Preheat the oven to 350 degrees F. Lightly, grease a 9-inch pie pan. In a large skillet, heat oil on medium heat. Add sweet potato noodles and cook for about 2-3 minutes. Add pears and cook for about 4-5 minutes. Remove from heat and keep aside. In a large bowl, add eggs, coconut milk and spices and beat till well combined. Stir in sweet potato mixture and cranberries. Transfer the mixture into prepared pie pan. Bake for about 35-40 minutes. Serve with the drizzling of melted honey.

APPLE PIE

Time: 50 minutes   Servings: 8

Ingredients:

2 refrigerated pie crusts
2½ pound honey crisp apples, spiralized
with Blade C
1 tablespoon fresh lemon juice
1 cup granulated sugar
¼ cup cornstarch
½ teaspoon ground cinnamon

½ teaspoon ground ginger
1 teaspoon vanilla extract
2 tablespoons unsalted butter, cut into 8
cubes
Cream, as required
Turbinado sugar, for sprinkling

Directions:

Preheat the oven to 375 degrees F. Unroll 1 prepared pie crust into a circle large enough to fit into a 9-inch pie dish. Arrange the crust in the pie dish, cutting and folding excess dough underneath the edges to create a scalloped crust edge. With a fork, prick the holes across the bottom of the crust. Freeze the pie dish for at least 15 minutes. In a bowl, add apple noodles and lemon juice and toss to coat. In another bowl, mix together sugar, cornstarch, cinnamon and ginger. Add the sugar mixture into the bowl of apple noodles and toss to coat. Transfer the apple filling into the prepared crust. Place the butter cubes over the filling evenly. Unroll the second round of pie dough and cut into 1-inch-wide strips. Top the pie with the strips in a lattice pattern, making slits in the crust so that steam can escape. Brush the top crust with cream and sprinkle with the sugar. Bake for about 45 minutes. Remove from oven and keep on wire rack to cool completely. Cut into desired slices and serve.

O-Bake Apple Pie

Time: 20 minutes   Servings: 2

Ingredients:

1 tablespoon cornstarch
¼ cup cold water
1 packet Truvia (artificial sweetener)
¼ teaspoon ground cinnamon

¼ teaspoon vanilla extract
Pinch of salt
2 medium Fuji apples, peeled, spiralized
with Blade C and chopped roughly

Directions:

In a bowl, dissolve cornstarch in cold water. Add sweetener, cinnamon, vanilla extract and salt and stir till well combined. Add apple noodles and toss to coat. Heat a greased skillet on medium heat. Add apple mixture, and cook for about 3-4 minutes, stirring occasionally. Serve warm.

Apple Crisp

Time: 1 hour 15 minutes   Servings: 12

Ingredients:

For Filling:

6 Granny Smith apples, peeled and
spiralized with Blade C
3 tablespoons brown sugar
1 tablespoon cornstarch
2 tablespoons fresh lemon juice
½ teaspoon ground cinnamon
Pinch of salt

For Topping:

1½ cups oats
1/3 cup brown sugar
½ cup almond meal
1 teaspoon ground cinnamon
½ teaspoon nutmeg
1 teaspoon pure vanilla extract
¼ cup butter, melted

Directions:

Preheat the oven to 350 degrees F. Grease a 13x9-inch baking dish. For filling in a large bowl, mix together all filling ingredients. Spread apple mixture into prepared baking dish. For topping in a large bowl, mix together oats, brown sugar, flour, cinnamon and nutmeg. Stir in the vanilla extract. Add the butter and mix till a crumbly mixture forms. Place the topping mixture over the apple mixture evenly. Bake for about 50-55 minutes.

pple & Rhubarb Crisp

Time: 50 minutes   Servings: 4

Ingredients:

3 gala apples, spiralized with Blade C
3 rhubarb stalks, sliced lengthwise and cubed
Honey, as required
½ cup vanilla granola of choice

Directions:

Preheat the oven to 350 degrees F. In a bowl, mix together apple noodles and rhubarb cubes. Place the apple mixture in 4 ramekins about ¾ full. Lightly drizzle the tops of each ramekin with honey. Bake for about 30 minutes. Remove from the oven and place granola over apple mixture in each ramekin evenly.
Bake for about 5 minutes.

MICROWAVE APPLE CRISP

Time: 25 minutes   Servings: 6

Ingredients:

4 medium tart cooking apples, peeled, spiralized with Blade C and chopped
2/3 cup old-fashioned oats
2/3 cup brown sugar

½ cup Bisquick mix
3 tablespoons butter, softened
¾ teaspoon ground cinnamon
¾ teaspoon ground nutmeg

Directions:

In the bottom of an ungreased 8-inch square microwavable dish, arrange apple noodles.
In small bowl, add remaining ingredients and mix till a crumbly mixture forms.
Spread the crumble mixture over apples evenly. Microwave, uncovered on High for about 7-10 minutes, rotating dish after 5 minutes. Serve warm.

PEAR & ORANGE CRUMBLE

Time: 55 minutes   Servings: 8

Ingredients:

For Filling:
9 medium pears, spiralized with Blade C
1/3 cup brown sugar
1 teaspoon ground cinnamon
3 tablespoons fresh orange juice
2 teaspoons fresh orange zest, grated finely

For Topping:
1 cup rolled oats
1 cup almond meal
1/3 cup brown sugar
1 teaspoon ground cinnamon
Pinch of ground nutmeg
Pinch of salt
¼ cup coconut oil, melted

Directions:

Preheat oven to 350 degrees F. Grease a 13x9-inch baking dish.
For filling in a large bowl, mix together appear noodles, sugar, cinnamon, orange juice and zest.
In another bowl, mix together oats, almond meal, sugar, cinnamon, nutmeg and salt.
Slowly, add coconut oil and mix till a crumbly mixture forms.
Transfer the pear mixture into the prepared baking dish evenly.
Top with crumb mixture evenly.
Bake for about 40 minutes.
Serve warm.

PPLE & YOGURT BOWL

Time: 20 minutes   Servings: 2

Ingredients:

1 medium apple, spiralized with Blade C   1 teaspoon unsalted butter
and chopped roughly   1 teaspoon brown sugar
1 teaspoon fresh lemon juice   ½ teaspoon ground cinnamon, divided
1 tablespoon old-fashioned oats   8 ounce Greek yogurt
1 tablespoon pecans, chopped

Directions:

In a bowl, add apple noodles and lemon juice and toss to coat well.

Heat a nonstick frying pan on medium heat.

Add oats and pecans and toast for about 2 minutes or till fragrant, stirring continuously.

Add butter, brown sugar and ¼ teaspoon of cinnamon and cook for about 2-3 minutes, stirring continuously.

Remove from the heat.

Stir the remaining cinnamon into yogurt.

Divide the yogurt into serving bowls and top with apple noodles and pecan mixture.

Serve immediately.

APPLE BARK

Time: 20 minutes   Servings: 24

Ingredients:

1 (10-ounce) package chocolate chips   3 teaspoons coconut flakes
2 medium honey crisp apples, spiralized   2 tablespoons almonds, sliced
with Blade C   Salt, to taste
1½ tablespoons almond butter

Directions:

Line a 17x11-inch baking sheet with parchment paper.

In a non-stick pan, place the chocolate chips on medium heat.

Cook for about 2-3 minutes or till melted completely, stirring continuously.

Transfer the melted chocolate into a large bowl.

Add apple noodles and stir till well combined.

Transfer the apple mixture into the prepared baking sheet in a thin layer.

Spread almond butter over apple mixture evenly.

Top with coconut flakes, almonds, and then sprinkle with a little salt.

Freeze the baking sheet for at least 1 hour or till set completely.

Cut into 24 equal sized squares and serve.

Zucchini Cookies

Time: 30 minutes   Servings: 12

Ingredients:

1 cup flour
1 teaspoon baking soda
¾ teaspoon ground cinnamon
Salt, to taste
¾ cup brown sugar
¼ cup apple butter

1 large egg
1 teaspoon vanilla extract
1 cup zucchini, spiralized with Blade C and chopped
2 cups rolled oats
½ cup white mini chocolate chips

Directions:

Preheat the oven to 350 degrees F. Line a cookie sheet with a parchment paper.

In a bowl, mix together flour, baking soda, cinnamon and salt.

In another bowl, add brown sugar and apple butter and beat till smooth.

Add egg and vanilla and beat till well combined.

Add flour mixture into egg mixture and mix till just combined.

Fold in the zucchini, oats and chocolate chips.

With 1 tablespoon, place the mixture onto prepared cookie sheet about 3-inch apart.

Bake for about 11-12 minutes or till the edges become golden brown.

Zucchini Muffins

Time: 45 minutes   Servings: 12

Ingredients:

½ cup coconut flour
¾ teaspoon baking soda
2 teaspoons ground cinnamon
½ teaspoon ground nutmeg
Salt, to taste
3 eggs
3 tablespoons maple syrup
2 tablespoons almond milk

1 tablespoon coconut oil, melted
2 teaspoons vanilla extract
1 ripe banana, peeled and mashed
1 medium zucchini, spiralized with Blade C, chopped and squeezed
½ cup pecans, chopped
¼ cup mini chocolate chips

Directions:

Preheat the oven to 350 degrees F.

Grease a 12 cups large muffin pan with cooking spray and then place parchment paper strips in each cup.

In a bowl, mix together coconut flour, baking soda, spices and salt.

In another bowl, add eggs, maple syrup, almond milk, coconut oil, vanilla and banana and beat till well combined. Add flour mixture into egg mixture and mix till smooth.

Fold in zucchini, walnuts and chocolate chips.

Transfer the mixture into the prepared muffin cups.

Bake for about 30 minutes or till a toothpick inserted in the center comes out

ZUCCHINI DONUTS

Time: 45 minutes

Servings: 6

Ingredients:

½ cup coconut flour
¼ cup tapioca flour
1½ tablespoons cacao powder
¾ teaspoon baking soda
¼ teaspoon salt
2 teaspoons ground cinnamon
3 eggs
3 tablespoons maple syrup
2 tablespoons almond milk

1 tablespoon coconut oil, melted
2 teaspoons vanilla extract
1 ripe banana, peeled and mashed
3 tablespoons maple syrup
2 teaspoons vanilla extract
1 medium zucchini, spiralized with Blade C
2 tablespoons unsweetened coconut, shredded

Directions:

Preheat the oven to 350 degrees F.

Grease a donut pan.

In a bowl, mix together coconut flours, cacao powder, baking soda, cinnamon and salt.

In another bowl, add eggs, maple syrup, almond milk, coconut oil, vanilla and banana and beat till well combined.

Add flour mixture into egg mixture and mix till smooth.

Fold in zucchini and coconut.

Transfer the mixture into the prepared donut pan.

Bake for about 30 minutes or till a toothpick inserted in the center comes out

CARROT PUDDING

Time: 35 minutes

Servings: 2

Ingredients:

2 tablespoons plus ¼ teaspoon coconut oil
2 cups carrots, peeled and spiralized with Blade C

2 tablespoons maple syrup
2 teaspoons plus 1 teaspoon ground cinnamon

Directions:

In a skillet, melt1/4 teaspoon of coconut oil on medium heat.

Add carrot noodles and cook for about 5 minutes.

Meanwhile in another pan, add remaining coconut oil, honey, and 2 teaspoons of cinnamon on low heat and cook for about 5 minutes, stirring continuously.

Remove sauce from the heat and pour over the carrots.

Return carrot mixture on medium heat and cook for about 15 minutes, stirring occasionally.

Serve warm.

7 Days Meal Plan

Day 1:
Breakfast: Potato Waffles
Lunch: Butternut Squash with Tomatoes
Dinner: Zucchini & Seafood Stew
Dessert: Microwave Apple Crisp

Day 2:
Breakfast: Zucchini with Scrambled Eggs
Lunch: Cheesy Potatoes
Dinner: Cabbage with Ground Pork
Dessert: Sweet Potato & Marshmallow Casserole

Day 3:
Breakfast: Squash & Spinach Frittata
Lunch: Zucchini with Broccoli
Dinner: Yellow Squash with Beef Meatballs
Dessert: Apple Pie

Day 4:
Breakfast: Beet Omelet
Lunch: Chilled Zucchini Soup
Dinner: Sweet Potato & Beans Chili
Dessert: Zucchini Donuts

Day 5:
Breakfast: Sweet Potato Pancakes
Lunch: Cucumber & Asparagus Salad
Dinner: Zucchini, Chard & Cod Parcel
Dessert: Apple & Yogurt Bowl

Day 6:
Breakfast: Broccoli & Tofu Scramble
Lunch: Zucchini in Creamy Sauce
Dinner: Carrot with Steak
Dessert: Pear & Orange Crumble

Day 7:
Breakfast: Zucchini & Sweet Potato Hash
Lunch: Apples with Spinach
Dinner: Sweet Potato with Cranberries & Turkey
Dessert: Carrot Pudding

Conclusion

Now that this book with healthy and deliciously tasting recipes has given you a good start with your vegetable spiralizer you can keep going on the healthy track smartly with no difficulties at all. The idea behind this book was to also target the novice and busy cooks who don't want to spend a lot of time in kitchen and still serve their families healthy and nutritious foods containing all important components of healthy diet. We hope you will like the recipes fastened with lots of love and affection for your loved ones. Stay Healthy!!

Thank you again for purchasing this book!

Finally, if you enjoyed this book, please take the time to share your thoughts and post a review on Amazon. It'd be greatly appreciated!

Feel free to contact me at emma.katie@outlook.com

Check out more books by Emma Katie at:

www.amazon.com/author/emmakatie